EXPLORATIONS IN CU

Ciara Moren

BIMM College
Dublin

EXPLORATIONS IN CULTURAL HISTORY

Edited by
T.G. Ashplant and Gerry Smyth

Pluto Press

LONDON • STERLING, VIRGINIA

First published 2001 by Pluto Press
345 Archway Road, London N6 5AA
and 22883 Quicksilver Drive, Sterling, VA 20166-2012, USA

www.plutobooks.com

British Library Cataloguing in Publication Data
A catalogue record for this book is available from the British Library

Library of Congress Cataloging in Publication Data
    Explorations in cultural history / edited by T.G. Ashplant and Gerry
Smyth.
    p. cm.
  ISBN 0–7453–1517–8 — ISBN 0–7453–1512–7 (pbk.)
  1. Culture—Study and teaching. 2. Culture—History. I. Ashplant, T.G.
II. Smyth, Gerry.
  HM101 .E97 2001
  306'.071—dc21
                                                        00–009907

ISBN 0 7453 1517 8 hardback
ISBN 0 7453 1512 7 paperback

Designed and produced for Pluto Press by Chase Publishing Services
Typeset by Stanford DTP Services, Northampton
Printed in the European Union by TJ International, Padstow, England

For Mike Pudlo

Contents

Preface and Acknowledgements

The last 20 years have seen far-reaching changes in the ways the humanities and social sciences have conceived of both their objects of study and their methodologies. The component disciplines have been challenged by the impact of feminist and postcolonial questionings, the rise of critical and cultural theory, and the alleged crisis in 'grand narratives' (Marxism, modernisation, the Enlightenment project). As a result, the internal structures and external boundaries of existing disciplines have been, to a greater or lesser extent, modified and their curricula expanded; new disciplines (women's studies, cultural studies) have emerged; and interdisciplinary exchanges between disciplines have become more common. These developments have of course had a differential effect in both timing and extent, being felt earlier or more extensively in some disciplines than others. Some traditional subjects have been radically reshaped, such as literary studies under the impact of the 'canon wars' and literary theory which together have greatly extended the range of texts studied and the modes of interpretation employed. Others have enjoyed a sudden rise to eminence, as with the emergence of cultural geography. Even in the venerable discipline of history – about which Dominick LaCapra could write in his *History and Criticism* as recently as 1985 that 'Historiography today is not in that state of fermentation to be found in fields such as literary criticism and Continental philosophy. Historians tend to pride themselves on their immunity to the wormlike doubt and self-reflective scrutiny that have appeared in other areas of enquiry, notably those infiltrated by recent French thought' (p. 46) – even here some sub-disciplines have felt the impact of the theory revolution, as with the 'linguistic turn' in social history.

The contributors to this volume have all worked during the past decade in the department of Literature and Cultural History at Liverpool John Moores University. During this period, the department has offered a BA degree in Literature, Life and Thought, a title borrowed from the post-1918 Cambridge English course (which became the dominant model for literary studies in Britain during the middle decades of the twentieth century), but reinscribed so as to allow a productive interdisciplinary exchange between literature, cultural history and critical and cultural theory. Stressing both the historical rootedness of all forms of writing, and the literary structuring of those texts historians have traditionally treated as sources, the degree has also engaged with contemporary theories as

themselves historically situated and textually constructed. The aim
has been to encourage fruitful dialogue between text, event and
theory, rather than to privilege any one of these terms. This work at
LJMU has its parallels in other humanities departments, especially
(though not only) in the new universities. Many of the curricular and
methodological developments pioneered in such departments are now
being absorbed into the mainstream of the respective disciplines.

This volume grows out of the experience of teaching, and related
research, just described. It outlines some of the methodological implications of these interdisciplinary encounters and offers examples of
the substantive research it has inspired. Part 1, entitled 'In Search of
Cultural History', offers an overview of the emergence of cultural
history in the 1980s as the locus for new research into the historical
construction and transformation of meanings. Chapter 1 traces
interacting developments within the discipline of history since 1945 in
Britain, France and America that have given shape to the new cultural
history. It focuses on the proliferation of sub-disciplines within history,
the influence of the French *Annales* historians and the British Marxist
historians and cultural theorists, and interdisciplinary exchanges with
literary and cultural studies and anthropology. It goes on to examine
the impact of key components within critical and cultural theory, in
particular poststructuralism and postmodernism, Foucault and new
historicism, and paradigms for the study of popular culture. As an
intervention in debates over the protocols of cultural history, it offers
a model for framing research into, and interpretations of, the
meanings of cultural artefacts in terms of three moments of analysis:
production, signification and reception. Part 2 comprises four case
studies of British and American cultural artefacts drawn from the last
two centuries. Each employs the cultural history frame introduced in
Part 1, adapted to both the specific type of artefact involved (a
political address, a polemical social investigation, a public monument,
a pop record), and to the research questions being posed.

Our former colleague Mike Pudlo was one of the pioneers in establishing and developing the Literature, Life and Thought degree, and
later the American Studies programme which grew out of it. Building
on his own training in American history and politics, he extended his
work into the fields of cultural history and historiographical theory.
His teaching communicated his own passion for history, at once
engaged and sceptical, while always setting exacting standards for his
students to aim at. It has been a privilege to work alongside Mike and
to benefit from the intellectual environment he helped to create. This
book is dedicated to him with respect and affection.

The authors would all like to express their gratitude to Sheena Streather and her colleagues at the Aldham Robarts Learning Resource Centre and the Inter-Library Loans Unit, LJMU, for their help in obtaining essential texts.

T.G. Ashplant wishes to thank the School of Media, Critical and Creative Arts, and the Literature and Cultural History Research Committee, Liverpool John Moores University, for the award of study leave during the preparation of this volume, and for undertaking consequential teaching and administrative duties; the staffs of the Upper Reserve, Upper Camera and Catalogue Desk, Bodleian Library, University of Oxford, for facilitating access to a wide range of research materials; Ursula Tarkowski for coffee and conversation; Sally Alexander and Daniela Koleva for encouragement at a crucial juncture; and especially Elspeth Graham for continuing support and apt advice throughout the project.

Joanna Price would like to thank her colleagues in American Studies, especially Ross Dawson, for making it possible for her to take the sabbatical leave during which she researched her chapter; Dr Patrick Hagopian for ideas and information; and Pete Morriss for his support, encouragement and critical contestation.

Note on Citations

All books cited in the bibliographies at the end of each chapter of this volume are published in London unless otherwise stated.

PART 1

IN SEARCH OF CULTURAL HISTORY

1 Schools, Methods, Disciplines, Influences

T. G. Ashplant and Gerry Smyth

1.1 Cultural History: Versions and Definitions

In the nineteenth century, the main focus of historical writing was the nation-state and its activities. Hence the core of the emerging historical discipline lay in the connected areas of political and constitutional history, with their necessary adjuncts of diplomatic and military history. The twentieth century has seen a massive diversification of the discipline. Starting with economic history, which became strongly established between the wars, this process has since 1945 seen the development of an ever-growing number of specialist subdisciplines – such as social history, labour history, family history, women's history, black history – between them tackling the history of ever more aspects of the human past. These sub-disciplines, which were defined initially by attention to hitherto neglected social groups, or aspects of society, have been complemented by a number of emergent specialisms that in the first instance were defined by their use of a specific technique of research (such as oral history or microhistory). Such distinctions have tended to blur, however, as the effort to investigate neglected aspects of the past has required the development of new methodologies; while innovative modes of investigation have brought fresh substantive questions into focus. Each of these sub-disciplines has developed a degree of institutionalisation, with the formation of national and international societies, and the publication of journals.

These sub-disciplines have shared, to varying degrees, certain common factors, including a shift of focus away from the activities of elites to those of wider sections of society; and a concern with (often enduring) social structures and transformations, rather than shortterm narratives of events. The expansion of the range of subject-matter of history was both spurred by, and in turn seemed to demand, a growing intellectual exchange of concepts and methodologies with the social sciences, beginning with economics and later extending to demography and sociology. This liaison reached its peak in the 1960s, with the enthusiastic adoption of quantitative techniques (in economic, demographic and social history), and the occasional assertion that such methodologies would place history on a scientific basis (Iggers, 1985). One result was an explosion of work in social history in Europe and America during the 1960s and '70s.

In common with other humanities disciplines, there has been a marked shift in orientation since the late 1970s. Considered from inside the discipline, this was an inevitable reaction to the sometimes inflated claims made for social scientific history. But it can also be contextually linked to felt crises in certain dominant intellectual paradigms, to what postmodernist theorists term the collapse of grand narratives, whether these be dominant stories of the triumph of modernisation, or counter-hegemonic accounts of intensifying class struggle. The focus of attention has shifted away from, for example, a working class supposedly growing in self-consciousness and social power, towards those disparate groups marginalised within dominant social orders (whether peasants during proto-industrialisation, or women within maturing capitalist societies).

Throughout these developments there have been recurring tensions within the models of investigation used by historians between certain (apparently) binary terms: narrative versus analysis, actor versus structure, interpretation versus explanation. In the heyday of social scientific history in the 1960s and early '70s, the second term in each pair was dominant: the task of the historian was to *analyse* historical *structures*, and *explain* their origins, persistence and change. With the passing of that intellectual moment, a return to narrative has been accompanied by a renewed emphasis on the capacity for action of individuals and groups, and a demand that the actors' perspectives be recovered hermeneutically rather than overlaid by later analytic categories. Accompanying this shift has been a redirection of interdisciplinary affiliations, towards anthropology, literary theory, gender studies, cultural geography and postcolonial theory. The general pattern of these developments has been international, although – as Iggers's survey (1997) makes clear – individual national traditions in history-writing still strongly inflect the timing and shape of disciplinary innovation.

Within these developments, cultural history has remained a marginal and elusive term. When first used, it referred primarily to the study of the (artistic or intellectual) products of high culture, and more broadly to the study of wider cultural traditions (often national, sometimes specific to a particular artistic or intellectual practice) which helped shape the character of those products. Burke (1997, pp. 1–22) has traced the origins of this sense of cultural history from the sixteenth century, culminating in the theorisings of culture by

Montesquieu, Herder and Hegel in the second half of the eighteenth century. With the rise to dominance of political history in the nineteenth century, cultural history tended to be marginalised. Though it was clearly an element in the work of the French historian Jules Michelet, and produced such influential works as Jacob Burckhardt's *Civilisation of the Renaissance in Italy* (1860), and Johan Huizinga's *The Waning of the Middle Ages* (1919), overall it represented a relatively weak and intermittent presence analogous to the much better established history of art, or history of ideas. In his recent, and aptly titled, *Varieties of Cultural History* (1997), Peter Burke commented: 'This classic model has not been replaced by any new orthodoxy' (p. vii). Hence there is 'no agreement over what constitutes cultural history' (p. 1); and so 'cultural history is not very firmly established, at least in an institutional sense' (p. 183; cf. Goodman, 1997, p. 792). It has not achieved the status of a broadly recognised, institutionalised sub-discipline of history, with the accompanying apparatus of learned societies and journals.

Instead, the term has been advanced by a variety of individuals and intellectual groupings, often within specific national contexts, as a convenient label under which to conduct a certain sort of enquiry into the social production of meanings. Three of the most significant of these claims to the title of cultural history were made during the 1980s in France and America, respectively in Roger Chartier's volume of essays *Cultural History: Between Practices and Representations* (1988), and in Robert Darnton's *The Great Cat Massacre and Other Episodes in French Cultural History* (1984) and Lynn Hunt's edited collection *The New Cultural History* (1989). In each case, this designation was adopted to signal a shift away from the earlier concerns of social history, and especially its focus on class, towards a more pluralist exploration of historical struggles to make and maintain meanings. Other historians following a similar path have also adopted the term.

This volume is offered as an intervention in this relatively fluid definitional field. Cultural history, as we define it, is concerned with the historical analysis of a range of cultural 'artefacts'. Such artefacts may be anything produced by human activity: written texts, but also visual texts, buildings, and other discrete material objects, as well as artefacts of greater complexity and more problematic identity, such as social practices and institutions, which require the historian first to reconstruct them as an object of knowledge before interpreting them (Spiegel, 1997, p. 196). Our understanding of culture is anthropological, so that any artefact is cultural insofar as it has become a source or locus of meaning. Distinctions of high and popular may be important in the course of interpretation, but cultural histories may be written of artefacts conventionally assigned to either category (Belsey,

1989, pp. 160–1). One result of the work in critical and cultural theory in recent decades has been to render the analysis of the production of meaning within culture considerably more complex. No longer is it possible to assume that meaning can be securely located within a cultural artefact itself, or in the intentions of its original producer(s). While such an investigation is still valuable, and may be sufficient for particular purposes, other aims may require an examination of the reception(s) of cultural artefacts, their appropriation in a range of diverse contexts in which they may help to produce quite different meanings.

Hence writing a cultural history of an artefact involves examining the systems of *production, signification* and *reception* that gave rise to the artefact and from which it derives its meanings. This methodology offers a way of framing the research, analysis and interpretation undertaken as part of any particular cultural history investigation. The terms 'production', 'signification', and 'reception' should be understood not as self-contained systems but as moments both in the making of the original artefact, and in the analysis of the meanings to which it has given rise. The production of an artefact includes its authorship (individual or collective), its mode of publication (that is, of bringing before the public), and its contemporary historical and cultural context. The systems of signification include the formal conventions within which the artefact was produced (such as literary language, style of painting, film genre). As LaCapra (1985, p. 127) comments: 'Contexts of writing include the intentions of the author as well as more immediate biographical, sociocultural, and political situations with their ideologies and discourses. They also involve discursive institutions such as traditions and genres.' Viewed from one perspective, signification is itself a constituent of production; formal conventions such as literary genre give shape to the artefact in the process of its making. The reason for treating signification as a separate moment is to highlight its importance within reception as well as production. Historians in particular have at times read the artefacts that they treat as sources as if they were transparent windows onto an aspect of the past, paying little or no attention to their generic construction.

The reception of the artefact involves study both of how it was received and 'read' by contemporaries, and of the various meanings attached to it later in changing historical circumstances. Though any particular cultural history investigation may focus on a discrete artefact, addressing questions of its reception necessarily extends the enquiry into a broader reconstruction of its historical impact. A study of reception involves attention to the specific contexts within which it takes place:

Contexts of reception pose the problem of how texts are read, used, and abused in different social groups, institutions, and settings. These may be institutions or settings such as trials, schools, and studies as well as social formations such as disciplines, parties, movements, and political regimes. Professional readers, for example literary critics, are a significant group in the reception of literature, for they help to shape judgement and to teach others how to read. (LaCapra, 1985, p. 129)

Again, production and reception are not entirely discrete. Reception may become part of the process of production of the initial artefact, as in the current Hollywood practice of trying out a trial cut of a film and reshaping it in the light of audience feedback. Moreover, much recent work in critical theory has stressed the dynamic, creative dimension of reception, to the point of preferring more active terms such as 'creative adaptation', 'cultural translation' (Burke, 1997, pp. 195–7), or displacing it altogether with 'productive activation' (Bennett, 1983, p. 214; see further pp. 20–7 below). Another important development has been the theorisation of the mechanisms of reception through key mediating figures within specific reception communities (see Rodden, 1989; and Chapter 3, below).

It is our contention that the use of such a model can help to clarify and render more precise the nature of any particular cultural history investigation, and the range of and the limits to the applicability of its findings. A concrete example will illustrate what we mean. In their study of *The Politics of War Memory and Commemoration*, Ashplant, Dawson and Roper (2000, ch. 1) traced two current paradigms in the study of war memory and commemoration: a political focus on the nation-state in its efforts to define and promote appropriate war commemoration; and a psychological emphasis on agencies of civil society in developing forms of commemoration which could enable mourning. While each of these paradigms has its value, they argue, in analysing the production and signification of particular war memorials, ceremonies or rituals, where both are inadequate is in their approach to reception. The former tends to assume the success of a given nation-state in securing the required identification of its population with the forms of commemoration it promotes; while the latter tends to elide specific responses into the psychic universalism of common human grief. Meanings are read off from public artefacts or memorial practices, or derived from the intentions of their producers, or inferred from claims made in public debate. To overcome the limitations of such analyses, Ashplant *et al.* invoke a third tradition of work on war memory that approaches reception through the methods of oral history and life stories, examining the meanings about war and its remembrance which people express for themselves in their own words. Thus the deployment of a cultural history model makes possible an assessment of the strengths and drawbacks of current approaches in this field, and the identification of other approaches which can enhance them. Chapter 4 below demonstrates how such a structured approach enriches understanding of war memorialisation.

The cultural history approach which we outline and exemplify in this volume is essentially interdisciplinary in its methodology. It represents the intersection of developments over the past four decades in several existing disciplines, especially history, literary studies and cultural studies, but including others such as art history and media studies. These developments have occurred on three levels. Firstly, those changes specific to each of these intellectual areas as an organised and institutionalised academic discipline, with its own history, methodologies and internal debates. Secondly, innovations and ruptures within broader theoretical and philosophical paradigms, which have had an impact across a wide range of humanities and social science disciplines. And thirdly, major shifts in the wider political and cultural context within which these academic disciplines are located, and which those theoretical paradigms have sought to address. The remainder of Part 1 traces developments at each of these levels, and suggests some of the connections between them. Since, as noted above, theories too are cultural artefacts, whose own geneses, conventions and receptions need to be explored textually and historically, such contextualisation works to avoid placing theory in a privileged analytical role.

Sections 1.2 and 1.3 locate the emergence of cultural history within the transformation of the discipline of history since 1945, focusing on interactions with the disciplines of literary studies, cultural studies and anthropology. They trace in particular two significant intellectual traditions, those of the British Marxist historians and cultural theorists, and of the French Annales historians. It will be apparent that both traditions shared certain concerns (especially with 'history from below', the recovery of the history and culture of non-elite social groups), and adopted interdisciplinary approaches involving borrowings from other disciplines. It will also be apparent that each tradition developed and modified its approach partly in response to wider political and intellectual shifts affecting the social sciences and humanities more broadly. As this body of historical writing and theorising itself becomes the object of historical and critical evaluation, it is increasingly possible to delineate and situate its characteristic concerns, questions and methods. Sections 1.4 to 1.6 examine the ways in which developments within broader theoretical paradigms (Poststructuralism and Postmodernism, Foucault and New Historicism, Popular Culture and Cultural Studies) have likewise helped shape the questions asked and the methods adopted within cultural history.

Part 2 consists of four case studies in which the cultural history model set out above is used to facilitate particular investigations into the historical creation of meanings. In Chapter 2 Helen Rogers engages with debates over the place of language in the formation of individual and collective identities in nineteenth-century British radical movements. In recent years, historians have stressed the role of language in constructing social identities, not merely expressing those already formed. Some have attributed to language the primary role in the process of individual and group identity formation. Rogers explores these issues with specific reference to radical women through consideration of a Chartist political document, the *Address of the Female Political Union of Birmingham to the Women of England* (1838). She considers the complex issues of authorship raised by this collective text, the gender of whose (unknowable) drafter is also undecidable; and situates it within the context of strenuous political debates. Attention is focused on the discourses deployed in the *Address* and in the wider political literature generated by those debates. Exploration of signification involves examining both the languages mobilised in these writings and speeches (including discourses of radical populism, evangelicalism, natural rights, respectability), and the performative dimensions of their delivery (including use of literary forms such as melodrama and autobiography, and linguistic registers such as hyperbole, parody and irony). Consideration of the historical context shows how and why at a certain moment this particular group of radical women were able to gain and then lose access to organisational and publicity resources for political struggle.

Chapter 3 explores the deeply divided contemporary and later reception of George Orwell's social investigation cum political polemic *The Road to Wigan Pier* (1937). T.G. Ashplant approaches the production of the text through an examination of Orwell's early career which situates him as one of many writers and activists attempting to understand and intervene in the deeply divided domestic and international politics of the late 1930s. An examination of how Orwell's multi-genred text has been understood to signify reveals the starkly differing readings which have been offered of its treatment of its most central issue: class relations and their impact on the possibility of socialist commitment. More recent interpretations have opened up a dimension of the text little commented on at the time of its publication: its implicit understanding of gender identities and roles. This focus on gender, together with a more theorised approach to signification via the concepts of voice and persona, has reinforced rather than resolved the division over meaning which *Wigan Pier* continues to provoke.

In Chapter 4 Joanna Price offers an account of the Vietnam Veterans Memorial in which the complex relations between the terms of this cultural history model may be seen especially clearly. Her chapter opens with an exploration of issues of production, considering the authorship of the Memorial in its cultural and historical context. Its origins in the private initiative of a Vietnam veteran, followed by its semi-adoption by the state through the provision of a site in a key location for national monuments, reveals the difficulty of finding any agreed version for the official commemoration of the Vietnam War in the face of the sharp divisions over its meaning. The character of the design chosen, and the subsequent debate over its suitability, trace this same conflict into the realm of signification. Price's analysis then turns to the reception of the Memorial. The immediate responses of the first visitors show it to be a site of pilgrimage whereby the Memorial has been appropriated for individual remembrance independent of any one specific stance towards the War. Price's chapter concludes with an analysis of subsequent cultural commentary over the meaning both of the Memorial itself, and of the uses to which it is being put. What is at stake in these debates, it would seem, is no longer the Memorial itself, nor the immediate responses to it, but the nature of the narratives into which both Memorial and responses are to be placed. Cultural histories of the Vietnam Veterans Memorial, then, may focus on the artefact itself, the relationship between the artefact and those who visit it, or the narratives that seek to attach it to wider claims about the development of American society since Vietnam.

Gerry Smyth's analysis of *Sgt. Pepper's Lonely Hearts Club Band* in Chapter 5 locates this enduringly popular record in terms of the model of historical production, textual signification and audience reception. The Beatles' *magnum opus* is revealed to be caught up in theoretical debates regarding the provenance and function of popular culture, the changes overtaking the category of 'youth' in postwar Britain, and wider institutional and aesthetic issues concerning the production and evaluation of pop music. The making of *Sgt. Pepper* in 1967 both signalled a new ambition for what popular music could achieve and formed an early moment in the oscillation between authenticity and irony which has become an enduring feature of the rock/pop musical genre then being consolidated. Through close analysis of a single song, set in the context of the pragmatics of recording and sequencing, Smyth explores the wider cultural meanings and the nature of the social impact that have been attributed to this landmark album.

1.2 Marxist Historiography and Cultural Theory

Marxists have taken an interest in the history and theorisation of culture primarily for political reasons. They have been concerned to establish the role of culture in political struggles and in particular the cultural roots of resistance and subordination among the subaltern classes; to explain the character and mechanisms of ideology; and to evaluate the effects of mass, commercial/commodified culture which has been such a major and distinctive feature of twentieth-century societies. The starting point for such analyses has traditionally been Marx's famous metaphor of base and superstructure.

> The sum total of [the] relations of production constitutes the economic structure of society, the real foundation, on which rises a legal and political superstructure, and to which correspond definite forms of social consciousness. The mode of production of material life conditions the social, political and intellectual life process in general. (Marx, 1859, p. 181)

Within this model/metaphor, culture has been seen as part of the superstructure, its character ultimately determined by the structure of the economic base of society. In the crudest versions of Marxist theory, the culture of a given society was seen merely as an automatic reflection of the prevailing political and economic system. Much Marxist theorising of culture in the later twentieth century has worked either to modify this model by loosening the ties supposed to bind base to superstructure, or – more recently and arguably more fruitfully – to challenge the very notion that culture is located in a separate superstructure (for a full discussion, see Rigby, 1998, pp. 175–298). While such modifications leave it doubtful how far Marx's original metaphor retains any value, they have arisen from the difficulties encountered, and the insights generated, during attempts to produce convincing analyses of specific instances of high or popular culture. Politically, the aim of such analyses has been to account for the unexpected (to Marxists) resilience of capitalist society, and the failure of revolutionary aspirations in advanced industrial societies; histor-ically, to explain how far and in what ways subaltern classes, numerically preponderant in any society, have been brought to accept their situation. Hence they have frequently focused on the relations between the resistant, rebellious or revolutionary, and the conserva-tive or conformist, aspects of popular and working-class culture (Dworkin, 1997, pp. 2, 141).

This section will trace one specific tradition within Marxism, that of the British Marxist historians and cultural theorists since 1945 (for the wider context of Marxist historiography, see Iggers, 1985, ch. 4; Iggers, 1997, ch. 7; Rigby, 1997, 1998). In dialogue with non-Marxist thinkers on the left they produced a pioneering body of writing in social and cultural history and literary studies, which worked across con-ventional disciplinary boundaries and in turn helped to create the new discipline of cultural studies. A survey of this tradition will show the impact of contemporary political and cultural changes on intellectual developments within this field, the conceptual and methodological innovations to which their inquiries gave rise, and the transformations within and exchanges between disciplines which resulted.

The origins of this tradition have been located partly in the work of the Communist Party Historians' Group (Dworkin, 1997, pp. 26–8; Gray, 1990, pp. 53–8; Goode, 1990; Schwarz, 1982). In their efforts to trace an indigenous British history of cultural and political radicalism (which could offer a historical lineage for the Marxist intellectual, and – until 1956 – Communist political traditions within which they worked), these historians drew connections between popular resistance to the advent of industrialisation, and the political and social critiques offered by the Romantic poets William Blake and William Morris. As Dennis Dworkin comments, 'when they examined historical forms of class struggle, they did so in terms that stressed consciousness, experience, ideas, and culture' (Dworkin, 1997, pp. 41–4; Higgins, 1999, p. 106). One of the striking characteristics of the Group was the extent of their interdisciplinary interests, embracing literature in particular; Edward Thompson, usually categorised as a historian, wrote his first and one of his last books on the literary figures of Morris and Blake (Thompson, 1955, 1993; Goode, 1990). This interest was to provide an important point of intersection with literary scholars.

The greatest impact on the discipline of history was made by Thompson with his *The Making of the English Working Class* (1963). Two related aspects of his work can be singled out. Firstly, he was one of the pioneers of the writing of 'history from below', a history that recognised the agency of subordinate social groups (cf. urban artisans in Rudé, 1959; peasants in Hobsbawm, 1959; cf. Sharpe, 1991). In Thompson's narrative the working class ceased to be an object of history, passively created from the labouring poor by the inexorable process of industrialisation; and became instead present at its own birth, an active agent with its own political and economic values (Eley, 1990, p. 15). In making this assertion, Thompson was engaged in combative debate with political enemies on both right and left. Rejecting what he saw as complacent models (whether conservative or Fabian socialist) in which social elites were the sole instigators and engineers of change, he was also reacting against the deformations of Stalinist Communism, with its mechanistic understanding of political change. At the same time, suggests Dworkin, he was also challenging some of the contemporary assumptions of both Labour revisionism and New Left rethinking of class (Dworkin, 1997, pp. 52–3, 96, 105–6; Sewell, 1990, pp. 52–4).

Secondly, Thompson's efforts to reconstruct that agency within a historical narrative led him to situate working-class political and economic struggles in the context of the values of their culture. 'The class experience is largely determined by the productive relations into which men are born – or enter involuntarily. Class-consciousness is the way these experiences are handled in cultural terms: embodied in traditions, value-systems, ideas and institutional forms' (Thompson, 1963, pp. 9–10). This culture had a history and was necessarily rooted in the relationships of daily living, in places of work, domesticity and leisure. The labouring poor and the urban artisans already had a political and associational culture formed by long resistance to agrarian capitalism, and struggles for political rights. These traditions had given them both institutions, and political and religious languages, with which to confront and struggle against increasingly rapid and radical social changes associated with industrialisation. Working-class history, which hitherto had largely meant the histories of labour institutions and leaders, Thompson now widened dramatically to embrace all those cultural elements through which groups of workers made sense of their experiences of class society and united in various ways to protect and advance their interests (cf. 1991, pp. 1–15).

A crucial contextual factor in shaping the work of the Marxist historians and cultural theorists was the attempt by a range of intellectuals, within the New Left which emerged after the events of 1956 (Khruschev's revelation of Stalin's crimes, the Soviet invasion of Hungary), to make sense of the changes in British society, and more broadly in postwar capitalism, that were starting to weaken the social and cultural solidarity of the 'traditional' working-class communities formed between 1880 and 1939 (Dworkin, 1997, pp. 3, 58, 62, 79, 99–101). Politically, these changes were registered in a crisis of the Labour Party in the late 1950s, as the apparent solidity of the working-class Labour vote began to crumble, and the prospect of any future electoral victory (let alone socialist advance) to recede. Culturally, what was apparent was a substantial intensification and acceleration of changes first clearly discernible in the interwar years: the growth of a youth culture, strongly influenced by American music and film, that rapidly became commodified; and the widening and deepening impact of the mass media. The attempt to understand the contemporary interrelationships of popular culture and oppositional politics led these historians and cultural theorists to an exploration of that same relationship in the past.

The interpretative approaches which developed in response to these changes reshaped the contemporary and historical study of culture. They originated within literary studies. In Britain, as Perry Anderson noted, the discipline of English, or literary studies, had since the nineteenth century taken on the role of offering an overview and critique of social and cultural developments which in other countries was more usually occupied by sociology or philosophy (Anderson, 1969; Mulhern, 1979; Baldick, 1983; Doyle, 1989). It was a non-Marxist literary scholar, Richard Hoggart, who brought this issue to the forefront of intellectual debate with his *The Uses of Literacy* (1957), which through close attention to the actions and stances of daily life powerfully evoked a picture of a distinctive working-class culture with deeply rooted values (Laing, 1986; Dworkin, 1997, pp. 83–5; see pp. 43–51 below).

If Hoggart's work opened the way for what would become cultural studies, it was Raymond Williams who through his retheorisation of culture and cultural production began to challenge the existing contours of English literary studies. Working at first independently of the Marxist historians, he was to provide an important link to their project. In *Culture and Society* (1958) he brought together, into what he termed the 'culture and society' tradition of cultural criticism, a series of literary figures stretching from Coleridge and Matthew Arnold to T.S. Eliot and F.R. Leavis. In doing so, he sought to recover that tradition from the conservative politics with which it had hitherto been to a significant extent associated (Dworkin, 1997, pp. 88–91). Two distinctive themes can be singled out in Hoggart's and Williams's work. Firstly, there was a redefinition of the term 'culture' in an inclusive anthropological, rather than an exclusive high-cultural, sense: culture comprised 'a whole way of life' (Williams, 1961; 1976, pp. 76–81; Dworkin, 1997, pp. 92–4). As a consequence, it became possible to study the complex values of working-class culture as it was actually lived. Secondly, the situating of particular elements of popular culture within this broader frame moved the emphasis of interpretation from isolated artefacts (or institutions or practices) to the meanings they generated in use.

While the historical mapping Williams had undertaken was recognised as significant, aspects of his interpretation of cultural debate and change were criticised by the Marxist historians. Thompson argued strongly that Williams's account was too eirenic, paid too little attention to class division; rather than a 'whole way of life', it was necessary to talk of a 'whole way of conflict' (Dworkin, 1997, pp. 101–3; Higgins, 1999, pp. 86–8). The development of Williams's thought over the next 20 years, John Higgins has suggested (1999, pp. 85–6, 172–3), can be seen as the outcome of a double struggle: with 'Cambridge English' (Williams's term for the dominant model of literary studies, the discipline in which he had been trained), and simultaneously with orthodox Marxist thinking about culture in general and literature in particular. At the same time, Williams was to absorb and integrate some of Thompson's criticism.

In the 1970s Williams began to engage more directly with classical and contemporary Marxist theorising, both absorbing some of its conceptualisations (especially Gramsci's model of hegemony; see pp. 49–50 below), and in turn critiquing it in the light of his own (Williams, 1977; Dworkin, 1997, pp. 150–2; Higgins, 1999; pp. 110, 113). In particular, he launched a thorough-going assault on the base/superstructure model (Williams, 1973). As Thompson had done in his analysis of the making of the working class (see above pp. 12–13), Williams argued that the economic base itself, the set of processes by which society maintained and reproduced itself, necessarily involved complex cultural relations, which were therefore not confined to the superstructure (Dworkin, 1997, p. 151; Higgins, 1999, pp. 112–13; Mukerji and Schudson, 1991, pp. 40–1). Cultural production (or the means and relations of communication) thus understood did not reside in some realm *separate from* the rest of society, whether it be from the material base (as in traditional Marxist theory), or from the market (as in liberal theory). Rather, he argued: '"Cultural practice" and "cultural production" ... are not simply derived from an otherwise constituted social order, but are themselves major elements in its constitution' (Williams, 1981, p. 160). In a related move, he developed a new approach to culture by taking the term *production* from its original Marxist application to the economy and applying it to intellectual or artistic work of all kinds, which he argued should also be seen as a form of production. 'We should look not for the components of a product, but for the conditions of a practice' (Williams, 1973, p. 16). Hence the focus should not be on cultural products as isolated artefacts, but rather on the practices of production (and relatedly signification and reception) through which they were constituted. At the same time, reworking his model of culture in the light of the concept of hegemony also meant a greater stress on the role of conflict, of the continuous struggle to maintain or challenge dominant meanings (Williams, 1984, p. 29; Dworkin, 1997, pp. 104, 152).

This way of thinking about cultural production in turn led Williams to two shifts in the terminology. He developed an extended notion of the concept of 'reading', applied now to social practices and social relations, as well as to artefacts; he practised this mode of reading himself most fully in his *The Country and the City* (1973). He also came to prefer the term 'writing' to 'literature'. Writing, as something anyone could do, fitted better with his more expansive and inclusive model of culture than did the narrower concept of literature. He traced (1977, pp. 45–54) the history whereby the meaning of the term 'literature' had been drastically narrowed to cover the limited portion even of imaginative writing that was admitted to the literary canon; the discipline of literary studies as currently constituted was complicit in this process of narrowing (Higgins, 1999, pp. 128–9).

Williams brought the ideas of culture and production together in the concept of 'cultural materialism', which he defined as 'the analysis of all forms of signification, including quite centrally writing, within the actual means and conditions of production' (Williams, 1984, p. 210; Dworkin, 1997, p. 150). In its embrace of all forms of writing (and indeed, all forms of signification), cultural materialism restated the rejection of the distinction between high and popular culture which Williams and Hoggart had developed in the late 1950s. A cultural materialist reading should *integrate* textual analysis with theoretical and historical modes of understanding, rather than privileging it as the then dominant paradigm in English demanded. As Higgins puts it:

> In this new paradigm of study, a text is read formally, in terms of the play of its generic and internal construction; it is located historically, both in terms of its means and conditions of original production, and also in relation to the history of its readings; and it is read theoretically, in terms of whatever questions can be productively put to it. (1999, p. 173; cf. pp. 134–5)

Williams's work contributed to the transformation of the discipline of literary studies from the mid-1970s following the rise of literary theory (though Higgins notes that some theorists borrowed Williams's term 'cultural materialism' while radically changing its content (1999, pp. 99, 137–8; 126, 171–2)). This self-questioning, self-deconstructing enterprise involved arguing for changes both in *what* texts could be read, a shift – summed up in the pun 'firing the canon' – that led to the inclusion of popular as well as high literature, of far more female, black and working-class writers, of a more diverse range of genres; and in *how* they could be read, shifting the focus onto readers rather than authors, onto collective discourses, onto reception by actual historical readers or reading communities (Showalter, 1978; Widdowson, 1982; Walder, 1990, pp. 9–41). The term 'text', covering any form of writing, increasingly displaced 'literature', which had been taken to designate a specific subset of writing alone worthy of study. These changes, as well as opening up links with some areas of philosophy, also brought literary studies closer to cultural studies (for example, in the study of popular fiction, or film). A new focus on the circulation and reception of texts of all kinds, and the ways they had been used to 'make meanings' in specific historical contexts, opened connections with the work of historians concerned to understand the generation of meanings in past societies.

This challenge to the validity of the high/popular distinction was sustained in a different way by research in both literary and cultural studies which demonstrated that what currently constituted high culture (often seen as timelessly valuable) had in fact been historically constructed, often by conscious efforts to demarcate specific areas within what had previously been more fluid fields of cultural practice (Mukerji and Schudson, 1991, pp. 16–17, 35–6; Levine, 1991; DiMaggio, 1991). Scholars traced the shifting contours of what had constituted the literary canon; while other research demonstrated the ways in which specific artefacts could shift location from high to popular culture or vice versa. This questioning of the previously taken-for-granted categories of literature (or serious music) compelled scholars to consider self-consciously their own, and their discipline's, roles in the processes of canon-(trans)formation (Mukerji and Schudson, 1991, pp. 52–3).

Tracing the intellectual trajectories of Thompson and Williams from the mid-1950s to the late 1970s reveals some interesting consonances. Each worked across the borders of his core discipline, in Williams's case to the point of ultimately rejecting the category of literature. Each emphasised that (in Williams's term) 'culture is ordinary', that creativity is evident in the daily lives and institutions (as well as writings) of those outside the political and literary elite. Each in the 1970s drew on Gramsci's theory of hegemony as a model for understanding the tension between determination (by economy, structures of power, language) and the available scope for action. Each at the end of the 1970s reacted (in Thompson's case violently) against the apparent dominance of Althusserian Marxist models which seemed to leave no scope for creative action, no place outside ideology (Thompson, 1978; Dworkin, 1997, pp. 211–15; Higgins, 1999, pp. 99, 113, 119–20, 131, 137–8).

In the wake of Thompson's pioneering book, and as part of the wider efflorescence of social history in the 1960s and '70s, there came a large body of work tracing the history of the British working class down to 1945 (Dworkin, 1997, pp. 182–3, 187–8; Sewell, 1990, pp. 50–1). In the course of this, both the substantive conclusions and the methodology of *Making of the English Working Class* have been challenged and modified. Firstly, it has become apparent that what Thompson described with memorable rhetorical power was only one, though a crucial, moment in the making of a class that has been continuously remade under the impact of successive waves of economic and technological change (Stedman Jones, 1974; Sewell, 1990, pp. 68–75). Secondly, Thompson had focused on a radical working-class tradition, which could be at least suggestively linked with the Romantic and anti-Utilitarian strands of bourgeois culture in the early nineteenth century, and from which connections could be drawn to later socialist and communist movements. Subsequently historians also began to explore other aspects of popular and working-class culture that are not assimilable into that lineage: defensive labourism, popular conservatism, anti-catholicism, anti-immigrant and racist outbursts (Gray, 1990, pp. 71–2). Thirdly, the rapid development of women's history since the early 1970s demonstrated the extent to which the world explored in *Making of the English Working Class* was predominantly a man's world; and that a fuller understanding of working-class culture, including its political and industrial dimensions, required equal attention to the specific position of women in that culture. This meant recognising not simply their place within the familiar contours of working-class history but also the complex and often opposed interests, in the workplace, within the family, and in the field of leisure, which might divide working-class women from men (Scott, 1988, pp. 68–90).

The theoretical concerns of the social and cultural historians of the 1960s and '70s had initially been focused on dialogue with Marxist conceptions of class, and on developments of social-scientific methodologies. This started to change from the later 1970s, as the rapid growth of critical and cultural theory in adjacent disciplines (especially those of literature and cultural studies) began to make a belated impact within history. The so-called linguistic turn in historical writing since the early 1980s can be understood as in part a determined effort to break completely with even revised Marxist models of culture, and to insist that there is *no* necessary or determinate relationship historically between social circumstances and political/cultural stance (Rogers, 2000, ch. 1). Rather, all such stances are mediated through language, which now came to be seen as the determining force; all social groups exist only as represented in discourse (see pp. 35–43 below). Gareth Stedman Jones's essay 'Rethinking Chartism' (1983, pp. 90–178) offered a powerful challenge to interpretations of the Chartist movement in terms of class, reading it instead as using a populist language of radicalism which deployed a 'vocabulary of political exclusion'. Patrick Joyce subsequently advanced a wider reinterpretation of nineteenth-century popular politics in which the language of radicalism displaced class consciousness as a crucial explanatory factor (Joyce, 1991). The new focus on language connects this shift in British historical writing with the concerns of *Annales*- and anthropology-influenced historiography (see pp. 20–7 below).

Again, the wider political context was relevant. The sequence of Conservative electoral victories from 1979 posed sharply the question Eric Hobsbawm had already formulated in 1978: 'The Forward March of Labour Halted?' (Hobsbawm, 1981); while the collapse of the regimes in the Soviet Union and Eastern Europe at the end of the 1980s signalled the end of the post-1917 Communist project. Together, these domestic and international developments called into question the viability of socialist (and even social-democratic) politics. A re-evaluation of the underlying premises of a generation of writing about working-class history and culture seemed necessary. Stedman Jones's *Languages of Class* included the essay 'Why is the Labour Party in a Mess?' (1983, pp. 239–56); whereas an earlier political generation had seen the emergence of a Labour Party as an important step in consolidating a working-class political identity, Biagini and Reid (1991, pp. 18–19), anticipating New Labour, argued for its return to the progressive liberal-radical tradition. This specifically British concern could be connected to the wider rejection of 'grand narratives' advanced by postmodernism. Such narratives, with their claims to certainty in discerning the teleological direction of history, were seen as having underpinned and rationalised historical atrocities: in the case of Marxism, Stalinism and the Gulag: in the case of what came to be termed 'the Enlightenment project', an imposition of (white Eurocentric) rationality implicated in racism and ecological catastrophe.

Criticisms have been made of this work. As historians have (belatedly) begun to engage with developments in literary studies and critical theory, they have had to recapitulate and assimilate key developments of the previous two decades explored above. Stedman Jones has been criticised for focusing on formal written texts and on a (rather literal) reading of words (Scott, 1988, pp. 53–67). More recently, historians – following Foucault's model (see pp. 27–32 below) – have tended to talk of discourses, seen as the product of specific historical and institutional practices. Attention has also shifted from static analyses of texts to the conflicts within them (the interaction of competing discourses, the tensions between different representational forms, and the spaces which these may create for different claims to be advanced); to the uses made by political actors of narrative modes and literary forms such as melodrama (Joyce, 1991, chs 9, 13; 1994, ch. 14); to performative elements of communication such as register; to situating the use of political language in the specific context of speaker, setting and occasion (Eley, 1990, pp. 26–35; Higgins, 1999, p. 94); and to the complexities of reception (see Chapters 2 and 3, below).

Furthermore it has been suggested that, in the polemical urging of a new approach, an inadequate and caricatured reading has been offered of the earlier extensive body of work in social history (Eley and Nield, 1997, pp. 68–70). As Sewell's (1990) critical re-reading of Thompson shows, the narrative of *Making of the English Working Class* clearly demonstrates the central role of what would now be termed the discourses of the radical political tradition in shaping artisan and worker responses to industrial and political change. Much of the social history written during the subsequent two decades can be seen to be shaped (as was Thompson's work) by a dialogue between, on the one hand formal Marxist-influenced models of class formation and class consciousness (whether explicitly invoked or not), and on the other an increasing awareness of the complex cultural resources on which working people drew in making sense of and responding to their circumstances.

One further change brought about by the impact of theory on historians may be noted: their growing recognition of the significance of their own rhetorical strategies in shaping the stories they tell. Influenced by Hayden White's analysis of literary tropes (see pp. 35–41), Renato Rosaldo has offered a valuable dissection of the ways in which Thompson's narrative structure tends to collapse the distance between past and present, historical subject and historian; and of the implications of his adoption of melodrama as the literary form within which to cast his account of *The Making of the English Working Class* (Rosaldo, 1990, pp. 110–20; cf. Cronon, 1992).

1.3 The *Annales* Historians, Anthropology and the New Cultural History

One of the most influential bodies of historical writing in the twentieth century has been that produced by the Annales group of historians (Burke, 1990; Green and Troup, 1999, ch. 4). (Their work is too diverse intellectually and methodologically for the term 'School', often applied to them, to be entirely satisfactory.) Their name derives from the journal *Annales: Economies, Sociétés, Civilisations*, founded in 1929 by Lucien Febvre and Marc Bloch, then teaching at the University of Strasbourg (original title – to 1946 – *Annales d'histoire économique et sociale*; current title – since 1994 – *Annales: Histoire, Sciences Sociales*). By commentators' conventional reckoning Annales historians have now reached their fourth intellectual generation. They raised the discipline of history to a prominent institutional and intellectual place within French academic life in the postwar period (Chartier, 1988, p. 2; Hunt, 1986); and have had an international impact on the practice of history, especially in America since the 1960s (Huppert, 1997, p. 73; for cultural history in Germany, see *New German Critique*, 1995; Iggers, 1997, pp. 113–16; Goodman, 1997, pp. 794–5). Their approach to the writing of history has been characterised by its ambition (to write *histoire totale*, total history); by the range of topics it has tackled, extending into every aspect of human life including many not previously thought to have a 'history'; and by its interdisciplinary methodologies (Huppert, 1997, p. 83; Iggers, 1985, ch. 2; Iggers, 1997, ch. 5). The engagement with a wide range of other disciplines began with the pioneering work of Febvre and Bloch, which made extensive use of both geography and anthropology (Burke, 1973; Huppert, 1997, p. 76). After 1945 this was joined by other disciplines, including economics and historical demography. While the postwar second generation of Annales historians had focused in particular on quantitatively based social history over the *longue durée* (lengthy periods, often of a century or more), the third generation in the 1960s and '70s took up anew and extensively developed one of Febvre's original interests – the history of *mentalités* (mentalities, belief systems) (Burke, 1997, ch. 11).

It was social historians of medieval and early modern Europe, both within and outside the Annales tradition, who were most active in borrowing from anthropology, a discipline that seemed to offer them pertinent concepts and methodologies. Anthropologists too studied societies that were predominantly preliterate, with cultures containing a strong performative element. At the same time, their disciplinary formation stressed the conscious effort required of anthropologists to see those societies as other, and to reconstruct their distinctive codes, rather than simply interpret them through the assumptions of their own culture (Medick, 1987, p. 84; Mukerji and Schudson, 1991, pp. 11–12, 20). This engagement with anthropology assisted two significant and related shifts, one of focus, the other of method. In terms of focus, these historians were particularly concerned with what had hitherto largely been ignored in medieval and early-modern historiography, the cultural activity of non-elite social groups (such as peasants and urban artisans). However, since such groups rarely left any written accounts of their own actions or purposes, it was necessary to develop new methods of reading popular practices via the records of them produced by literate elites (Mukerji and Schudson, 1991, p. 8). One approach, developed by some third-generation Annales historians, adapted the quantitative methods so successful in economic and social history. By assembling statistics of quantifiable information about popular practices preserved in series of bureaucratic documents (for example, about religious invocations in wills), it was possible to trace changes over time in popular devotional practice and hence at least to hypothesise about popular religious attitudes (Mukerji and Schudson, 1991, pp. 8–9; Huppert, 1997, pp. 80–1). Darnton (1984, p. 258) later criticised this approach for its false homogenisation into uniform series of what were in fact cultural objects imbued with (potentially differentiated) meaning, which 'need to be read, not counted' (cf. Chartier, 1988, pp. 95–6, 101–2; Levi, 1991, pp. 97–8).

A different, qualitative, approach – and the one advocated by Darnton (1984, p. 259) as necessary to link social and cultural history – was to borrow and deploy anthropological concepts and models

(Green and Troup, 1999, ch. 7). In the early 1970s, as Lynn Hunt (1989, p. 11) notes, historians such as Natalie Zemon Davis drew on the work of a diverse range of anthropologists to examine the role of ritual in social life, whether in routine events (annual carnivals) or extraordinary ones (riots). Davis, and other historians such as Edward Thompson, focused in particular on developing readings of protest actions that would reveal the agency and intentions of those who took part in them, even when their politics could be expressed only symbolically (Thompson, 1971; 1972; Davis, 1975; Desan, 1989; Rosaldo, 1990).

More recently, however, the work of the American Clifford Geertz has tended to become the dominant reference point for historians engaging with anthropology – to the extent of obscuring the degree of conceptual and methodological debate within that discipline (Hunt, 1989, pp. 12–13; Biersack, 1989; Goodman, 1997, pp. 788–9). Geertz pressed strongly the 'text analogy' for reading the meanings of social actions; the 'thick description' of key events which he advocated anthropologists should produce 'examines public behaviour for what it *says* rather than what it does. It 'reads' the symbolic content of action, interprets it as sign' (Biersack, 1989, pp. 74–5). In his famous essay 'Deep Play: Notes on the Balinese Cockfight', Geertz offered a dense and sophisticated interpretation of the cockfight and the gambling surrounding it, on the Indonesian island of Bali, as a dramatisation of status alignments, tensions and psychological predispositions among male Balinese. By provocatively comparing participation in such a fight to seeing a Shakespeare play or reading a Dickens novel, he cut across the high/popular culture divide; these brief and bloody avian battles equally had the capacity to symbolise, and thereby render knowable, deep-rooted structures and conflicts within social identity (Geertz, 1975; Mukerji and Schudson, 1991, pp. 20–2).

While often admiring of the rich descriptions Geertz produced, critics have pointed out important limitations to his approach, in particular its collapse of history, politics and social conflict into aesthetics. His account of the cockfight presented a rather timeless picture, removed from any evident connection with specific social conflict or change. He read it as symbolic of Balinese identity *tout court*, while his own account made it very clear that the key actors were men of standing within the village; more marginal men, and all women, were excluded from participation (Geertz, 1975, p. 435). Moreover, his own text noted the repression of the cockfight by both Dutch colonial and Indonesian state authorities, suggesting but not exploring its implication in political processes (Biersack, 1989, p. 80). Rather than maintaining the tension between cause and meaning, the social and the textual, Geertz has collapsed the former into the latter.

The elucidating of meaning has become an end in itself, at the cost of exploring whose meanings these are, and in what context of power they are asserted and maintained (Levi, 1991, p. 105). Biersack, quoting back at him Geertz's own assertion that 'man is an animal suspended in webs of significance he himself has spun', suggests that the focus of his attention in this analogy has fallen entirely on the text, not on the process of textualising (Biersack, 1989, p. 80; cf. Spiegel, 1997, pp. 185–7).

A striking example of anthropologically influenced cultural history addressing an incident of symbolic protest, directly influenced by Geertz but sensitive to some of the criticisms of his approach, is to be found in an essay by Darnton. His studies of eighteenth-century French cultural history (his translation of the Annales term *histoire des mentalités*) lay great emphasis on broadening the focus of inquiry away from elite to popular culture. He rejects 'the high road of intellectual history' in favour of a 'history in the ethnographic grain', which 'treats our own civilisation in the same way that anthropologists study alien cultures' (Darnton, 1984, p. 3). In 'The Great Cat Massacre of the Rue Saint-Séverin', Darnton (1984, pp. 75–104) examines an incident in a Parisian printing shop in the late 1730s, when the apprentices and journeymen tricked the master of the shop and his wife into allowing them to round up and kill the local cats, including several domestic pets. This 'massacre' was decked out in ritual, the cats hanged in the workshop after being subjected to a mock trial. Subsequently, the massacre was often theatrically re-enacted by the workers for their own uproarious entertainment. In seeking to make sense of this, at first sight bizarre, incident Darnton first sets it in the context of tense relations between journeymen printers and masters in mid-eighteenth-century France. Journeymen felt their traditional prospects, of rising to become masters in their own right, blighted by a limit on the number of masters; while their conditions were threatened from below by increasing use of unqualified printers. In this particular shop, the apprentices, as well as seeing fewer opportunities ahead of them once they became journeymen, were poorly treated as regards food and housing – worse, in fact, than the cats who were the master's and especially the mistress's pets. Darnton then explores the general rituals of charivari and carnival, the journeymen's own trade rites involving mock trial, and the folklore surrounding cats and their relationship to the Devil in early-modern France, for clues to decipher the ritual slaughter enacted. He suggests that the massacre can be read as a coded means of expressing violence, against the master (who is symbolically murdered) and the mistress (who is symbolically raped). This sick joke, Darnton suggests, is worth interpreting 'because it can help one to see how the workers made their experience meaningful by playing with themes of their culture'.

(Chartier (1988, p. 109) in his review of Darnton, accepts the interpretation of the incident as an example of the workers' anger at their
ill-treatment, while querying 'the full repertory of diabolical and
carnival motifs' that Darnton suggests.)

This qualitative approach to interpreting the ritual dimension of
public events has frequently invoked the notion of 'reading' which is
implicit in the text analogy. However, one crucial difference between
the historian's and the anthropologist's task is that while the latter has
direct access to the event studied (Geertz had to flee a cockfight when
the police raided it), the former can approach such events only via the
intermediary of those texts (what historians traditionally term
'sources') that recorded them. Since such texts are usually (though
not always) written from an elite perspective, they too require an interpretative process of 'reading' before the actions they describe can be
reconstituted in a way which might allow access to the actors' perspectives (Chartier, 1988, pp. 105–7; LaCapra, 1988, pp. 98–100;
Spiegel, 1997, p. 196). Hence, in addition to making interdisciplinary
borrowings from the methodology of anthropology, historians have
been compelled also to refine their own traditional disciplinary skill in
the critical reading of documents (Hunt, 1989, p. 14). In particular,
they have had to become more sensitive to the literary and linguistic
structuring, the conventions and tropes, of even repetitive bureaucratic documents (LaCapra, 1985, pp. 62–3; 1988, p. 102; Medick,
1987, pp. 92–3; Hunt, 1989, pp. 19–20; Laqueur, 1989).

This effort to read source texts more critically has in turn involved
an effort to situate their authors and first readers more precisely.
Mukerji and Schudson (1991, pp. 9–10) point out that this led some
historians to intensive investigation of literacy in early-modern
Europe, its extent and its cognitive effects. Davis in particular
explored the complexities of what was meant by literacy: to be able to
read did not necessarily imply having access to literate culture, while
texts of literate culture could circulate among those who were illiterate
by being read aloud. She also began to analyse reading as an active
process, of translating the texts read, of cutting, editing and adapting
them for the readers' own particular purposes. As Mukerji and
Schudson comment, this approach links some Annales and related
historiography with slightly later developments in literary theory, so
that substantive historical investigation intersects with, and questions
or is questioned by, wider methodological assumptions. Carlo
Ginzburg, in *The Cheese and the Worms* (1980), used Inquisition
records to explore the ways in which a literate Italian miller of the
sixteenth century, Menocchio, read the Bible and various theological
texts through inherited patterns of oral culture, producing via the
'explosive mixture' of these two codes a cosmogony far removed from
orthodox Christianity. Tony Bennett (1983, pp. 214–18) subsequently

used Ginzburg's analysis of Menocchio's reading practices to support his own retheorising of the relationship between reader and text; while Dominick LaCapra (1985, pp. 45–69) questioned the adequacy of some aspects of Ginzburg's understanding of Menocchio's ways of reading, as well as his own reading practice as a historian.

This approach has been further inflected, in response to the work of, among other theorists, Michel Foucault (see pp. 27–32 below), Norbert Elias and Pierre Bourdieu, by Chartier. In *Cultural History: Between Practices and Representations*, he offered a statement of his own approach to cultural history, as developed in response to dissatisfactions with the earlier Annales-influenced historiography of the 1960s and '70s (1988, pp. 1–2). Chartier's aim was to uncover how, in specific times and places, people conceived of their social reality and interpreted it to others, appropriating and making varied use of the available 'intellectual motifs or cultural forms' (1988, pp. 4, 102). The approach he formulated was one that reflected the debates around the work of Geertz and others in its awareness of the ways in which representations are shaped by power, conflict and division; they are 'always captive within a context of rivalries and competition' in which 'power and domination' are at stake (1988, p. 5; cf. pp. 102–4). In similar vein, Hunt too has emphasised the importance for cultural historians of seeing communities as differentiated or divided, and ritual as able to transform as well as consolidate community identity (1989, pp. 11–12). Such a cultural history, Chartier urged (1988, pp. 11–13), required investigation of the ways in which meanings had been historically produced by specific social groups. A study of 'appropriation', he argued, 'really concerns a social history of the various interpretations, brought back to their fundamental determinants (which are social, institutional and cultural), and lodged in the specific practices that produce them'.

Several of the themes just outlined – the focus on popular rather than elite culture, the use of both qualitative and quantitative methods, the effort to reconstruct the historical actor's perspective – are well sketched in another of Darnton's essays (1991) that gives an overview of his studies of eighteenth-century reading. He did not confine his attention to elite readers, or to the reading of canonical texts. Rather, he sought to establish – using such sources as publishers' and library catalogues, and wills – *who* read *what*. He also examined *where* reading took place: often not in privacy at home, but in libraries, or communally in workplace groups or reading clubs (1991, pp. 142–51). What proved hardest to uncover is *what meanings* those readers derived from their texts; only a limited quantity of sources survive (letters, life-writings) that narrate an individual's reading, and only rarely do these record that reader's interpretation of what he or she read (1991, pp. 140–2). What the historian can do, however, Darnton suggests, is to seek to reconstruct the horizon of expectations of such historical readers, drawing on empirical research (such as an examination of how people learned to read, and of the ideals and assumptions underlying the practice of reading), informed by current theoretical debate (such as reader-response theory) on how texts seek rhetorically to construct and guide their readers (1991, pp. 152–5).

The transition from social to cultural history, and the accompanying shifts in subject-matter and method, are responses not only to the internal developments of history as a discipline, but also to wider political and intellectual trends. The work of the historians considered above has been concerned, where possible, to reconstruct and depict vividly the complex agency of individuals outside the social elites of medieval and early-modern society, and their capacity to win a degree of freedom within powerful religious or political systems. As several commentators have suggested, the widespread choice to research these periods, the focus of the best-known and most influential of such anthropologically influenced works, may have rested in part on a wish to challenge the empirical and evaluative limitations of what an earlier generation of social scientists and historians had taken to be the central story of modern economic and social history, that of industrialisation and modernisation (Medick, 1987, pp. 82–3; Iggers, 1997, pp. 63–4, 97–9).

Thus on the one hand, anthropology gave warrant for a concern with issues (such as women's history, and the history of the family) that in the 1950s and '60s were commonly seen as marginal to that story; in Davis's terms, liberation from the disciplinary metanarrative of what was important (Goodman, 1997, p. 786). In fact, subsequent research was to show that the sexual division of labour, the structure of the household and patterns of family formation were all crucial to a full understanding of this transition (Levi, 1991, pp. 95–8). On the other hand, anthropologically influenced interpretations opened the possibility of re-evaluating dominant postwar narratives of progress, whether these were drawn from liberal or conservative theorists of 'modernisation' (who largely discounted the costs of transition to a capitalist mode of production) or from Marxists (who, though emphasising those costs, still regarded that transition as essential for the development of a more fully human society). This body of work, notes Medick (1987, p. 82, citing Davis), has called into question unilinear schemes of the transition to modernity in which markets replaced custom and history myth. It has led to a greater awareness of losses associated with modernisation and indeed destabilised simple notions of loss and gain (though both Medick (1987, p. 83) and Iggers (1997, pp. 112–13), in relation to Annales historiography and microhistory, note the dangers of romanticisation in this negative evaluation).

This emphasis among Annales historians was paralleled by the emergence in the 1970s and '80s of what came to be termed 'micro-history' in Italy (Iggers, 1997, pp. 107–13). Its practitioners had also been affected by the crisis in Marxist politics and theory (which had a strong political and cultural presence in Italy), as well as more broadly in the so-called 'grand narratives' of progress (Levi, 1991, pp. 93–4). The intention of microhistory, Giovanni Levi has claimed (1991, pp. 95–7), was to narrow the historian's analytical focus onto a tightly defined aspect of the past – perhaps a single document or individual (Ginzburg, 1980), or a key event (cf. Le Roy Ladurie, 1981) – so as to investigate it in greater depth. Microhistorians used an action/conflict model in order to understand how great was the margin of freedom available to people within dominant normative systems and the ways in which they struggled and negotiated over definitions of meaning (Levi, 1991, pp. 94–5; cf. Medick, 1987, p. 91). As with many of those who engaged critically with Geertz, they emphasised that public symbols were differentiated between different social groups; their concern was with 'defining the ambiguities of the symbolic world, the plurality of possible interpretations of it and the struggle which takes place over symbolic as much as over material resources' (Levi, 1991, pp. 95, 103–5).

These concerns have also led such historians to question the way in which terms such as 'industrialisation', understood in purely economic terms, could become reifications, obscuring the question of human agency. It is here that work on pre-industrial societies connects with that discussed on the world of industrialisation (pp. 12–13 above).

1.4 Foucault and New Historicism

The work of the French philosopher/historian Michel Foucault has had an important influence on modern ways of thinking about history and historiography. The awkward designation – 'philosopher/ historian' – is indicative, however, of many of the problems that Foucault presents. Much of the commentary on this imposing intel-lectual figure specifically addresses the issue of situating his work in terms of established disciplines: was he a philosopher interested in history, or an historian concerned with philosophy? This is less of an issue in France, where boundaries between disciplines are not so stringently observed and where intellectuals tend to assume a different socio-political role to their Anglo-American counterparts (O'Farrell, 1989; Merquior, 1991, pp. 11–13). Foucault certainly undertook research that was 'historical' in nature, albeit in areas relatively uncharted within the Western academy. Besides writing histories of medicine, madness and the penal system, he was at the time of his death embarked on a major (some have said impossibly ambitious) project to research a history of human sexuality. At the same time, Foucault was careful always to distance himself from the characteristic methodologies of 'traditional history', claiming at one point that he was interested in the past only in so far as it enabled him to write 'the history of the present' (1977a, p. 31). His troubled relationship with the established discipline is reflected by the fact that Foucault's influence tends to be in areas addressed to broader issues of method and the philosophy of history, rather than in actual empirical debates concerning the subjects about which he wrote.

Foucault researched in many areas, and changed methodological emphasis frequently during his career. A number of concerns remained constant, however, one of which was his ambition to track the rise of 'reason' in Western history. This involved identifying the ways in which human experience has been ordered and classified throughout history, and how these processes continue to impinge on life in the late twentieth century. Like Friedrich Nietzsche, the philosopher to whom his work is most indebted, Foucault was concerned to discover how the idea of the human subject had evolved, and in what ways that subject could know itself and, more importantly, differentiate itself from others. The modern Western subject, he suggested, is not a self-conscious, immutable, centred being possessed of certain qualities and emotions that remain constant over time and space; it is, rather, the result of very particular, and relatively recent, changes in the ways knowledge and power function within society.

In his *The Order of Things* Foucault speculated that Western history was made up of a series of distinct 'epistemes'. An episteme denotes the historical conditions that, 'in a given period, [delimit] in the totality of experience a field of knowledge, [define] the mode of being of the objects that appear in that field, [provide] man's everyday perception with theoretical powers, and [define] the conditions in which he can sustain a discourse about things that is recognized to be true' (1970, p. xxii). Foucault adapted the term 'archaeology' to describe the method whereby these different epistemes could be researched and identified. Each historical episteme, moreover, gives rise to a particular 'politics of truth', a system for organising the ways in which knowledge functions and circulates in society. Such systems are fundamentally linked to power, and this is because knowledge – and more specifically control of what *counts* as knowledge – sets the limit on how subjects can locate themselves in relation to other subjects and to society as a whole. Even those who claim to oppose certain systems of knowledge (and the uses of power to which they give rise) are obliged to traffic in the particular 'politics of truth' of a given episteme. Thus, Marx obviously objected to certain aspects of the Enlightenment and the capitalist politics of truth to which it had given rise, yet he could only imagine that objection in terms of a transcendental subject – the proletariat – progressing through history towards its class destiny. The idea of history advancing in this fashion according to some over-arching idea or human-centred narrative was anathema to Foucault, and part of his project at this time was 'to define a method of historical analysis freed from the anthropological theme' (1972, p. 16).

According to Foucault, identifying and accounting for the changes that have overtaken the human subject should be the historian's real task. As two sympathetic commentators put it: 'He sees the job of the intellectual as one of identifying the specific forms and specific inter-relationships which truth and power have taken in our history' (Dreyfus and Rabinow, 1986, p. 116). This was a task, however, for which the traditional discipline of history was hopelessly unequipped. Invented in the early nineteenth century, institutional history was itself a reflex of particular changes in human understanding that took place during the eighteenth century. Founded on the Enlightenment principles of order, reason and progress, and with the human subject placed firmly at the centre of history, its early practitioners felt that knowledge of the past should be ordered along the same rational, anthropocentric lines as every other field of knowledge (Marwick, 1989, pp. 38–71). And because it was itself so informed by notions of order, reason and progress, professional history was incapable of his-toricising the evolution of these values, or of the modern human subject who constituted the discipline's central concern. History claimed to be *the* pre-eminent humanistic discipline, utilising techniques both from art (for example, the technique of explanation by narrative – that is, telling stories) and science (for example, explaining past occurrences according to certain laws) (Atkinson, 1978). Far from representing history's 'natural' fusion of the aesthetic and the scientific, however, this was an example of the discipline's opportunism and bad faith, its inability to account for its own historical constitution, methods or subject-matter.

Historicism in itself was not a problem for Foucault. In fact, the trouble with the traditional discipline of history as it had been inherited from the nineteenth century was that it was not historicist enough. Unlike traditional historians and philosophers, Foucault does not address variations on the 'great' questions accruing from Enlightenment reason: ethico-political questions such as 'What should I do?'; epistemological questions such as 'What can I know?'; or libidinal-aesthetic questions such as 'What do I want?' Such questions all seem to operate on the very *un*historical assumption of a transcendent subject, an 'I' who remains constant over time with regard to these issues of ethics, knowledge and desire. Foucault, on the other hand, wishes to study the regimes of truth under which such issues have been legitimately engaged. Thus a different set of questions is posed: How do I become a subject with the ability to choose *this* rather than *that*? How do I become a subject with the ability to identify and differentiate between different kinds of knowledge? How do I become a subject who desires and receives pleasure from a range of different practices? As Foucault himself puts it: 'This is my question: at what price can subjects speak the truth about themselves?' (quoted in Merquior, 1991, p. 17).

To answer these questions Foucault moved on from 'archaeology' to what he termed 'genealogy', a term derived from the writing of Nietzsche (1956). In Foucault's adaptation, genealogy

> opposes itself to the search for origins ... if the genealogist refuses to extend his faith in metaphysics, if he listens to history, he finds that there is 'something altogether different' behind things: not a timeless and essential secret, but the secret that they have no essence or that their essence was fabricated in a piecemeal fashion from alien forms. (1984, pp. 77–8)

Genealogy gives rise to what Foucault calls 'effective' history, about which he has this to say:

> Nothing in man – not even his body – is sufficiently stable to serve as the basis for self-recognition or for understanding other men. The traditional devices for constructing a comprehensive view of history and for retracing the past as a patient and continuous development must be systematically dismantled. Necessarily, we must dismiss those tendencies that encourage the consoling play of recognitions ... History becomes 'effective' to the degree that it introduces discontinuity into our very being – as it divides our emotions, dramatizes our instincts, multiplies our body and sets it against itself. 'Effective' history deprives the self of the reassuring stability of life and nature, and it will not permit itself to be transported by a voiceless obstinacy toward a millennial ending. It will uproot its traditional foundations and relentlessly disrupt its pretended continuity. (1984, pp. 87–8)

Foucault's 'effective' history draws on Nietzsche's critique of historicism in so far as both take as their target that strand of Enlightenment thinking which supports the notion of a rational, transcendent human subject located both at the beginning and the end of history, and by virtue of whom history has both meaning and direction. In place of the 'consoling play of recognitions' traditionally sought by both dominant and oppositional ideologies (for example, capitalism and Marxism) as part of their bid for power, Foucault offers discontinuity, division, drama, disruption and conflict. And against an understanding of 'history given as continuity or representative of a tradition' – even a marginalised or oppositional tradition – effective history gives rise to 'countermemory', that is, a kind of memory not mortgaged to the search for truth or knowledge but which aims to effect 'a transformation of history into a totally different form of time' (1984, p. 93).

In terms of its general anti-humanist ethos, subject-matter and distinctive methodologies, Foucault's work has impacted on a wide range of intellectual and institutional practices. Perhaps the first major initiative to engage with his thought was Edward Said's groundbreaking work on what he termed 'Orientalism' – the representation of the East by the West (1985). Said's study was typically Foucauldian in its interdisciplinary approach to the history of East–West relations and in its emphasis on 'discourse' – the key methodological figure of Foucault's later career. Many also acknowledge Said's book as the basis for the highly successful field of postcolonial theory which impacted so strongly on humanistic scholarship across the planet towards the end of the millennium. Despite Said's subsequent unease with many of the implications of Foucault's work (1986) (and the concomitant rise of deconstruction and psychoanalysis as the primary methodological motors of postcolonial theory), the field may be said to have been initially 'enabled' by Foucault's model of discourse as a specific historical configuration of power/knowledge.

The unease with Foucault's work felt by a generally sympathetic figure such as Said points to the ambivalence with which that work has been greeted across the spectrum of political and intellectual thought. For many, Foucault is the arch anti-humanist and irrationalist, postulating a ubiquitous system of power/knowledge which is then made to serve as a foil for constant yet doomed resistance (Eagleton, 1990, pp. 384–97). He is also dubbed a 'neo-conservative' who, while insisting that the power which ensues from humanistic knowledge and its 'consoling play of recognitions' should be resisted, was infamously reluctant to offer any form of counter-knowledge around which resistance could mobilise (Habermas, 1987). Many now feel that the Enlightenment (which for Foucault, as for so many postwar French intellectuals, constitutes the root of all contemporary misfortunes) should not be dismissed so easily; for its single most important characteristic – rational critique – provides the best available means to comprehend power and resistance during the modern era.

At the same time, Foucault has been widely criticised by the practitioners of the 'traditional' disciplines he looked to fuse. As many historians have pointed out, his research is frequently erroneous and always tendentious – as one critic says, 'just tall orders largely unsupported by the facts' (Merquior, 1991, p. 144). There appears to be an inconsistency in Foucault's method whereby, implicitly refusing the legitimacy of 'facts', he nevertheless has constant recourse to them – in the shape of primary and secondary sources – to support his various theses. Meanwhile, the inheritors of the analytical tradition in philosophy – instigated by Wittgenstein and Russell, and arguably the greatest development in twentieth-century thought – scoff at the supposed 'radical' scepticism of modern French philosophy. Many resent the dogmatism, bad faith and ahistoricism of late twentieth-century philosophical scepticism, the convenience with which it forgets a 2500-year-old tradition, and the arrogance with which Foucault in particular was wont to browbeat 'traditional' scholars and intellectuals.

Although there is no school dedicated to carrying on Foucault's work, the adjective 'Foucauldian' is widely used with reference to certain applications and adaptations of his thought. However, since the early 1980s there has been one critical practice, American in origin and especially concerned with the field of early modern literature, that has been particularly associated with Foucault: the practice called 'new historicism'.

The term 'new historicism' was coined in 1982 by the literary critic Stephen Greenblatt, and he has gone on to become its foremost advocate and practitioner. New historicism connotes a way of thinking about the relations between texts and contexts; which is to say, it combines formalist (text) and historicist (context) methodologies. Like every other field of modern critical enquiry, that is, new historicism engages with the classic methodological binary (text/context) which has set the limits on scholarly endeavour since the Enlightenment. The challenge of new historicism, however, lies in its refusal to prioritise either element of the binary – its refusal, in fact, to differentiate between the received categories of 'text' and 'context'. Time and again in his writing, Greenblatt points out that the text/context binary is in itself historically contingent, and that what modern critics or historians might consider to be a text or a context – as well as the systems of knowledge used to differentiate between these categories – is in fact the result of historical changes in which the modern critic and/or historian is still caught up. There is no 'natural' or logical reason, he argues, for analysing the 'literary text' of a Shakespeare play in terms of its relation to the 'context' of Elizabethan-Jacobean England; the notion of 'literary text' is in fact an ideal invented at a much later time and would have been irrelevant

to Shakespeare or to his audience, whereas the notion of 'context' has
no material reality beyond its representation in various contemporary
textual traces (1980, pp. 1–9; 1988, pp. 1–20; 1990, pp. 1–15).

In a key essay entitled 'Towards a Poetics of Culture' (1990,
pp. 146–60) (this being his preferred designation), Greenblatt tried
to describe the theoretical and critical genealogy of new historicism.
He locates it somewhere between the two dominant critical paradigms
of the late twentieth century: poststructuralism and Marxism
(represented in his essay respectively by the French cultural analyst
Jean-François Lyotard and the American aesthetic theorist Fredric
Jameson). Both poststructuralism and Marxism oppose capitalism;
because each construes capitalism in a different way, however, each
also offers a different diagnosis of the relations between cultural texts
and historical contexts. Greenblatt argues that Jameson wishes to
destroy the notion (fostered under capitalism) 'of a separate artistic
sphere and to celebrate the materialist integration of all discourses';
whereas Lyotard seeks 'to celebrate the differentiation of all discourses
and to expose the fallaciousness of monological unity' (1990, p. 150).
For Marxism, in other words, capitalism fosters difference (between
discursive fields) where there should in fact be unity; while for poststructuralism, capitalism fosters unity where there should in fact be
difference.

The problem, Greenblatt argues, is that neither of these critical
practices has 'come to terms with the apparently contradictory
historical effects of capitalism' (1990, p. 151). He understands
capitalism as a discourse characterised by its ability to operate flexibly
along a continuum between complete unity and complete difference,
depending on the disposition of the relevant economic and cultural
factors. 'Capitalism', writes Greenblatt, 'has characteristically
generated neither regimes in which all discourses are co-ordinated,
nor regimes in which they seem radically isolated or discontinuous,
but regimes in which the drive towards differentiation and the drive
towards monological organization operate simultaneously, or at least
oscillate so rapidly as to create the impression of simultaneity' (1990,
p. 151). Cultural texts, he then goes on to suggest, are caught up in
these rapid oscillations between different spheres and different
systems of valuation, so much so that it becomes entirely inappropri-
ate to address the cultural text in terms of any pre-formulated theory
or set of assumptions. The text is not a stable vessel containing *a*
meaning which the critic must recover; it is neither the (Marxist)
repository of hidden or unconscious subversion nor the (poststructuralist) exemplification of anti-monological playfulness. Rather, the
text is a dynamic entity capable of producing and sustaining a range
of meanings, depending on the current capitalist disposition. And this

dynamic and radically unstable entity is the 'text' to which new historicism addresses itself.

Discovering that traditional literary history did not possess a critical language to describe the ways in which cultural texts move between different discursive regimes, Greenblatt was obliged to invent one. The typical new historicist essay is peppered with terms such as 'manipulation', 'circulation', 'currency', 'energy', 'negotiation' and 'exchange' – terms deliberately chosen to communicate both the contingency of historical meaning and the underpinning of cultural practices by capitalism since the early modern period. Changing the language of literary history puts pressure on the discipline itself and new historicism has been responsible for the opening up of the discourse to traditionally uncountenanced forms and practices. Two frequently remarked innovations are the use of the anecdote as inter-pretative key, and the critic's invocation of autobiographical material. But perhaps the terms which best convey the specificities of new historicism are those described by Greenblatt in his essay 'Resonance and Wonder' (1990, pp. 161–83):

> By resonance I mean the power of the object displayed to reach out beyond its formal boundaries to a larger world, to evoke in the viewer the complex, dynamic cultural forces from which it has emerged and for which as metaphor it may be taken by a viewer to stand. By wonder I mean the power of the object displayed to stop the viewer in his tracks, to convey an arresting sense of uniqueness, to evoke an exalted attention. (1990, p. 170)

Here, in a nutshell, the concerns of new historicism are adumbrated: power and pleasure.

Because of its intellectual debt to Foucault, new historicism has attracted criticisms similar to those directed at his work. Other approaches which have invested heavily in either formalism or historicism attack new historicism's refusal of the text/context binary. Marxists, especially, discern little resonance and less wonder in a critical practice they characterise as politically quietist, if not reactionary. Critics such as Terry Eagleton and Frank Lentricchia claim that, for all its interest in those who have been condemned to the margins of history, new historicism communicates a profound scepticism towards the possibility of intended, organised, effective resistance to power – what Eagleton calls its 'feckless sub-Nietzschean defeatism' (1991). Dissent is always anticipated, 'a prearranged theater of struggle set upon the substratum of a monolithic agency which produces "opposition" as one of its delusive political effects' (Lentricchia, 1989, p. 235). From a poststructuralist point of view, on the other hand, new historicism's claim to short-circuit the traditional text/context binary seems naive in the extreme, and it remains (like Foucault's work) caught up within the systems and traditions it ostensibly opposes. In fact, 'it would seem [that] the new historicists are both too historical and not historical enough; they are too formalist and nor formalist enough, depending on which variety of historical theory or of literary theory is taken as the basis for criticizing them' (White, 1989, p. 296). Nevertheless, the richness and ingenuity of the interpretations produced by Greenblatt and other new historicist critics go some way towards accounting for its attraction as an intellectual exercise and its success as an institutional practice.

1.5 Poststructuralism and Postmodernism

Poststructuralism and postmodernism are related though distinct 'movements' in the humanities and social sciences which emerged in the last four decades of the twentieth century. Taken together for the purposes of this section, they represent an assault upon traditional humanistic paradigms of knowledge, and in particular upon what they take to be the epistemological indefensibility of the West's great traditional 'master narratives'. Denis Cosgrove and Mona Domosh put it like this: 'Postmodern deconstruction of the idea of a progressive historiography of scientific knowledge produces a relativism which rejects all forms of totalizing discourse and denies any possibility of constructing a meta-language for intellectual communication' (1993, p. 28). Which is to say, poststructuralists and postmodernists argue that the stories traditionally told about how humans live in the world are clearly arbitrary, relative and self-contradictory and are as a consequence incapable of serving as the basis for a coherent politics, culture or ethics. In other words, history in all its forms – global or local, conservative or progressive – *is* bunk, mere stories with greater or lesser rhetorical force contained in texts which are as deconstructable as any other human artefact. As might be expected, such arguments have generated great debate, not only about their initial methodological rectitude but about their subsequent political and cultural implications.

The figure most closely associated with the emergence of post-structuralism as an intellectual-institutional force is the French philosopher Jacques Derrida. There is no space here for an engagement with Derrida's vast and complex *oeuvre* but because he remains such an important figure in contemporary intellectual debate (including history) it is worthwhile outlining what he is generally perceived to represent. The structuralism against which Derrida and other (mostly French) intellectuals found themselves reacting during the 1960s represented an influential method for understanding how texts created and communicated meaning. Now, besides other things, structuralism was often held to be essentially ahistorical. This was because it focused critical attention not on how meanings emerged and altered over time, but on the structure of meanings as generated in particular textual instances. *Post*structuralism did not represent so much a return to history, however, as a means of demonstrating that all meanings (including the ones identified by structuralist analysis) function in terms of binary oppositions – for example, relevant and irrelevant, articulated and absent, meaningful and meaningless – and that these oppositions are organised into hierarchies with reference to an idea of *presence* located outside the text. Every human artefact contains a trace of this *presence*, a moment in which the discourses of the text – revealed to be insufficient unto themselves – require the tacit importation of a non-historical, absolutely originary word around which a range of meanings may be ordered. Every text, in other words, is an exercise in privilege and bad faith, generating meanings based upon hierarchical oppositions which the text itself is incapable of justifying. That justification always comes from outside the text, and the task of the critic is to trace the moments in which this extra-textual presence makes itself felt. This is the critical method that has become known as 'deconstruction', the essential feature of which, according to Christopher Norris, 'consists not merely in *reversing* or *subverting* some established hierarchical order, but in showing how its terms are indissociably entwined in a strictly undecidable exchange of values and priorities' (1987, p. 56, original emphases).

If structuralism was felt to be ahistorical, Derrida's version of post-structuralism rapidly came to be seen as a virulent form of *anti*-historicism. When combined with other strands of poststructuralist critique (such as the post-Freudian psychoanalysis of Jacques Lacan), its effect, as Antony Easthope points out, has been 'to throw in question the whole enterprise of conventional empiricist history (including much Marxist history)' (1988, p. 105). All the basic assumptions underpinning traditional (liberal or Marxist) historiographical discourse – the (human) 'subject' of history, the perception of meaning and change over time, a transparent language through which the historian could communicate interpretations of the past – all these could be deconstructed to reveal a fatal ambivalence at the heart of the text, an ambivalence which was itself the articulation of a fundamentally decentred human consciousness.

Given this situation, it is perhaps not surprising that no 'poststructuralist' or 'deconstructionist' school of historiography has emerged, although individual historians have attempted to address various aspects of these challenging theories. One such historian (or, perhaps, philosopher of history would be a better designation) is the American Hayden White who has written a number of books which attempt to register the impact of structuralist and poststructuralist theories on traditional historiographical practices. In his first major intervention, *Metahistory* (1973), White drew attention to the fact that historiography – the writing of history – had both its own particular history and a set of highly prescriptive generic and social conventions within which it was expected to function. 'Metahistory' describes a process in which the critic takes a backwards step so as to perceive the principal ways in which history has been written in the modern period. Metahistorical analysis can reveal how the supposedly 'real' events of human history may be represented in any number of different ways, depending on a range of factors such as narrative trajectory, language and rhetorical tenor. These factors are social in provenance and ideological in impact, constituting a range of story-telling conventions that circulate in different kinds of society and which are amenable to study and classification.

White has pursued this theme in each of his subsequent books. In a famous essay entitled 'The Fictions of Factual Representation' included in *Tropics of Discourse* (1978), he draws attention to the similarities between fictional representations of the past – novels, for example – and the supposedly 'real', 'true' or 'factual' accounts that circulate in modern Western societies as 'history':

> Although historians and writers of fiction may be interested in different kinds of events, both the forms of their respective discourses and their aims in writing are often the same. In addition, in my view, the techniques or strategies that they use in the composition of their discourses can be shown to be substantially the same, however different they may appear on a purely surface, or dictional, level of their texts. (p. 21)

In emphasising the links with fiction, White's subject here is 'narrative', the apparently universal human reliance on story-telling as a means of communicating – in effect, surviving – in the world. 'History', he reveals, developed alongside the realist novel, each genre licensed to represent the past, but in different ways. Institutional historiography emerged during the nineteenth century as a discourse founded on the belief that with the right attitudes, protocols and tools – as well as full access to the traces of the past – it could produce a truthful narrative of the way things really were in the past. In typical poststructuralist fashion, however, White emphasises that the past is only knowable through discursive representations in the present, and that the notion of a straightforward encounter with the past described in a transparent language and structured in terms of an 'empty' genre is a myth, an ideological construction. Although apparently withdrawing from a full-blooded relativism (Chase, 1996, p. 70), the implication of White's work is that the idea of 'history' as such is untenable (we can never access the past), and that historiography (the means of representing the past) is subject to the ideological structuring of society but can in itself provide no logical basis for any kind of political or ethical vision.

While poststructuralism has been undermining the claims of traditional institutional history, 'postmodernism' has also emerged as an influential critical-cultural model. As a description, 'postmodern' carries both temporal and evaluative resonances, referring to methods of understanding and paradigms of knowledge that come *after* (and in some respects *against*) modernism – that particular Western cultural paradigm which lasted from about 1880 to 1930. But it also refers to a range of attitudes, styles and effects that circulate in the contemporary world. One influential strand of postmodernism is associated with the work of the French philosopher Jean-François Lyotard. In his *The Postmodern Condition* Lyotard delivered 'A Report on Knowledge' (the text's subtitle) which considered the changes overtaking the West in the latter half of the twentieth century. What he found was a growing technologisation of discourse and a concomitant diminishing of the power of history to explain the causes of change. The late twentieth-century subject occupies many different temporalities and trajectories, each possessing its own specialised knowledges and languages. No one narrative – whether political, religious or scientific – could possibly explain the multitude of causes and effects that impinge upon the formation and/or function of that subject, or the society in which he/she lives; no one 'big' story could hope to encompass the multitude of 'small' stories that make up the postmodern condition. It was in this context that Lyotard could write: 'The grand narrative has lost its credibility, regardless of what mode of unification it uses, regardless of whether it is a speculative narrative or a narrative of emancipation' (1984, p. 37).

Lyotard's scepticism with regard to the 'grand narratives' of history has led to him being designated (like Foucault) 'neo-conservative' by some commentators (Sarup, 1993, pp. 145–6). Lyotard's postmodernism is an escape from an historicism he understands to be repressive and authoritarian; for him, the so-called 'narrative of emancipation' in fact represents the violent imposition of a particular way of seeing the world, one that becomes as limiting in its prescriptions as any system it opposes. This is what he calls the 'modern' – that which attempts to 'master' history by narrating it within the terms of a specific 'universal' language. As we shall go on to see, for many this represents a traducement of traditional emancipatory critique. In the meantime, Lyotard's case is not helped when one notes the manner in which 'postmodernism' has been co-opted by conservative critics to argue, for example, that since we no longer live in a uniformly capitalist society, Marxism as an explanatory system is itself outmoded and should be discontinued as a viable socio-political goal (of which more below). In a related twist, the American neo-conservative commentator Francis Fukuyama (1992) agrees with the postmodernists when he argues that 'history' – which he defines as the strife between various social and political systems – has indeed ended but only because Western liberal democracy clearly emerged at the end of the twentieth century as the victor over competing (or frankly *wrong*) political ideologies.

Many of these issues regarding the influence of poststructuralism and postmodernism upon historiography emerged in a debate conducted in the pages of the English historical journal *Past and Present*. This debate was initiated by a short piece written by the distinguished historian Lawrence Stone first published in May 1991, warning against various threats (from deconstruction, structural anthropology and new historicism) to the discipline. Stone's initial attitude – a combination of dismissal and panic – elicited responses from those within the British historical community who felt that it was time the challenge of modern European theory was confronted and positively engaged rather than (as with Edward Thompson's (1978) notorious demolition of the work of the French Marxist Louis Althusser) ignored or traduced – the perennial English response. Patrick Joyce, for example, wished to retain notions such as the 'social' (a vital category for any engaged historiography) but at the same time to insist upon its 'irreducibly discursive character' (1997, p. 247) – that is, its dependence not upon some 'real' masternarrative outside history (such as economics, religion or science) but upon specific effects produced in specific textual instances. Echoing Lyotard, Joyce wrote:

> There is no overarching coherence evident in either the polity, the economy or the social system. What there are are instances (texts, events, ideas and so on) that have social contexts which are essential to their meaning, but there is no underlying structure to which they can be referred as expressions or effects. Thus with the notion of social totality goes the notion of social determination, so central to 'social history'. The certainty of a materialist link to the social is likewise broken. Gone too are the grand narratives that historicized the notion of social totality. (1997, p. 247)

Responding, Stone adopted a typically English liberal humanist position, calling for the discovery of some 'common ground' (1997b, p. 257) and 'a common position of moderation' (p. 258) between 'proper' historians (such as himself) and 'the more cautious of the postmodernists' (p. 257). At the same time, he remained adamant about the need to retain the distinction between fact and fiction, a distinction which (he perceived) poststructuralists and postmodernists were trying to erase. Another 'real' historian opting for the 'middle ground' (1997, p. 265) between (what she understands to be) the complete discursive constructivism of postmodernism and the complete discursive transparency of traditional positivist historiography is Gabrielle Spiegel. Advocating 'a "mixed" kind of reading' (p. 268), Spiegel advised historians to 'reject the tendencies of an extreme poststructuralism to absorb history into textuality', but at the same time to 'learn to appreciate and employ what it teaches us by and in its enactment of the complex tensions that shape the postmodern world' (p. 269).

If traditional historians were not about to take the twin assaults of poststructuralism and postmodernism lying down, then neither was the field with ostensibly the most to lose from the advent of these theories: Marxism. As one of the classic Western 'meta-narratives' – that is, a 'big' story about capitalism that could explain all the 'small' stories comprising Western social and cultural history – and as a discourse relying heavily on the notion of change through time, Marxism became one of the principal targets for postmodernist and poststructuralist critiques. Indeed, in some respects, both Derrida and Lyotard may be regarded as 'spoiled' Marxists, disillusioned by the failure of the radical movements of the 1960s and determined not to be fooled again by any romantic theories of oppression and resistance. For them, Marxism came to be seen as equally oppressive and epistemologically partial as the bourgeois formations it ostensibly opposed.

However, although reeling after events in Eastern Europe and the supposed collapse of international communism, Western Marxism has rallied in the years since and continues to refine a critique of bourgeois economics and its attendant politico-cultural discourses. Many of Marxism's doubts concerning poststructuralism are voiced in an article by Bob Chase, in which he argues for some kind of leap of faith over the poststructuralist abyss into the realm of concerned intervention beyond. Whilst acknowledging the force of poststructuralism's critique of Marxist humanism, Chase fears that 'the dissolution of all perceived realities into sheer discursivity would leave us with no reason or motivation whatsoever to raise objections to suffering and oppression' (1996, p. 61). Focusing on the work of (poststructuralist) Hayden White and (Marxist) Fredric Jameson, Chase sees the debate as one centred on meaninglessness or meaningfulness in history. While conceding poststructuralism's claims regarding the unknowability of the past, he maintains that both in practice and in theory humans work with historical representations around which they organise their social, political and moral lives:

Even though historical representations can never correspond to some hypothetical extra-discursive reality, surely we know enough about reality through experience (however culturally specific the construction of that experience may be) to allow us to speculate that some representations may be better than others and may approximate sufficiently to general truths about oppression and exploitation to justify employing them as starting points for our approach to the question of history. (p. 65)

As Geoff Bennington and Robert Young point out in the introduction to their influential book *Post-structuralism and the Question of History*, there is of course a certain irony here in as much as 'it is surprising to find that the attack mounted on poststructuralism in the name of history should be so confident in its reliance on precisely what is in question' (1987, p. 4). However, for Chase and like-minded commentators, it would ultimately appear to be a question not of truth but of plausibility. He concedes that after Derrida, Lyotard, Foucault, White and others, there can be no return to a naïve, representationalist view of history and struggle. But given that humans need narratives to survive in the world, the issue of whether a particular story can ever fully (or truthfully) represent reality or not is less relevant than its capacity to generate forms of collective and individual identity capable of recognising the disposition of an unevenly empowered world. The issue is not one of epistemology but of survival:

A story of humankind which represents human beings as creating their own 'nature', through material practice, over time, and arriving at the grand denouement of a communitarian, co-operative, non-antagonistic mode of living, in harmony with nature, must surely have more survival-value than does an embrace of chaotic discontinuity and meaninglessness. (Chase, 1996, pp. 73–4)

Chase's position is of a kind categorised by Keith Jenkins as 'left-wing traditionalist': 'This is a group which can accept the fact that anti-foundational philosophy has brought a new awareness as to the ways narrative structuring, emplotment and metaphor enter into our readings of the world ... But ... postmodernism's undercutting of any principled grounds for truth disables their attempts to resist capitalist practices and alternative scenarios' (1997, p. 23). Derrida has recognised the force of these 'left-wing traditionalist' criticisms of deconstruction and has attempted to effect a rapprochement with Marxism. In his *Specters of Marx* (1993), he argues that although it is no longer possible to embrace Marxian discourse in this postmodern, post-narrative age, we are, and should remain, 'haunted' by its possibility. Marxism is predicated on certain notions such as the centred subject, linear narrative, a range of stable oppositions and so on (notions that it shares with its ostensible enemy: bourgeois liberalism) that poststructuralism has revealed to be philosophically untenable. Yet its ethical dimension – the exposure of practices that contribute to an unjustly organised society – provides an element of critique which poststructuralism, with its scepticism towards all foundationalist discourses (including ethics), cannot. Just as the ghost is a reminder of somebody who is actually missing – an absent presence, simultaneously there and not there – so Derrida's 'hauntology' (a play on the philosophical term 'ontology') aims to invoke an ethico-political dimension without actually affiliating to any system. This enables deconstructionists to criticise bourgeois social practices but at the same time saves them from implication in Marxism's potentially repressive ethical system. Derrida thus tries to retain both a secure platform from which to engage in ethically grounded criticism, and at the same time the freedom to float above those same discourses which in another move he reveals to be fundamentally flawed and incoherent. This precarious balancing act has by and large failed to impress, as Kate Soper explains:

> Ready though he may be to accept that a deconstructive critique only makes sense against the background, or within the context, of a certain ethical commitment, Derrida still seems very loath to endow it with any content. For when it comes down to it, the prevailing message is still to the effect that we must never ontologize, must remain no more than haunted by the spirit of an emancipatory politics, must never seek to incarnate it in any set of goods, institutions or strategies, since to do so – it is implied – is inevitably to betray the spirit itself. (1996, p. 27)

In the meantime, the British philosopher Christopher Norris has taken it upon himself to save Derrida from the poststructuralists and postmodernists. Norris has attacked the 'sophistical chicanery' (1994, p. 115) and 'new obscurantism' (1997, p. 2) which passes for post-modernist analysis as well as the 'widespread and damaging misperception' (1997, p. 79) that construes Derrida's work as the fountainhead of a supposedly radical relativism. Although initially regarded as an advocate of fashionable continental philosophy himself, Norris has of late emerged as a fierce opponent of what he terms 'anti-realism' – that is, any critical system which looks to suspend the difference between reality and representation. He insists that 'the distinction between historical fact and literary or fictive representation has been vital to the entire post-Renaissance enterprise of enlightened secular critique' (1994, p. 112), and that critical systems which deny this distinction are incapable of articulating 'an ethics and a politics of genuine emancipatory values' (1994, p. 125). Norris seems keen to differentiate between a 'good' poststructuralism and a 'bad' postmodernism – between those (like Derrida) who articulate their critical systems in terms of an ethically driven notion of change in the real world, and those (like Lyotard) who encourage the 'facile or factitious paradox-mongering to be found (very often) on the woollier fringes of literary academe' (1997, p. 2).

All these issues are of seminal importance for any engaged notion of cultural history. Poststructuralism and postmodernism teach us to doubt any correspondence between discursive representation (the historiographical text) and non- or extra-discursive reality (the past). These lessons cannot be unlearned except in the context of a political denial of difference and a concomitant insistence upon the absolute union of image and reality, a context that (as Lyotard warns, 1984, p. 81) would be symbolically fascist in ethos and terrorist in method. At a more practical level, postmodern approaches to the study of history are also vindicated, as Keith Jenkins points out, in so far as they 'enable historians to be increasingly reflexive as to what they think history is, and to explicitly position themselves within and/or against traditional discourse' (1997, p. 2). At the same time, writing from an historical materialist perspective, Bob Chase warns that '[somehow] we must hold on to the notion of continuity whilst still realizing that the past remains other' (1996, p. 80). The past may be a foreign country, in other words, but it is one with which we need to become familiar (while accepting all the dangers implicit in the notion of 'familiarity') if we are to equip ourselves to resist certain exploitative tendencies in the present. The cultural historian cannot resolve these issues. However, every time we confront an historical artefact or event, we are obliged to address a tension between representational status – that is, the *construction* of that artefact or event in terms of certain discursive determinants such as narrative genre or context of narration – and the function of such artefacts and events in the real (*sans* scare quotes) world of knowledge and experience.

1.6 Popular Culture and Cultural Studies

It will be noted that the four case studies undertaken in the second part of this book focus on texts that might in some or other sense be considered 'popular'. This is indicative of significant changes that have overtaken the study of both history and culture in the late twentieth century. The fact that it is not possible to refer to a single sense of the 'popular', however, is itself the result of a complex disciplinary history. As a number of commentators have pointed out, the term has gone through a number of shifts and emphases since it first

impacted on the critical and cultural imagination of the industrialis-
ing world at the beginning of the eighteenth century (Shiach, 1989,
pp. 19–34; Mukerji and Schudson, 1991, pp. 1–62). Nonetheless, the
'popular' has emerged at the beginning of the twenty-first century as
a crucial category of social and cultural analysis, one with which any
account of the rise of Cultural History is obliged to engage.

A number of critical schools, predominantly Marxist in derivation,
have focused upon popular culture as a key element of contemporary
cultural analysis. One of the most influential engagements emerged
in the earlier part of the twentieth century in the work of the German
cultural critic Theodor Adorno. Adorno was a member of the
Frankfurt Institute of Social Research (*Institut für Sozialforschung*)
founded in that city in 1923. The Frankfurt School (as this group of
theorists is commonly referred to) was a sort of think-tank dedicated
to redeveloping Marxist analysis in the light of the social and technological developments that had overtaken the world since Marx first
formulated his theory of capital in the mid-nineteenth century. One of
the most important such developments, according to Adorno and his
fellow scholars, was the emergence of Western mass popular culture.

Adorno argued that 'authentic' art (by which he meant works of
'high' culture) articulated a creative and original tension between the
individual vision of the artist and a range of formal, social and
historical constraints (Middleton, 1990, pp. 3ff). It was with reference
to this tension that the Marxist critic could expose the contradictions
of capitalist society. For Adorno, the last artist to achieve a truly
authentic articulation of personal voice and social vision was the
German composer Beethoven, at the beginning of the nineteenth
century. Since then, however, there had been a decline in European
culture, a loss of balance in which either individual voice came to
dominate and the social dimension was lost (this was the case with
early twentieth-century Modernism and many of its *avant garde* sub-
sidiaries); or the social dimension came to dominate and culture
became simply a reflex of its own context rather than a subjective
articulation of much larger historical tensions.

According to Adorno, the reason for this lapse was the onset of
the age of mass popular culture. In Marxist discourse, authentic
culture had a 'use-value'; it was capable of producing certain kinds
of effects and insights for certain kinds of subjects within Western
industrial societies. Mass popular culture had only an 'exchange-
value' in which those effects and insights could be calculated
according to their material worth, and reproduced to order with
reference to certain recognised formulas and conventions. Modern
cultural producers were alienated from the kind of creative, organic
tension between vision and form that had characterised Beethoven's
music, and were only capable of producing isolated effects and

images which echoed art's true potential. At the same time, there no longer existed a public capable of appreciating anything that might constitute an authentic modern culture, which has consequently declined into *avant-garde* posturing.

Adorno encapsulated many of these criticisms in his essay 'On the Fetish-character in Music and the Regression of Listening'. The people who listen to popular music are described as childish, primitive and culturally retarded. The problem with popular music, as indeed with other mass cultural forms such as cinema and sport, is that it robs us of our right to authentic cultural experience, replacing it with mere effects, just an impotent echo of the real thing. From a Marxist perspective, it is politically retrograde in that it produces only the *effect* of creative interaction between consumer and text, and in so far as it attempts to separate those effects of aesthetic vision, formal integrity and subjective insight (which had characterised true cultural value) into small undemanding packages intended for immediate consumption and immediate disposal. Popular cultural production is overwhelmingly market-driven as society and culture becomes more and more integrated. Musical form, for example, is formulaic and technology-driven, incapable of being integrated into an organic vision or statement. Musical listening becomes a constant search for quicker and simpler gratification, for the aesthetic high which had once been available only though concentration and sustained effort. Altogether, for Adorno, modern music (as an exemplary form of modern mass popular culture) represents the prostitution of authentic art's liberating potential in the cause of capitalism's never-ending, ever-expanding drive for profit.

While Adorno's pessimism has been influential on both left- and right-wing accounts of popular culture, it has also been the subject of much criticism. In an essay entitled 'The Work of Art in the Age of Mechanical Reproduction' (1936), another German cultural critic, Walter Benjamin, refused to accept Adorno's nostalgia for some kind of golden cultural age in which supposedly 'authentic' cultural texts were produced for an audience capable of discerning 'the real thing'. Benjamin also doubted the proposition that, because modern cultural discourse had been so fully determined by capitalism, the only form of contemporary critique available was a negative one. He believed that contemporary Marxist critics should accept that they had been born into a highly technological age, and that as committed intellectuals they should try to discover ways in which to seize and re-articulate the discourses of mass popular culture for a liberatory politics.

Benjamin's main contention in this essay was that the new mass media (such as cinema, photography and popular music) constituted an attack upon the 'aura' of traditional works of art (such as painting, literature and classical music). During the nineteenth century the 'aura' of the original art work encapsulated the ideology upon which traditional capitalist formations relied, fostering certain effects and practices such as individualism, authority, leisure and privilege. Works like Beethoven's symphonies were fetishised into depoliticised rituals, rituals which despite their revolutionary posturing in fact underpinned the social and political *status quo*. The new mass media, however, threatened this aura; one could hear snatches or adaptations of Beethoven's music anywhere at any time, and this (Benjamin suggested) undermined culture's claim to be a reflection of a reality 'naturally' organised in certain stratified ways: bourgeoisie and proletariat; capital and labour; producers and consumers. Exposing the arbitrary, contingent nature of the art work would be the first step in exposing the arbitrary, contingent nature of all social and political effects, and was thus a potentially revolutionary act. The mass com- modification of the text was a blow against the formerly sacred work of art, and therefore could teach people to question the things they were encouraged to accept as normal.

Benjamin's critique feeds into the position of a later Marxist theorist, Tony Bennett, who opines that Adorno did not go far enough in his analysis of the relations between the popular and the canonical. The Frankfurt scholar's mistake, according to Bennett, was to accept the division – a division instigated and maintained by bourgeois ideology – that already existed between the canonical and the popular, between the valuable and the merely ephemeral. Bennett says:

> [The] point that Marxist critics have ... merely mirrored bourgeois criticism, accepting its valuations and duplicating its exclusions, remains valid ... The result has been, for a science which claims to be revolutionary, a highly paradoxical history in which Marxist criticism has functioned largely corroboratively in relation to the distinctions forged by bourgeois criticism: approving of the same body of canonized works but for different reasons, and disapprov- ing of the rest – lumped together as a residue – but, again, for different reasons. Bourgeois criticism has thus been simultaneously patted on the back for having recognized which works are truly great and taken to task for having misrecognized the reasons for their greatness ... Marxist criticism's basic orientation in relation to bourgeois criticism has been to compete with it on its own ground rather than to dispute or displace that terrain. (1986, pp. 241–2)

Bennett's point here is that Marxist critics who accept the division between the valuable and the valueless, between Beethoven and the Beatles, collude with the ideology they ostensibly oppose. Instead, he suggests, radical critics should use the analysis of popular culture as a starting point for exploding the categories of high and low culture, of canonical and popular, of the intrinsically valuable and the irre-deemably worthless. If we start with popular texts such as *Sgt. Pepper*, he suggests, we might end up with a different kind of analysis altogether, one in which we can stop deliberating about received categories and values, and start thinking instead about struggle and strategy.

Parallel to the continental European interest, there was a concern – indeed, almost a fixation – in the Anglo-American world with the impact and effects of mass popular culture. In Britain, writers and critics such as Matthew Arnold, T.S. Eliot and F.R. Leavis (in the 'culture and society' tradition, see pp. 10–20, above) worried about the social implications of popular culture, seeing it as some kind of dilution of the national essence – at best an earthy reflection of the experiences of the labouring classes, at worst an expression of a crudity (of both reason and emotion) that was threatening to swamp proper 'culture'. During the 1950s, however, popular culture came to be seen as a significant practice wherein both individual and social identities were made and contested. The work of Raymond Williams and Richard Hoggart is considered significant in this respect. Hoggart's pioneering *The Uses of Literacy* (1957) proved contradic-tory. On the one hand, he offered a powerfully positive evaluation of working-class culture as embodied in the actions and stances of everyday life. His arguments drew on innovative analyses of the (normally overlooked) textures and tokens of daily, and especially domestic, living: the clichés of conversation, women's weekly magazines, the lines on the face of a working-class mother. By teasing out the meanings implicit in these ways of living, he was able to offer a powerfully positive evaluation of traditional working-class culture built up since the late nineteenth century. On the other hand, Hoggart found it impossible to respond positively to the emergent youth culture of the mid- and late 1950s, seeing it simply as threatening the strenuously constructed and maintained value system that had been built by working people intent on survival. Moreover, as socialist com-mentators were quick to stress, even the working-class culture which Hoggart celebrated he simultaneously separated from the activities of political activists (whom he saw as a distinct earnest minority within the working class).

In terms of history, the key moment in the arrival of popular culture as a serious scholarly subject was the publication in 1963 of Edward Thompson's groundbreaking study of *The Making of the English Working Class*, a process of conscious construction – 'making' – by subjects who perceived themselves to be in a certain disadvantaged relationship with history and acted accordingly (see pp. 10–20, above). Thompson's insistence on the popular as a legitimate arena of cultural practice in which social and political power is contested constitutes his major contribution to the academic field that claims him (as well as Williams and Hoggart) as one of its founding fathers: Cultural Studies. This term describes a set of academic practices, institutional locations and scholarly concerns that combined to form perhaps the most successful and influential 'discipline' of the 1980s and 1990s. This is reflected in the work of certain high-profile practitioners, as well as the field's generation of a number of dedicated national and international journals, readers and textbooks, standing conferences and symposia. The continuing success of Cultural Studies is all the more remarkable because of its uncertain intellectual identity and the process of constant self-examination undertaken by its adherents. No other modern academic 'movement' appears to be so concerned with its own emergence and evolution, nor so suspicious of 'success', academic, institutional or otherwise (Ferguson and Golding, 1997, pp. xiii–xxvii).

Cultural Studies is a notoriously difficult term to engage. In part, this is because it encompasses a subject-matter, a methodology, an ideological bias and an institutional dimension. This is complicated still further by the peculiarities of the various national schools, so that for example Australian, American and British Cultural Studies are all intricately enmeshed with one another yet significantly different at the same time. The roots of the field are usually located in the Centre for Contemporary Cultural Studies (CCCS), founded at the University of Birmingham in 1964. It was there that the work of Hoggart (who was the Centre's first director) and Stuart Hall (the crucial figure in the subsequent emergence of Cultural Studies) began to develop a recognisable intellectual profile. The key feature of this profile might be described as a concern with the ways in which contemporary popular culture is used – by producers, institutions, and consumers – as part of the social contestation of power. Drawing on the 'culturalism' of Williams and Thompson (who had no official links with the CCCS but were crucial to its intellectual imagination), the CCCS began to foster and undertake research which took as its founding assumption the signal importance of culture – used in its widest anthropological sense – as a key element in the production and reproduction of society.

Two key developments continue to determine the focus and the direction of Cultural Studies. The first was the emergence of 'structuralism' during the 1960s. This was a continental European movement in the humanities and social sciences that grew from the work earlier in the century of the Swiss linguist Ferdinand de Saussure. Its adherents attacked what they saw as the 'bourgeois' notions of authorship, individualism and agency which underpinned most cultural and critical works, and stressed instead the abstract systems that set the limits on both human activity and its interpretation. These systems, it was claimed, functioned like a language, and could be studied as such without distracting critical energy towards largely irrelevant methodological issues such as the intentions or self-consciousness of historical subjects. Although practitioners such as Roland Barthes (1957) insisted otherwise, structuralism was widely perceived as a sophisticated formalism and condemned as being ahistorical and reactionary. Nevertheless, despite the 'humanist' assumptions underpinning the work of all the major founders of Cultural Studies (and the antipathy of Thompson in particular), structuralism won much support for its provision of a level of theoretical analysis by and large absent from traditional studies of culture in general, and popular culture in particular. As noted in the previous section, structuralism itself has been superseded in the humanities and the social sciences by poststructuralism, which assumes a fundamental scepticism towards the basic assumptions of the culturalism-structuralism debate.

The second key factor bearing on the development of Cultural Studies was the dissemination during the 1970s of the work of the Italian Marxist theorist Antonio Gramsci. The cultural and political theories developed by Gramsci during his time in a Fascist prison in the 1920s and 1930s significantly modified and developed classical Marxist thought, offering a sophisticated analysis of the means by which social consent was created and resisted. According to him, social and political power is not a matter of straightforward confrontation between clearly recognisable and rigidly formed categories, such as capital and labour, or bourgeois and proletariat. A group vying for dominance of a particular society needs to be able to command the 'intellectual and moral leadership' of other groups within that society – what Gramsci termed 'hegemony'. Leadership is never finally 'won', it is only ever 'held', or 'held together' with the consent of subjects who perceive themselves and the groups to which they affiliate to be in a strategic relationship with another, temporarily dominant, group. Thus, power is a matter of negotiation and strategic alliance, compromise and temporary association – in short, a matter of politics.

One of the principal ways in which social leadership is contested is through the meanings represented in popular culture. The characterisations, idioms, narrative plots and resolutions deployed in popular cultural texts are a major source of the 'commonsense' assumptions through which social groups attempt to validate their positions. It seems clear, for example, that the individualism extolled in many contemporary Hollywood films – encapsulated in the figure of the lone hero – encourages values and perceptions of the world supportive of a particular political ideology stressing self-responsibility and resourcefulness, while casting doubt on the advisability, or indeed the possibility, of collective social action. At the same time, the meanings 'encoded' in such texts will be 'decoded' differently in a range of consuming contexts dispersed over time and space (Hall, 1980). Not only will different 'meanings' be taken from the same text, but the same 'meanings' will be activated for different reasons and towards different ends. Such films are thus part of an ongoing contest for the 'intellectual and moral leadership' of the various societies in which they are consumed.

Popular culture, as well as the institutions and policies which bear on both its production and consumption, is thus of particular interest to a Cultural Studies inspired by Gramsci. To a large extent, hegemony resolves the stand-off between culturalism and structuralism in so far as it provides a theory of human action *within* specific systems. As John Storey argues:

> Neo-Gramscian hegemony theory at its best suggests that there is a dialectic between the processes of production and the activities of consumption. The consumer always confronts a text or practice in its material existence as a result of determinate conditions of production. But in the same way, the text or practice is confronted by a consumer who in effect *produces in use* the range of possible meaning(s) – these cannot just be read off from the materiality of the text or practice, or the means or relations of its production. (1996, p. 9, original emphasis)

Human action, it would appear, is neither entirely free nor entirely structured; systems are neither entirely absent nor entirely determining. A popular cultural text is to a large extent a reflex of the generic and institutional systems within which it is articulated. At the same time, it possesses the capacity to produce meanings which challenge currently dominant positions, and thus shift the balance of leadership within any social context. It is perhaps ironic that although working in circumstances so much less auspicious than his contemporary Adorno, Gramsci should have developed a theory that was so much more optimistic with regard to popular culture and its ability to be harnessed for emancipatory ends.

Although Cultural Studies has focused predominantly on modern (nineteenth century onwards) and contemporary culture – or perhaps even more specifically on contemporary media and communications – the emergence of the field is clearly of major significance for Cultural History. There remains much mutual suspicion, not to say resentment, between the discipline of History (even one reinvigorated by the culturalist emphasis of Thompson) and a Cultural Studies tormented by its uncertain disciplinary status (Turner, 1990, pp. 68–72; pp. 180–9). Despite moments of overlap and cross-fertilisation, the fields regularly accuse each other of naïve empiricism and institutional isolation on the one hand, and effete theoreticism and modishness on the other (Steinberg, 1996). Nowhere are these differences more apparent than in the divergent attitudes to the phenomenon of popular culture, both in its pre-industrial and its modern mass forms. Much of the controversy centres on the status of the popular cultural text and its function within analysis. When historians criticise Cultural Studies for its apparent unwillingness to engage with the wider institutional and contextual factors bearing on the production of such texts, the latter points to historians' apparent inability to 'read' – that is, engage formally – with the texts that form the basis for their historical claims. It would appear that Cultural History, infused with the empiricism of its parent discipline History, yet sympathetic to the intellectual and methodological eclecticism of its near relation Cultural Studies, must attempt to heal the family feud by building upon those moments of overlap and cross-fertilisation, and by contributing to the development of a popular cultural analysis which is both theoretically refined and historically alert.

Bibliographies

Preface and Acknowledgments

LaCapra, D. *History and Criticism* (Ithaca, NY: Cornell University Press, 1985).

1.1 Cultural History: Versions and Definitions

Ashplant, T.G., G. Dawson and M. Roper (eds) *The Politics of War Memory and Commemoration* (Routledge, 2000).

Belsey, C. 'Towards Cultural History – in Theory and Practice', *Textual Practice* 3.2 (1989), pp. 159–72.

Bennett, T. 'Texts, Readers, Reading Formations', *Literature and History* 9.2 (Autumn 1983), pp. 214–27.

Burke, P. *Varieties of Cultural History* (Cambridge: Polity Press, 1997).

Chartier, R. *Cultural History: Between Practices and Representations* (Cambridge: Polity Press, 1988).

Darnton, R. *The Great Cat Massacre and Other Episodes in French Cultural History* (Allen Lane, 1984).

Goodman, J. 'History and Anthropology', in M. Bentley (ed.) *Companion to Historiography* (Routledge, 1997), pp. 783–804.

Hunt, L. (ed.) *The New Cultural History* (Berkeley, CA: University of California Press, 1989).

Iggers, G.G. *Historiography in the Twentieth Century: From Scientific Objectivity to the Postmodern Challenge* (Hanover, NH: Wesleyan University Press, 1997).

LaCapra, D. *History and Criticism* (Ithaca, NY: Cornell University Press, 1985).

Rodden, J. *The Politics of Literary Reputation* (New York: Oxford University Press, 1989).

Spiegel, G.M. 'History, Historicism and the Social Logic of the Text in the Middle Ages', in K. Jenkins (ed.), *The Postmodern History Reader* (Routledge, 1997), pp. 180–203.

1.2 Marxist Historiography and Cultural Theory

Anderson, P. 'Components of the National Culture', in A. Cockburn and R. Blackburn (eds) *Student Power* (Harmondsworth: Penguin, 1969), pp. 214–84.

Baldick, C. *The Social Mission of English Criticism, 1848–1932* (Oxford: Clarendon Press, 1983).

Belsey, C. 'Towards Cultural History – in Theory and Practice', *Textual Practice* 3.2 (1989), pp. 159–72.

Biagini, E.F. and A.J. Reid 'Currents of Radicalism, 1850–1914', in E.F. Biagini and A.J. Reid (eds), *Currents of Radicalism: Popular Radicalism, Organised Labour and Party Politics in Britain 1850–1914* (Cambridge: Cambridge University Press, 1991), pp. 1–19.

Cronon, J. 'A Place for Stories: Nature, History, and Narrative', *Journal of American History* 78.4 (1992), 1347–76.

DiMaggio, P. 'Cultural Entrepreneurship in Nineteenth-century Boston: Creation of an Organizational Base for High Culture in America', in Mukerji and Schudson (eds) (1991), pp. 374–97.

Doyle, B. *English and Englishness* (Routledge, 1989).

Dworkin, P. *Cultural Marxism in Postwar Britain: History, the New Left, and the Origin of Cultural Studies* (Durham, NC: Duke University Press, 1997).

Eley, G. 'Edward Thompson, Social History and Political Culture: the Making of a Working-Class Public, 1780–1950', in Kaye and McClelland (eds) (1990), pp. 12–49.

Eley, G. and K. Nield 'Starting Over: The Present, the Post-modern and the Moment of Social History', in K. Jenkins (ed.) *The Postmodern History Reader* (Routledge, 1997), pp. 366–79.

Goode, J. 'E. P. Thompson and the "Significance of Literature"', in Kaye and McClelland (eds) (1990), pp. 183–203.

Gray, R. 'History, Marxism and Theory', in Kaye and McClelland (eds) (1990), pp. 153–82.

Higgins, J. *Raymond Williams: Literature, Marxism and Cultural Materialism* (Routledge, 1999).

Hobsbawm, E. *Primitive Rebels: Studies in Archaic Forms of Social Movement in the Nineteenth and Twentieth Centuries* (Manchester: Manchester University Press, 1959).

— 'The Forward March of Labour Halted?', in M. Jacques and F. Mulhern (eds) *The Forward March of Labour Halted* (Verso, 1981), pp. 1–19.

Hoggart, R. *The Uses of Literacy* (Macmillan, 1957).

Iggers, G.G. *New Directions in European Historiography* (rev. edn., Methuen, 1985).

— *Historiography in the Twentieth Century: From Scientific Objectivity to the Postmodern Challenge* (Hanover, NH: Wesleyan University Press, 1997).

Joyce, P. *Visions of the People: Industrial England and the Question of Class, 1840–1914* (Cambridge: Cambridge University Press, 1991).

— *Democratic Subjects: The Self and the Social in Nineteenth-century England* (Cambridge: Cambridge University Press, 1994).

Kaye, H.J. and K. McClelland (eds) *E.P. Thompson: Critical Perspectives* (Cambridge: Polity Press, 1990).

Laing, S. *Representations of Working Class Life, 1957–64* (Macmillan, 1986).

Levine, L.W. 'William Shakespeare and the American People: a Study in Cultural Transformation', in Mukerji and Schudson (eds) (1991), pp. 157–97.

Marx, K. 'Preface to *A Contribution to the Critique of Political Economy*' (1859), in K. Marx and F. Engels, *Selected Works in One Volume* (Lawrence & Wishart, 1968), pp. 180–4.

Mukerji, C. and M. Schudson (eds) *Rethinking Popular Culture: Contemporary Perspectives in Cultural Studies* (Berkeley, CA: University of California Press, 1991).

Mulhern, F. *The Moment of 'Scrutiny'* (New Left Books, 1979).

Radway, J. *Reading the Romance: Women, Patriarchy, and Popular Literature* (Chapel Hill, NC: University of North Carolina Press, 1984).

Rigby, S.H. 'Marxist Historiography', in M. Bentley (ed.) *Companion to Historiography* (Routledge, 1997), pp. 889–928.

— *Marxism and History: A Critical Introduction* (2nd edn., Manchester: Manchester University Press, 1998).

Rogers, H. *Women and the People: Authority, Authorship and the English Radical Tradition in the Nineteenth Century* (Aldershot: Ashgate, 2000).

Rosaldo, R. 'Celebrating Thompson's Heroes: Social Analysis in History and Anthropology', in Kaye and McClelland (eds) (1990), pp. 103–24.

Rudé, G. *The Crowd in the French Revolution* (Oxford: Clarendon Press, 1959).

Schwarz, B. '"The People" in History: the Communist Party Historians' Group, 1946–56', in R. Johnson *et al.* (eds), *Making Histories: Studies in History Writing and Politics* (Hutchinson, 1982), pp. 44–95.

Scott, J.W. *Gender and the Politics of History* (New York: Columbia University Press, 1988).

Sewell, W.H. 'How Classes are Made: Critical Reflections on E.P. Thompson's Theory of Working-class Formation', in Kaye and McClelland (eds) (1990), pp. 50–77.

Sharpe, J. 'History from Below', in P. Burke (ed.) *New Perspectives on Historical Writing* (Cambridge: Polity Press, 1991), pp. 24–41.

Showalter, E. *A Literature of Their Own: British Women Novelists from Bronte to Lessing* (Virago, 1978).

Stedman Jones, G. 'Working-class Culture and Working-class Politics in London 1870–1900: Notes on the Remaking of a Working Class' (1974), in Stedman Jones (1983), pp. 179–238.

— *Languages of Class: Studies in English Working-class History 1832–1982* (Cambridge: Cambridge University Press, 1983).

Thompson, E.P. *William Morris: Romantic to Revolutionary* (Lawrence & Wishart, 1955).

— *The Making of the English Working Class* (Gollancz, 1963).

— *Customs in Common* (1991; Harmondsworth: Penguin, 1993).

— *Witness against the Beast: William Blake and the Moral Law* (Cambridge: Cambridge University Press, 1993).

Walder, D. (ed.), *Literature in the Modern World: Critical Essays and Documents* (Oxford: Oxford University Press, 1990).

Widdowson, P. (ed.) *Re-reading English* (Methuen, 1982).

Williams, R. *Culture and Society 1780–1850* (Hogarth Press, 1958).

— *The Long Revolution* (Chatto & Windus, 1961).

— 'Base and Superstructure in Marxist Cultural Theory' (1973), in his *Problems in Materialism and Culture* (Verso, 1980), pp. 31–49.

— *The Country and the City* (Chatto & Windus, 1973).

— *Keywords: a Vocabulary of Culture and Society* (Glasgow: Fontana, 1976).

— *Marxism and Literature* (Oxford: Oxford University Press, 1977).

— *Culture* (Glasgow: Fontana, 1981).

— *Writing in Society* (Verso, 1984).

1.3 The *Annales* Historians, Anthropology and the New Cultural History

Bennett, T. 'Texts, Readers, Reading Formations', *Literature and History* 9.2 (Autumn 1983), pp. 214–27.

Biersack, A. 'Local Knowledge, Local History: Geertz and Beyond', in Hunt (ed.) (1989), pp. 72–96.

Burke, P. *A New Kind of History: from the Writings of Febvre* (Routledge, 1973).

— *The French Historical Revolution: the Annales School, 1929–89* (Cambridge: Polity Press, 1990).

— *Varieties of Cultural History* (Cambridge: Polity Press, 1997)

Burke, P. (ed.) *New Perspectives on Historical Writing* (Cambridge: Polity Press, 1991).

Carrard, P. *Poetics of the New History: French Historical Discourse from Braudel to Chartier* (Baltimore: Johns Hopkins University Press, 1992).

Chartier, R. *Cultural History: Between Practices and Representations* (Cambridge: Polity Press, 1988).

Darnton, R. *The Great Cat Massacre and Other Episodes in French Cultural History* (Allen Lane, 1984).

— *The Kiss of Lamourette: Reflections in Cultural History* (Faber, 1990).

— 'History of Reading', in Burke (ed.) (1991), pp. 140–67.

Davis, N.Z. *Society and Culture in Early Modern France* (Duckworth, 1975).

Desan, S. 'Crowds, Community, and Ritual in the Work of E.P. Thompson and Natalie Davis', in Hunt (ed.) (1989), pp. 47–71.

Geertz, C. 'Deep Play: Notes on the Balinese Cockfight', in his *The Interpretation of Cultures: Selected Essays by Clifford Geertz* (Hutchinson, 1975), pp. 412–53.

Ginzburg, C. *The Cheese and the Worms: the Cosmos of a Sixteenth-century Miller* (Routledge, 1980).

Goodman, J. 'History and Anthropology', in M. Bentley (ed.) *Companion to Historiography* (Routledge, 1997), pp. 783–804.

Green, A. and K. Troup (eds) *The Houses of History: A Critical Reader of Twentieth-century History and Theory* (Manchester: Manchester University Press, 1999).

Hunt, L. 'French History in the Last Twenty Years: The Rise and Fall of the *Annales* Paradigm', *Journal of Contemporary History* 21.2 (1986), pp. 209–24.

Hunt, L. (ed.) *The New Cultural History* (Berkeley, CA: University of California Press, 1989).

Huppert, G. 'The *Annales* Experiment', in M. Bentley (ed.) *Companion to Historiography* (Routledge, 1997), pp. 873–88.

Iggers, G.G. *New Directions in European Historiography* (rev. edn., Methuen, 1985).

— *Historiography in the Twentieth Century: from Scientific Objectivity to the Postmodern Challenge* (Hanover, NH: Wesleyan University Press, 1997).

LaCapra, D. *History and Criticism* (Ithaca, NY: Cornell University Press, 1985).

— 'Chartier, Darnton, and the Great Symbol Massacre', *Journal of Modern History* 60.1 (March 1988), pp. 95–112.

Laqueur, T.W. 'Bodies, Details, and the Humanitarian Narrative', in Hunt (ed.) (1989), pp. 176–204.

Le Roy Ladurie, E. *Carnival in Romans: A People's Uprising at Romans 1579–1580* (Harmondsworth: Penguin, 1981).

Levi, G. 'On Microhistory', in P. Burke (ed.) (1991), pp. 93–113.

Medick, H. '"Missionaries in the Row Boat"? Ethnological Ways of Knowing as a Challenge to Social History', *Comparative Studies in Society and History* 29.1 (1987), pp. 76–98.

Mukerji, C. and M. Schudson (eds) *Rethinking Popular Culture: Contemporary Perspectives in Cultural Studies* (Berkeley, CA: University of California Press, 1991).

New German Critique Special Isssue on 'Cultural History/Cultural Studies', 65 (Spring/Summer 1995).

Rosaldo, R. 'Celebrating Thompson's Heroes: Social Analysis in History and Anthropology', in Kaye and McClelland (eds) (1990), pp. 103–24.

Spiegel, G.M. 'History, Historicism and the Social Logic of the Text in the Middle Ages', in K. Jenkins (ed.), *The Postmodern History Reader* (Routledge, 1997), pp. 180–203.

Thompson, E.P. 'The Moral Economy of the English Crowd in the Eighteenth Century', *Past & Present* 50 (1971), pp. 76–136.

— 'Anthropology and the Discipline of Historical Context', *Midland History* 1 (1972), pp. 41–55.

— *The Poverty of Theory and Other Essays* (Merlin, 1978).

1.4 Foucault and New Historicism

Atkinson, R.F. *Knowledge and Explanation in History: An Introduction to the Philosophy of History* (Basingstoke: Macmillan, 1978).

Colebrook, C. *New Literary Histories: New Historicism and Contemporary Criticism* (Manchester: Manchester University Press, 1997).

Dreyfus, H.L. and P. Rabinow 'What is Maturity? Habermas and Foucault on "What is Enlightenment?"', in Hoy (ed.) (1986), pp. 109–21.

Eagleton, T. *The Ideology of the Aesthetic* (Oxford: Basil Blackwell, 1990).

— 'The Historian as Body-snatcher', *Times Literary Supplement* (18 January 1991), p. 7.

Foucault, M. *The Order of Things: An Archaeology of the Human Sciences* (1966), trans. A. Sheridan-Smith (Tavistock, 1970).

— *The Archaeology of Knowledge* (1969), trans. A. Sheridan-Smith (Tavistock, 1972).

— *Discipline and Punish: The Birth of the Prison* (1975), trans. A.M. Sheridan-Smith (Allen Lane, 1977a).

— *Language, Counter-Memory, Practice: Selected Essays and Interviews*, ed. D.F. Bouchard, trans. D.F. Bouchard and S. Simon (Oxford: Blackwell, 1977b).

— 'Nietzsche, Genealogy, History' (1971), reproduced in P. Rabinow (ed.) *The Foucault Reader: An Introduction to Foucault's Thought* (Penguin, 1984), pp. 76–100.

Goldstein, J. *Foucault and the Writing of History* (Oxford: Basil Blackwell, 1994).

Greenblatt, S.J. *Renaissance Self-fashioning from More to Shakespeare* (Chicago and London: University of Chicago Press, 1980).

— *Shakespearean Negotiations: The Circulation of Social Energy in Renaissance England* (Oxford: Clarendon Press, 1988).

— *Learning to Curse: Essays in Early Modern Culture* (New York and London: Routledge, 1990).

Habermas, J. *The Philosophical Discourse of Modernity: Twelve Lectures*, trans F. Lawrence (Cambridge: Polity Press, 1987).

Hawthorne, J. *Cunning Passages: New Historicism, Cultural Materialism and Marxism in the Contemporary Literary Debate* (Edward Arnold, 1996).

Hoy, D.C. (ed.) *Foucault: A Critical Reader* (Oxford: Basil Blackwell, 1986).

Lentricchia, F. 'Foucault's Legacy – A New Historicism?', in Veeser (ed.) (1989), pp. 231–42.

Marwick, A. *The Nature of History* (3rd edn., Basingstoke: Macmillan, 1989).

Megill, A. 'Foucault, Structuralism, and the Ends of History', *Journal of Modern History* 51.3 (1979), pp. 451–503.

Merquior, J.G. *Foucault* (2nd edn., Fontana, 1991).

Montrose, L. 'New Historicisms', in S. Greenblatt and G. Gunn (eds) *Redrawing the Boundaries: The Transformation of English and American Literary Studies* (New York: Modern Language Association of America, 1992), pp. 392–418.

Montrose, L. and J.E. Howard (eds) *English Literary Renaissance* 16 (Winter 1986).

Nietzsche, F. *The Birth of Tragedy [1872] and The Genealogy of Morals [1887]*, trans. F. Golffing (New York: Doubleday Anchor Books, 1956).

O'Farrell, C. *Foucault: Historian or Philosopher?* (Basingstoke: Macmillan, 1989).

Poster, M. *Foucault, Marxism and History: Mode of Production versus Mode of Information* (Cambridge: Polity Press, 1984).

— 'Foucault, Poststructuralism, and the Mode of Information', in M. Krieger (ed.) *The Aims of Representation* (New York: Columbia University Press, 1987), pp. 107–30.

Roth, M.S. 'Foucault's "History of the Present"', *History and Theory* 5.2 (1981), pp. 111–34.

Ryan, K. (ed.) *New Historicism and Cultural Materialism: A Reader* (Edward Arnold, 1996).

Said, E.W. *Orientalism* (1978; Penguin, 1985).
— 'Foucault and the Imagination of Power', in Hoy (ed.) (1986), pp. 149–56.
Veeser, H.A. (ed.) *The New Historicism* (Routledge 1989).
White, H. 'New Historicism: A Comment', in Veeser (ed.) (1989), pp. 293–302.

1.5 Poststructuralism and Postmodernism

Bennington, G. and R.Young 'Introduction: Posing the Question of History', in D. Attridge, G. Bennington and R.Young (eds), *Poststructuralism and the Question of History* (Cambridge: Cambridge University Press, 1987), pp. 1–9.
Chase, B. 'History and Poststructuralism: Hayden White and Fredric Jameson', in B. Schwarz (ed.) *The Expansion of England: Race, Ethnicity and Cultural History* (Routledge, 1996), pp. 61–91.
Cosgrove, D. and M. Domosh 'Author and Authority: Writing the New Cultural Geography', in J.S. Duncan and D. Ley (eds) *Place/Culture/Representation* (Routledge, 1993), pp. 25–38.
Derrida, J. *Of Grammatology* (1967), trans. Gayatri Chakravorty Spivak (Baltimore: The Johns Hopkins University Press, 1976).
— *Specters of Marx: The State of the Debt, the Work of Mourning and the New International* (1993), trans. Peggy Kamuf (Routledge, 1994).
Easthope, A. *British Post-structuralism since 1968* (Routledge, 1988).
Fukuyama, F. *The End of History and the Last Man* (Penguin, 1992).
Jenkins, K. (ed.) *The Postmodern History Reader* (Routledge, 1997).
Joyce, P. 'History and Postmodernism', in Jenkins (ed.) (1997), pp. 244–9.
Lyotard, J-F. *The Postmodern Condition: A Report on Knowledge* (1979), trans. G. Bennington and B. Massumi (Manchester: Manchester University Press, 1984).
Norris, C. *Truth and the Ethics of Criticism* (Manchester: Manchester University Press, 1994).
— *New Idols of the Cave: On the Limits of Anti-realism* (Manchester: Manchester University Press, 1997).
Sarup, M. *An Introductory Guide to Post-structuralism and Postmodernism* (2nd edn., Hemel Hempstead: Harvester Wheatsheaf, 1993).
Soper, K. 'The Limits of Hauntology', *Radical Philosophy: A Journal of Socialist and Feminist Philosophy* 75 (January/February 1996), pp. 26–31.
Spiegel, G. 'History and Postmodernism', in Jenkins (ed.) (1997), pp. 260–73.

Stone, L. 'History and Postmodernism', in Jenkins (ed.) (1997a), pp. 242–3.

— 'History and Postmodernism', in Jenkins (ed.) (1997b), pp. 255–9.

Thompson, E.P. *The Poverty of Theory and Other Essays* (Merlin, 1978).

White, H. *Metahistory: The Historical Imagination in Nineteenth-century Europe* (Baltimore: Johns Hopkins University Press, 1973).

— *Tropics of Discourse: Essays in Cultural Criticism* (Baltimore: Johns Hopkins University Press, 1978).

— *The Content of the Form: Narrative Discourse and Historical Representation* (Baltimore: Johns Hopkins University Press, 1987).

1.6 Popular Culture and Cultural Studies

Adorno, T.W. 'On the Fetish-Character in Music and the Regression of Listening' (1938), in A. Arato and E. Gebhardt (eds) *The Essential Frankfurt School Reader* (New York: Urizen Books, 1978), pp. 270–99.

Barthes, R. *Mythologies* (1957), trans. A. Lavers (Jonathan Cape, 1972).

Benjamin, W. 'The Work of Art in the Age of Mechanical Reproduction' (1936), in M. Solomon (ed.) *Marxism and Art: Essays Classic and Contemporary* (New York: Alfred A. Knopf, 1973), pp. 550–7.

Bennett, T. 'Marxism and Popular Fiction' (1981), in Humm, Stigant and Widdowson (eds) (1986), pp. 237–65.

Brantlinger, P. *Crusoe's Footsteps: Cultural Studies in Britain and America* (New York and London: Routledge, 1990).

Chaney, D. *The Cultural Turn: Scene-setting Essays on Contemporary Cultural History* (Routledge, 1994).

Ferguson M. and P. Golding (eds) *Cultural Studies in Question* (Sage, 1997).

Gramsci, A. *Selection from Prison Notebooks*, trans Q. Hoare and G. Nowell-Smith (Lawrence & Wishart, 1971).

Hall, S. 'Encoding and Decoding', in S. Hall *et al.* (eds) *Culture, Media, Language* (Hutchinson, 1980), pp. 128–38.

Hoggart, R. *The Uses of Literacy* (1957; Harmondsworth: Penguin, 1990).

Humm, P., P. Stigant and P. Widdowson (eds) *Popular Fictions: Essays in Literature and History* (Methuen, 1986).

McCabe, C. (ed.) *High Theory/Low Culture* (Manchester: Manchester University Press, 1986).

Middleton, R. *Studying Popular Music* (Buckingham: Open University Press, 1990).

Mukerji, C. and M. Schudson (eds) *Rethinking Popular Culture: Contemporary Perspectives in Cultural Studies* (Berkeley: University of California Press, 1991).

Nelson, C. and D. Parameshwar Gaonkar (eds) *Disciplinarity and Dissent in Cultural Studies* (Routledge, 1996).

Shiach, M. *Discourse on Popular Culture: Class, Gender and History in Cultural Analysis, 1730 to the Present* (Cambridge: Polity Press, 1989).

Steinberg, M.P. 'Cultural History and Cultural Studies', in Nelson and Parameshwar Gaonkar (eds) (1996), pp. 103–29.

Storey, J. 'Mapping the Popular: The Study of Popular Culture within British Cultural Studies', *The European English Messenger* 3.2 (Autumn 1994), pp. 47–59.

— (ed.) *Cultural Theory and Popular Culture: A Reader* (Hemel Hempstead: Harvester Wheatsheaf, 1994).

— (ed.) *What is Cultural Studies? A Reader* (Edward Arnold, 1996).

Turner, G. *British Cultural Studies: An Introduction* (Unwin Hyman, 1990).

Williams, R. *Culture and Society 1780–1950* (Harmondsworth: Penguin, 1958).

PART 2

CASE STUDIES

2 'What right have women to interfere with politics?': The Address of the Female Political Union of Birmingham to the Women of England (1838)

Helen Rogers

The role of language and culture in the formation of individual and collective identities has been one of the major preoccupations of historians of society and politics since the 1960s. At the heart of this enquiry lie the questions: are political and social discourses shaped by the relations of power which structure society; or, conversely, are power relations themselves the effects of those discourses? In British histori-ography, nowhere have these questions been the subject of more debate and controversy than in the study of nineteenth-century popular culture and politics and especially the language and meanings of radicalism. Historians have contended that radical movements offered their followers political languages which enabled them to understand their world and thus constituted them as political subjects or agents with the capacity to act in and reshape their world (Vernon, 1993; Joyce, 1994; Epstein, 1994). However, the 'subjects' of radicalism were often positioned in very different ways, and this was particularly the case for women. At certain moments, some radicals appealed directly to women but often, when they addressed 'the People', they spoke specifically to men (Rogers, 2000). Under what conditions, therefore, did women come to see themselves not simply as the subjects of radicalism but as authors of radicalism, and is it possible to identify a peculiarly female radical voice? These questions will be explored through an examination of the political dialogue between the women and men of the Birmingham Political Union in their campaign for universal manhood suffrage between 1838 and 1839.

The Birmingham Political Union (BPU) was one of the political associations that in 1838 initiated a national campaign to petition parliament for the six points or demands of the People's Charter:

universal manhood suffrage; equal electoral districts; the abolition of property qualifications and the introduction of payment for Members of Parliament; and an annual and secret ballot. The demands were designed not only to allow equal representation for all men but also to ensure that working-class men could stand for parliament, and that political representatives would be held accountable to their electors. In the decade between the raising of the first national petition of 1839 and the presentation of the third and last petition of 1848, the Chartists, as they began to call themselves, mobilised the largest popular political movement of the first half of the nineteenth century, composed predominantly of working-class people, extending across most of Britain. As part of its efforts to create a national movement, the Birmingham Political Union established an allied Female Political Union (FPU), the first of nearly 150 female Charter associations formed in the decade. Though historians have referred extensively to the history of the BPU, the participation of women was almost entirely omitted from their accounts before the 1980s (Tholfsen, 1958; Briggs, 1959, pp. 18–28; Behagg, 1990). In his history of the BPU, Carlos Flick overlooked the Female Union altogether, except for a dismissive reference to its first meeting as 'The most curious public event to occur in Birmingham during this period' (1978, p. 134). An analysis of the sexual politics of the two Birmingham Unions draws our attention, therefore, to the gendered making of historical as well as political knowledge.

The examination of the gendered construction of Chartist discourse has been central to the investigations of women's participation in the movement and reflects some of the major developments in feminist historiography since the 1980s. The first detailed study of female Chartism was undertaken by Dorothy Thompson (1983 and 1984). Thompson's role in complementing and extending the work of her husband Edward Thompson is often overlooked, for if Edward Thompson sought to demonstrate the role of radical culture in the self-making of the working class from the 1790s through to the 1830s (see pp. 12–13, 17–18 above), Dorothy Thompson argued that with the beginnings of the Chartist movement working-class politics had come of age. It constituted a genuinely popular, community-based politics embracing women and children as well as men, new and old trades, skilled and unskilled, across regions with diverse cultural and occupational traditions: 'divisions of sex and gender did not, any more than divisions of religious adhesion and ethnicity, inhibit the prevailing class loyalties, at any rate in the earlier years of the movement' (1984, p. 121). Few female societies appeared to sustain their organisation, however, and their numbers dwindled dramatically in the 1840s. For every eight societies active in 1839, there was only one in 1848, when there were also fewer reports of female participation in the Chartist crowd (Schwarzkopf, 1991, p. 199; Thompson, 1984, p. 122). Thompson provided a number of speculative answers as to why women had effectively 'disappeared' from working-class politics, including the proposition that in the 1840s Chartist men seem to have expressed with growing fervency and in a 'thoroughly middle-class manner' the view that women's place was in the home (1984, p. 131). The articulation of a language of female domesticity suggested to Thompson the assimilation of middle-class ideals of 'respectability' in working-class culture and indicated the increasingly reformist nature of working-class politics. For Thompson, then, the history of women could be incorporated into existing chronologies of working-class politics, while at the same time throwing light on their changing dynamics.

Subsequent feminist investigations of the sexual politics of radical and working-class community, trade and political organisations have argued that the appeal to domesticity did not simply reflect the adoption of 'middle-class values' but rather marked the attempt by working men to bolster the authority that they had traditionally exerted in the family and workplace. These studies have provided a stringent critique of the Thompsons' accounts of the formation of working-class consciousness. Anna Clark contends that from the eighteenth century plebeian culture was riven with sexual antagonism. Reacting to state measures to discipline the working-class family in the 1830s and 1840s, radicals demanded the breadwinner wage to enable working men to keep their wives and children out of the labour market. This was not the only alternative, argues Clark, for more egalitarian strategies were proposed in freethinking, republican and Owenite-socialist movements. The political choices made by radical men 'were determined', she claims, 'not by the dominance of discourse, but by the realities of power: their lack of political clout, and working men's desire to retain control over women at home and at work' (1995, pp. 9–10). Clark rewrites Edward Thompson's heroic account of working-class formation as a 'tragedy' in which 'The fatal flaws of misogyny and patriarchy ultimately muted the radicalism of the British working class' (1995, p. 271).

With her contention that political strategies were determined by the 'realities of power' rather than 'the dominance of discourse', Clark provided an important rejoinder to those who have emphasised the determining role of political rhetoric. In their examinations of the political addresses composed by female Charter societies, and the occasional reports of women's intervention in political debates, Clark and others have contended that Chartist women articulated their own understanding of their experience and interests as working-class women. Women's marginalisation and exclusion should be attributed therefore to the exclusive practices of male radicals, who failed to provide women with the resources to participate fully in the movement, rather than to women's lack of political ambition. However, if political interests and ideals are the product of particular movements and traditions, then how far can the political addresses of Chartist women be read as authentic and unmediated accounts of women's 'lived experience' or 'real interests'? In response to Edward Thompson and to historians of women, Joan Scott has asked:

> Can we assume a pre-existing common self-understanding on the part of women, or of all women of the same class? Was there an objectively describable working-class women's 'interest' in nineteenth-century England? How did the politics and the appeals of particular political movements figure in the definitions of such interest? (1988, p. 90)

This chapter explores these questions by examining how experience and interest were signified in the 'Address of the Female Political Union of Birmingham to the Women of England' that was printed in the *Birmingham Journal* on 6 October 1838.

The political addresses published in the Chartist press provide one of the few sources for the examination of women's participation in the movement, for there are few other records of the activities of many female societies. However, as Michelle de Larrabeiti has argued, the address was a highly stylised form of political rhetoric and cannot be seen as revealing in any straightforward way the complexities of women's political aspirations or intentions (1998, p. 108). The extensive reports on the Birmingham Female Political Union in its first year of existence provide a rare opportunity to contextualise the Union's political rhetoric in terms of the wider development of Chartist organisation and policy at local and national level. By reading the Address intertextually alongside other contemporary writings and speeches it is possible to analyse the strategic and performative aspects of political statements or utterances. The first part of this chapter considers how the Address was formulated within the conventions of radical discourse and representation and how these conventions may have shaped the potential meanings of the text. Although political actors may deploy an established political vocabulary, the meanings of words are rarely stable but rather are understood and redefined in the course of debate, dispute and struggle. In order to examine the changing inflections of political discourse, the chapter traces the production of the Address through the formation of the Union under the mentorship of its founding father, the Birmingham radical Thomas Clutton Salt. By examining the political dialogue of Chartist women, the chapter considers how the members received, utilised and reworked Salt's initial conception of women's political 'mission'.

Gender does not merely denote the different social roles ascribed to men and women for, as Scott has contended, it also operates as a primary signifier of other forms of political, cultural or social differentiation (1988, p. 45). The final part of the chapter explores how the ideas of sexual difference articulated by the Birmingham reformers were deployed, and acquired new meanings, in the context of heated disputes about political strategy, organisation and leadership.

What Right Have Women to Interfere with Politics? Political Rhetoric and the Construction of Identity

ADDRESS OF THE FEMALE POLITICAL
UNION OF BIRMINGHAM
TO THE WOMEN OF ENGLAND

Dearest Countrywomen!

We address you at the present crisis with mingled feelings of joy and sorrow – with joy, to see the united bands of English and Scotchmen determined to throw off that yoke of bondage which has so long cruelly impoverished them, pressed upon their energies, and almost driven them to despair – with sorrow, to see men so devoid of every feeling of humanity and justice, as to set at naught the petitions and the remonstrances of the people, and who, for their own aggrandisement and to gratify their own ambition, have not hesitated to make the people drink the cup of misery to the very dregs – with sorrow that we have to call you from your domestic duties to assist your fathers, sons, and brothers, in driving those factions from power, who, like the locusts of old, have devoured up everything and left the people to perish!

Dearest Countrywomen!

As you love your husbands, fathers, sons, and brothers, we implore you not to hesitate one moment, but immediately to co-operate with us in an endeavour to obtain those blessings, which God, in the fullness of his mercy, has conferred upon the land; but which our mis-governors have made of none effect, yea, in some instances turned into a curse.

Some may ask, what right have women to interfere with politics; let this be your answer –

"Those who call themselves our governors have brought misery to our dwellings, desolation to our hearths, and want, with all its concomitants, to ourselves and our families, by their accursed acts, which make our FOOD DEAR and our LABOUR CHEAP. If they have usurped the power, and arrogated to themselves the right of committing all these evils, surely we have a right to use those energies which God has given us, to alter that system which has so long oppressed us."

Dearest Countrywomen!

As you value the peace, the happiness, and the prosperity of yourselves and families, raise in every town, village and hamlet, the standard of liberty! Your husbands, sons, and brothers, with you will rally round it. Determine never to cease your exertions till your husbands, sons, and brothers, are placed upon an equal footing, in respect of political rights, with their richer neighbours. Then will England soon become, indeed, what it now is in name only – "the envy of surrounding nations and the admiration of the world." Then may we boast, in the language of the Spartan mothers of old – none but English women could produce such men!

These are the things we aim at, and these things, with the help of God, we will accomplish.

We call upon you to join us in the glorious struggle, to assist us in the noble task of raising our country from the present degradation and misery, to which the infamy of faction has reduced it. We aim at the possession of power, for the purpose of abolishing all unjust laws, but especially those laws that press upon honest industry – the Corn-laws, and that infamous law, the Poor Law Amendment act, which violates every feeling of humanity, sets aside the law of God, by which after they have taken from the honest workman the means of supporting himself and family by his own industry, and he is driven to the workhouse for relief, they place the husband and father in one place, the wife and mother in another, and their offspring in a third; regarding not the despair and wretchedness of the man, nor the heart-rending anguish of the bereaved mother, nor the tearful supplication of their children, not to be taken away from that protection which nature has given them a right to.

We appeal from the authors of misery, who have sacrificed every feeling of humanity at the shrine of avarice and ambition, to you, our countrywomen. We appeal to you, to save yourselves and families from these miseries, by joining with us and our now aroused countrywomen, in obtaining universal suffrage; for without that you can do nothing, with it everything. That is what we must obtain first, and then, when we have the power, we shall speedily get rid of those unjust laws we complain of.

We appeal to you, as wives, mothers, daughters, and sisters, to stand by us at the present crisis. Be united! be firm! be determined! and you must – you shall be free and happy!

CAROLINE BRADBURY
Presidentess.

The Address appeared in the *Birmingham Journal* without editorial comment. This in itself is significant, suggesting that the Female or Women's Political Union needed no introduction. Since its formation at the end of August, the FPU's weekly meetings had been reported regularly by the newspaper. These reports tended to be published alongside those of the Birmingham Political Union, which currently was co-ordinating support for the Charter in the town, and the national petition campaign. Though women did attend BPU functions, it was led by an all-male Council, and only men spoke formally at its meetings. The Women's Political Union had been established as a quasi-autonomous adjunct to the BPU, a status clearly approved by the *Birmingham Journal*, the official organ of the BPU, edited by a member of its executive Council, R.K. Douglas. The newspaper distinguished between the meetings of the respective organisations by the headings 'Political Union' and 'Women's Union', a naming device that tellingly indicated the anomalous status of the FPU as a political association. Nonetheless, that the Birmingham movement had its own journal which was sympathetic to female organisation is the main reason why the Women's Union would be the most extensively and consistently reported of all female Chartist associations.

Though the Address is signed by the Union's 'Presidentess', [Miss] Caroline Bradbury, this is by no means an indication of authorship. Quite possibly, it was written by one of the Union's male supporters who often led discussion at the Women's meetings. Neither do any of the reports in the *Birmingham Journal* mention discussion or adoption of the Address by the women members. If it was not written by the Union's founder, Salt, the Address certainly rehearsed his earlier appeals to the 'Women of Birmingham'. Since the question of authorship is probably unresolvable, the various addresses and statements of the Union and its male advocates will be examined below in terms of a political dialogue rather than as discrete texts. In some respects, however, the preoccupation with authorial identity is misleading, for the point of political addresses was to articulate a collective rather than an individual voice. It was fairly standard for addresses of political societies to be published unsigned, or to list the names of the society's executive. The political address was one of the most important forms of radical representation, circulated to sympathetic local newspapers and to the reform press. John Collins, a tool-maker, leading working-class Chartist, and consistent advocate of and speaker at the Women's Union, informed a subsequent meeting that the address would be forwarded to the *News* and the *True Sun* (*Birmingham Journal*, 13 October 1838, p. 3).

Political addresses were also designed to be delivered in public, for oral communication was as important as the written word in popular reform movements which aimed to include the illiterate and semi-literate. A rousing address provided a rhetorical high point for public meetings and demonstrations. The Female Union's Address was probably read out at meetings of women in other towns, held by Salt,

Collins and the BPU 'missionaries' on their lecture tours to promote the Charter; and the Birmingham women would discuss with delight the addresses from other female organisations. Political addresses had been one of the main forms of radical representation adopted by female reform societies since the earlier movement for universal manhood suffrage in the late 1810s (Rogers, 2000, pp. 11–23). They would provide a channel of communication between female Chartist societies, enabling their members to feel part of a national movement of women, for although a few women would become Chartist lecturers, they rarely spoke in public outside their own locality.

By adopting the format of the political address, the Birmingham women clearly identified themselves with a radical tradition with firmly established rhetorical conventions. Though theirs was the first address published by a female Chartist society, its language and imagery would be familiar to all reformers. At their meetings, the Birmingham women would refer to themselves as members of the working classes, but 'class' is not an identity used in their address. As many historians have demonstrated, the discourse of radical movements in nineteenth-century Britain was primarily populist in its appeal, invoking inclusive imagined communities, most commonly 'the people', 'the nation', and 'humanity' (Stedman Jones, 1983; Belchem, 1981; Joyce, 1991). When radicals used the term 'class' to describe themselves it was often in the expansive sense of the 'industrious' or 'producing classes' which could include everyone involved in the creation rather than the consumption of wealth, and even when they referred to the 'working' or 'middle classes' it was almost always in the plural. 'The people' were defined by their love of liberty, fairness and care for their fellow beings, and by their difference from those who acted in the interests of selfish and exclusive elites: 'the factions' and 'mis-governors' condemned by the FPU. This was a radical analysis of society in which the relationships of political exclusion and inclusion were seen as determining social as well as political power. Oppressive legislation was at the root of their misery, alleged the Birmingham women, and therefore they demanded universal suffrage, 'for without it you can do nothing, with it everything ... when we have power, we shall speedily get rid of those unjust laws we complain of'.

The radical analysis outlined by the FPU employed a primarily 'political vocabulary' that had been articulated by political reform movements since the 1790s but which drew eclectically from older political and intellectual traditions, including seventeenth-century radical dissent, Lockean natural rights, eighteenth-century civic humanism and constitutionalism (Stedman Jones, 1983). However, as Anna Clark has shown, these traditions retained 'a patriarchal notion of the masculine head of household as the proper elector' (1996b, pp. 232–3). Many political reformers grounded this masculine entitlement in a mythic history of the 'ancient constitution' of Anglo-Saxony when, before the imposition of the Norman yoke, all male householders earned the entitlement to vote because they bore arms in their country's defence. In the 1790s plebeian reformers, influenced by the democratic claims of the French Revolution and by Thomas Paine's *Rights of Man*, began to appeal to the ideal of fraternity, rather than the more exclusive definition of householder, a position that many working men could not attain. The universalism of Paine's natural rights discourse offered an even more inclusive identity, 'humanity', one which, as Clark notes, was invoked both by Mary Wollstonecraft in her effort to claim the innate capacity of both sexes for reason and virtue and by plebeian reformers to emphasise 'empathy, derived from one's hardships, [and] for the sufferings of others' (1996a, pp. 267–9). Both of these rhetorical developments enabled conceptions of 'the People' that included both sexes.

In common with female reform societies since the late 1810s, the Birmingham Chartists sought to show how the humanity of the people was signalled by their deference to the gendered and familial roles allotted to them by divine and natural law. The effects of oppressive legislation, they contended, were experienced and felt as members of families:

the Poor Law Amendment act, which violates every feeling of humanity, sets aside the law of God, by which after they have taken from the honest workman the means of supporting himself and family by his own industry, and he is driven to the workhouse for relief, they place the husband and father in one place, the wife and mother in another, and their offspring in a third; regarding not the despair and wretchedness of the man, nor the heart-rending anguish of the bereaved mother, nor the tearful supplication of their children, not to be taken away from that protection which nature has given them a right to.

For the Birmingham Chartists, the differing political capacities of the people are determined by their responsibilities and duties as family members. They advise their 'Countrywomen' that their role is to inspire and 'assist' their menfolk:

As you value the peace, the happiness, and the prosperity of yourselves and families, raise in every town, village and hamlet, the standard of liberty! Your husbands, sons and brothers, with you will rally round it. Determine never to cease you exertions till your husbands, sons, and brothers, are placed upon an equal footing, in respect of political rights, with their richer neighbours.

Some of the early studies of female Chartism argued that by emphasising their respectability and by positioning themselves in a supportive role to men, Chartist women placed a 'self-imposed limitation on the female contribution' (Thomis and Grimmet, 1982, p. 114). Subsequently, feminist analyses have contended that the auxiliary role permitted to and claimed by Chartist women was itself indicative of Chartist formulations of sexual difference which inflected the rhetoric and the organisational forms developed by the movement. In one of the first attempts to investigate the implications of the language of sexual difference in radical politics, Sally Alexander claimed that 'natural rights and Biblical law ... together with the evocation of a golden age always prove insecure foundations for equality between the sexes', for women tend to be placed 'closer to nature and the animal world, distancing them from human law and knowledge ... Women's exclusion from independent subjectivity is then a consequence of their different capacity and place. Valued for their household skills and domestic virtue as part of the family under the protection of men', concludes Alexander, 'independence is almost inconceivable' (1984, pp. 141–2). Chartism, in this interpretation, is acknowledged as permitting women to speak about and to politicise their experience of the family but also seen as limiting that enquiry by appealing to a nostalgic past and the divine and natural truths of sexual difference.

In what ways, then, might the radical discourses inherited by the Birmingham Female Political Union have contained or enabled the self-representation of its members? Working with a Foucauldian model of subject formation, the philosopher Judith Butler has challenged the idea that the subject exists prior to discourse but rather argues that the subject is brought into being through a 'regulated process of repetition'. '[A]ll signification', she suggests, 'takes place within the orbit of the compulsion to repeat' and therefore constitutes a performance or re-enactment (Butler, 1990, p. 145). Repetition may be subversive, however, if it draws attention to the *act* of repetition to reveal the performative rather than innate or natural status of identity. For Butler, subversion is likely to take a parodic form: 'there is a subversive laughter in the pastiche-effect of parodic practices', she argues, 'in which the original, the authentic, and the real are themselves constituted as effects' (1990, p. 146). As 'the effects of a subtle and politically enforced performativity' Butler contends that gender itself is an 'act' that 'is open to splittings, self-parody, self-criticism, and those hyperbolic exhibitions of "the natural" that in their very exaggeration, reveal its fundamentally phantasmatic status' (1990, pp. 146–7). In Butler's much discussed example, drag potentially can constitute subversive repetition by drawing attention to the manufactured and performative nature of gender identity.

Butler's formulations of performativity and subversion are both helpful and problematic in examining the self-representation of Chartist women. Their assertion of their careful observation of their natural duties as women can be seen as constituting an act of reiteration. Could their use of hyperbolic rhetoric and extravagant imagery be seen as an exaggerated performance that signals the performative nature of femininity? Though, as will be discussed below, there are specific instances where radical women used parody to ridicule the pretensions of their political opponents, or even men within their own movements, parody was, in general, a very difficult mode for them to inhabit. Since the French Revolution, the public appearance of the female reformer had been marked by the publication of grotesquely sexualised and animalistic caricatures that defamed the reputation of radical women and, by extension, 'henpecked' radical men who had lost mastery to their women. Alternatively, women who pursued their own political rights were represented as un-sexed spinster blue-stockings, who had lost both common sense and common feeling for those of whom they should take care. Throughout the 1830s, the working woman, particularly the factory woman, with her alleged lack of domestic skills and attachment, was held by a whole array of 'experts' and opinion-makers to be the source of family disintegration and hence social degeneration (Hamilton, 1998). With so many people speaking in derogatory terms about them, and so few opportunities to speak for themselves, female reformers, especially from the lower classes, were unlikely to opt for self-criticism or self-parody as a rhetorical device. It may be useful to qualify Butler's model by distinguishing between hyperbolic and parodic forms of representation. Why should we assume that the hyperbolic enactment of gender roles indicates an ironic and self-conscious rejection of those roles? For radical women the claim to speak 'the truth' may have been as subversive as any act of mockery or parody. Moreover, the *assertion*, rather than the *subversion*, of femininity may, in their terms, have been an act of political defiance.

The 'experience' recounted by the Birmingham Chartists was the product of a highly stylised, melodramatic rhetoric: 'the factions' have forced 'the people to drink from the cup of misery to the very dregs'; have 'like the locusts of old ... devoured up everything and left the people to perish!' As a number of historians have shown, melodrama saturated radical discourse. The conventions of melodrama invoked a world of moral absolutes in which good struggles with evil. Through its use of exaggerated imagery, gesture and prose, melodrama made those truths accessible and understandable to all; but 'truth' was also seen as manifested in the world itself: no one with a heart could deny the suffering of a mother separated from her children. Melodrama, therefore, was an inclusive medium, which might be particularly appealing to those with little social status, such as poor women. But melodrama was also a drama of restoration rather than of revolution and therefore could have conservative as well as radical implications (Brooks, 1976; Joyce, 1994, pp. 161–75). Within the political imagination of the Chartists, it has been argued, melodrama entailed the restoration of lost constitutional rights and the return to the 'natural order' of the family (Clark, 1995, pp. 221–6).

However, the meanings of texts do not lie merely in their form, and hyperbolic or melodramatic representations of truth and reality jostled with and were inflected by other modes of representation, often within the same text (Rogers, 2000, pp. 10–11, 21). In particular, Chartists used the form of the manifesto: a statement of demands based on the natural rights discourse of the Enlightenment which released reformers from the dictates of custom and precedence. If the Birmingham women desire to speak as mothers, it is 'in the language of Spartan mothers of old'; but this appeal to a historic model of republican motherhood is accompanied by their perception of the present struggle of their countrywomen who are *already* 'now aroused, in obtaining universal suffrage; for without that you can do nothing, with it everything'. Is it significant that the Address omits the qualifier *manhood* in its demand for the suffrage? Although the Birmingham women announce their intention of supporting men, their address oscillates between identifying the political rights of 'their' men and a more open and inclusive assertion of 'our rights': 'We aim at the possession of power', they claim. The 'we' here seems to refer both to 'we, women' and 'we, the people'. With other Chartists, the Birmingham Address distinguished between different bodies of the people: the suffering community; the women who can testify on behalf of a people in suffering; and the men who could represent the rights of the people before the political nation. The presence of women in reform culture, however, could both signal and confuse these distinctive conceptions of the people. In posing the question 'What right have women to interfere with politics?', does the Address leave open the possibility that women might become fully independent political subjects? If the populist tradition deployed a highly changeable and ambiguous meaning system, this was never more so than in the Chartist decade; but in order to explore more fully the potential meanings that may have been intended by or imputed to the Address, we need to move beyond the text itself, to examine the conditions of its existence.

'Women Have Thought so Little Upon Politics': The Political History of Women in Birmingham

With the question 'What right have women to interfere with politics?', the Birmingham Address can be seen as 'repeating' or 'answering' not only its potential critics, but also the question posed by Thomas Clutton Salt, the founder of the Women's Union. In his 'Address to the Women of Birmingham', published on 16 August 1838 and distributed in the weeks preceding the formation of the Union, Salt provided the female Chartist with an extended riposte to the question 'Wherefore are Women made to meddle with politics?':

> Let this be your reply:–
> The Idle have legislated for the Industrious, the Wealthy for the Poor ... They dragged the Wife from her home, the Child from its sport, to break down the wages of the Husband and Father ... Therefore do the people gather together, and therefore do the Women leave their homes to attend political meetings ...

Salt's Address was reprinted and given a national readership by the *Northern Star,* the widest circulating Chartist newspaper (25 August 1838, p. 8). Salt was a prominent middle-class radical and a leading member of the Birmingham Political Union. Jutta Schwarzkopf, author of the fullest examination of female Chartism to date, contends that Salt's eulogising of female domesticity exemplified his 'middle-class thinking' and that by appealing themselves to 'woman's mission' – a 'ruling-class ideological device' – Chartist women laid themselves open to 'increasing pressure to conform to middle-class standards' (1991, p. 122). Significantly, though, Salt always spoke to the FPU as a body of poor women and seems to have made no appeal to women of the higher classes. The middle classes had abandoned the working classes in 1832, he advised the FPU (*Birmingham Journal*, 27 October 1838, p. 3), and he warned one Chartist that 'From the middle classes, I expect nothing until virtue becomes with them a necessity, and they see the people strong in their union; then they will begin to seek shelter in their ranks' (*Northern Star*, 5 May 1838, p. 3). Salt explained his own commitment to the Chartist cause in terms of his response to the deprivation faced by labouring women the previous year: 'He had never forgotten the scene last winter, when respectable matrons stood exposed to the scorn and pity of their fellow creatures, almost fighting for a piece of flannel' (*Birmingham Journal*, 27 October 1838, p. 3). Salt's use of the word 'scene' tellingly indicates the ways he dramatised the 'experience' of poor women, acting as scriptwriter for their collective voice. His Address offered a template for female

Chartist representation that could be adopted by subsequent societies, including that of the Birmingham Union.

Salt's identification with working-class women indicates the changing class alliances within the town's reform movements. Since its formation to campaign for a Reform Bill in January 1830, the BPU had appealed to all classes but especially to the industrious working and middle classes, in order to build a popular movement with a national reach. The members of its Political Council, on which Salt sat, believed that the interests of 'the People' could be represented by the enfranchisement of property-holding, rate-paying men and they suspended the Union in the aftermath of the 1832 Reform Act which extended the suffrage to the £10 male householder, effectively enfranchising middle-class men. Working-class radicals in Birmingham refused to accept this limited suffrage, which reduced the number of working-men voters in many areas (Behagg, 1990, pp. 158–83). Their calls for full manhood suffrage intensified in response to the 'class legislation' passed by the so-called 'Reformed Parliament'. Political radicalism was accompanied by workplace radicalism (Behagg, 1990, pp. 104–57).

Birmingham's manufacturing base was mainly in small- to medium-scale workshop production, and large-scale capitalists like Salt, a lamp manufacturer, were exceptional. Both workers and established manufacturers like Salt felt the effects of aggressive competition from smaller and newer capitalists who sought to undercut prices by forcing down wages. In a good year, Salt explained to a parliamentary select committee in 1833, he could make profits of £3000, but in a bad year like the current one, he made none at all; he had once employed upwards of 120 men, but now only 60 (1833, qq. 4538 and 4556). Birmingham was at the centre of attempts to form general unions across the trades in the period 1833–4; while, concurrently, the merchants and larger manufacturers, who had dominated the BPU, began to pursue currency reform as a means of increasing and cheapening the supply of money (Behagg, 1990, pp. 178–83). By 1837, these middle-class radicals resumed their efforts to build alliances with working-class radicals, partly to promote currency reform and to provide a popular base in their bid for local leadership of the town, as it obtained new powers of local government through a Charter of Incorporation (Behagg, 1990, p. 185). As a Guardian of the Poor charged with overseeing the administration of poor relief, Salt claimed intimate knowledge of the immiseration of the working classes (1833, q. 4590). He began to back the calls of working-class radicals for universal manhood suffrage as the only means of securing the political representation of the poor. When the BPU resumed its political activities in 1837, Salt lobbied for a mass campaign based around the raising of a national petition that would be signed by 2 million men and women (Flick, 1978, pp. 129–30).

The 1832 Reform Act was significant in gender as well as class terms because, for the first time in statute, the vote was defined as applying to 'male persons' only. A few contemporary feminists, such as John Stuart Mill, realised that this specification further secured women's customary exclusion from the franchise; and it would take almost a century before advocates of women's suffrage obtained equal voting rights for both sexes (Clark, 1996b). William Lovett claimed that he had included the provision for female suffrage in his original draft of the Charter but dropped the clause when other reformers advised that it might discourage support (Thompson, 1984, p. 124). Salt never intimated in public that women might be entitled to the franchise, but rather called on women to defend their own and their families' interests by supporting the right of their husbands, fathers and sons to vote. One life-long advocate of women's political rights, the Birmingham co-operator George Jacob Holyoake, recalled that Salt was one of the first men to actively encourage women's political participation; for he had written a pamphlet in 1832 that repeatedly called on women to 'meddle with politics' (1906, p. 29). Though women had attended reform demonstrations in 1832, they had not established their own societies and, as Salt would tell the women of Birmingham in 1838, the men had made a 'bungling job' of the Reform Bill, for 'nothing was done well but what was done by women' (Lopatin, 1999, p. 168; *Birmingham Journal*, 14 July 1838, p. 4). Salt set out to formalise and extend the participation of women by launching the Birmingham Female Political Union that would stand as a model for similar associations across the country (*Northern Star*, 5 May 1838, p. 3). His plan for the national organisation of women began with 'a Public Meeting of the Women of Birmingham' at the Town Hall on 7 April 1838. Both the venue and composition of the meeting were highly significant. Twelve thousand women were reported as filling to capacity the central building of local government.

The assembled women passed three resolutions that very probably were drafted by Salt. As expressed in the subsequent Address of the Union, the meeting agreed that parliament had passed 'corn-laws to make food dear, and money-laws to make money dear' and had combined 'with free trade to make labour cheap; giving MONOPOLY to the wealthy, and COMPETITION to the poor', and that only universal suffrage would ensure the overthrow of the iniquitous New Poor Law. The first resolution called into being a new political subject, the female Chartist:

> The Women of Birmingham, not forgetful that the proper sphere of women's virtue is in the performance of their important domestic

duties, have nevertheless thought it incumbent on them to hold a great public meeting, to consider the increasing difficulties to which they find themselves and their families exposed; difficulties which have destroyed the happiness of their homes, and forced them from that retirement and those duties to which they are so much attached, and on the due performance of which the welfare of their families so materially depends, to undertake labours in workshops unsuited to their sex, and further, to consider that even this resource has become less secure in its continuance, and more scanty in its remuneration. (*Birmingham Journal*, 7 April 1838)

That Salt prepared a justification of women's right to protest in public may well have been a calculated move to anticipate and deflect criticism of women's intrusion in the political arena. Encouraging the Sheffield radical Ebenezer Elliot to hold a similar meeting of women, Salt boasted that, 'I alone of Birmingham reformers, dared convene or attend it.' The step was necessary, however, for he claimed:

I believe (I might say I know) that hitherto, the women have thought so little upon politics, and being so utterly ignorant of the connection of our system with their poverty and degradation, that they have either not interfered, or persuaded their husbands from meddling with politics, as a thing of no profit. We cannot afford their neutrality or hostility; they must be our enthusiastic friends. (*Northern Star*, 5 May 1838, p. 3, repr. Frow, 1989, pp. 192–3)

Women's political ignorance was a familiar charge. The political body that cooperated with the BPU in drafting and promoting the Charter, the London Working Men's Association, encouraged its members to involve their wives in their political concerns in order to combat the reactionary influence women were believed to exert over men (Lovett, 1920, vol. 1, p. 98). However, Salt carefully prescribed the limits of women's political engagement. At a second public meeting of women in July, he reassured the assembly that he would not appeal to the 'influence' of women 'upon ordinary occasions': 'There was a sacredness about the character of woman in the retirement of her home, that must not be lightly trespassed upon' and he 'was the last that would wish to see her habitually taking part publicly in angry political discussions' (*Birmingham Journal*, 14 July 1838, p. 3).

Salt ascribed women's newly acquired sense of political identifica- tion to their 'deeply felt' and 'religious' resolution to protect their children, and it was to the history of women's participation in Christian and philanthropic missionary work that Salt looked for a legitimising precedent (*Northern Star*, 5 May 1838, p. 3). 'The agency of Women sent the Missionary on his christian pilgrimage; it redeemed the slavery of the Negroes! It has ever triumphed!', he proclaimed (*Northern Star*, 25 August 1838, p. 8). Throughout the 1830s women's domestic, Christian and political duties were all formulated around the ideals of 'woman's mission' and 'female influence'. These terms resonated with specifically evangelical conceptions of mission that, since the beginning of the century, had been assimilated by dissenting and secular discourses. They depended for their meaning on a notion of sexual differentiation, denoting the distinctive capacities of women for moral and spiritual sensibility, empathy with others, and nurturance; and yet they could also be mobilised spectacularly to widen the accepted sphere of female activity (Davidoff and Hall, 1987). In the name of women's Christian duty to relieve the suffering and to accept everyone as an equal child of Christ, the Birmingham Female Society for the Relief of the Negro Slaves, the first female abolitionist society in the country, instigated the popular campaign for immediate rather than the gradual abolition of slavery. The 'truths' of sexual difference were confirmed by women anti-slavers when they strove as Christian daughters and mothers not only to eliminate slavery but to make the Christian family the bedrock of post-Emancipation society (Midgley, 1992).

The philanthropic and Christian missionary work celebrated by Salt was very much associated with the activities of middle- and upper-class women. The language of 'woman's mission' and 'female influence' was, however, highly contested. In the 1830s it had been deployed with very different meanings and effects by radicals in the freethought and Owenite-socialist movements, which were socially mixed, and included plebeian women (Taylor, 1983, pp. 30–1). Far from women in Birmingham being entirely ignorant of politics, there was in fact a history of women's political activism within the decade that Salt's contention obscured. Throughout the 1820s and the 1830s women had participated in the campaign for press freedom and for the repeal of the stamp duties on newspapers, or the 'taxes on knowledge'. In 1833, 150 women from Birmingham signed their names and addresses when they volunteered in Richard Carlile's campaign for press freedom and political reform (*Gauntlet*, 25 August 1833; repr. Frow, 1989, pp. 50–5). 'Some men may ask, why do women make [freedom] their business?' they remonstrated, professing that:

> Our reasons are two: first because Englishmen have neglected theirs; and, secondly, because our interests are inseparably connected with the welfare of men: and, being so, we are bound to co-operate with them for the general good. Others may ask, what can women do? To such we would reply by asking, what have women not effected? None but a novice can doubt our ingenuity, and none but a fool would set our power at naught.

With 'the "Rights of Man" enclosed in our hands' they denounced the exploitation of the working classes by the middle classes and the machine, along with the national church and the boroughmongery. Their declaration of support for 'Equal Rights and Equal Laws' was no doubt informed by their reading of the *Gauntlet* in which Carlile expounded the rights of women to free marriage and divorce, as well as to education and political representation (*Gauntlet*, 25 August 1833; repr. Frow, 1989, pp. 50–5). In their political addresses, women in freethinking, republican movements tended to be considerably less deferential to their male allies than other female reformers and often, like the Birmingham volunteers, criticised the intellectual and political condescension of radical men towards women (McCalman, 1980; Rogers, 2000, pp. 48–79).

It had been customary in the Black Country for women to work in many of the numerous branches of the metal trades, usually in small- to medium-sized workshops or as outworkers in the home (Pinchbeck, 1985, pp. 270–81). With the introduction of machinery in the early decades of the nineteenth century, many trades formerly dominated by men transferred to female labour. There is a certain historic irony in Salt's repeated protest that women had been dragged from their homes to labour in unnatural occupations. In 1833 he had testified to the parliamentary select committee on manufactures that, as a consequence of falling prices, he had resorted to the 'screwing system' in his own brass manufactory, undercutting the wages of skilled male artisans with non-apprenticed cheap labour: 'There are many inferior parts of the work that used to pass through the men's hands; we take as much of this as we can off the men, and have it done in parts by the boys or the women, and then give it to the men to finish; which, while the trade was good, men would not submit to.' Women workers queued outside his factory to receive employment at half the pay received by men (1833, qq. 4565 and 4564). The gendered employment practices of manufacturers like Salt had not gone without criticism. The Owenite-socialist newspaper the *Pioneer*, edited in Birmingham by James Morrison, urged trade unions to defend equal wages for men and women, and the unionisation of both sexes (Taylor, 1983, pp. 83–117). Writing as the 'Bondswoman of Birmingham', his wife Frances Morrison pointed out to her 'sister bondswomen' that:

In manufacturing towns, look at the value that is set on woman's labour, whether it be skilful, whether it be laborious, so that woman can do it [*sic*]. The contemptible expression is, it is made by woman, and therefore cheap? Why, I ask, should woman's labour be thus undervalued? Why should the time and ingenuity of the sex, that could be so usefully employed otherwise, be monopolized by cruel and greedy oppressors, being in the likeness of man, and calling themselves masters? (*Pioneer*, 8 February 1834; repr. Frow, 1989, pp. 141–2)

Like the Birmingham volunteers, the Bondswoman criticised men who 'in general, tremble at the idea of a reading wife'. By dedicating a 'Page to the Ladies' the *Pioneer* actively promoted the self-organisation and self-expression of working women, subsequently dropping the 'aristocratical' term 'Lady' in favour of 'Woman'. It provided a forum for information about the organisation of women in trades unions and for wide-ranging discussion about marriage, the relations between the sexes, education and culture.

Several feminist historians have argued that by championing the male breadwinner and the domestic wife, the Chartist movement retreated from the more progressive and egalitarian strategies developed within the freethinking, republican and Owenite communities (Taylor, 1983, pp. 265–75). Schwarzkopf contends that, like Salt, Chartist men welcomed women's participation with the proviso that they accepted the 'supportive' and 'subordinate' role allotted to them, and sanctioned a 'clearly demarcated sexual division of labour' (1991, pp. 209–12). In 1833, when Salt had complained to the select committee that he had been forced to undercut the wages of skilled men, he had spoken only of the dire effects of low wages and unemployment on the working man and made no comment on the position of the woman worker. He proposed, then, that currency reform was *the* solution to the 'continual degradation of both parties' – manufacturers and working men (1833, qq. 4667 and 4760). As the conflicts between masters and men intensified in the 1830s, it seems that the removal of female labour became an issue around which men of different social classes could unite. Yet did the aspiration for a male 'family wage' that would enable women to withdraw from paid work outside the home necessarily involve the subordination of women as political subjects? Even the Bondswoman of Birmingham, we should note, asked, 'Why should the time and ingenuity of the sex, *that could be so usefully employed otherwise*, be monopolized by cruel and greedy oppressors?' (my emphasis). Rather than being seen as a form of 'false consciousness', perhaps it is more helpful to analyse the aspirations of working people for the family wage and female domesticity as a 'rational' response to the organisation of productive and reproductive labour (Rose, 1993, pp. 186–7; Rogers, 2000, p. 26). To consider these questions, I now move from the formal political texts produced by the Birmingham reformers to the debates and discussions that they generated, and consider whether these betray the traces of alternative political traditions or forms of expression.

'Let This be Your Reply': The Political Discussions of the Female Political Union

While Schwarzkopf emphasises the restrained nature of female self-representation in the movement, other historians argue that Chartist women manipulated the language of domesticity to articulate a defiant, political voice that spoke for working-class women (de Larrabeiti, 1988, p. 111). Clark claims that Chartist women developed their own conception of 'militant domesticity' that 'differed subtly from the flowery rhetoric of the Chartist men' as well as from middle-class conceptions of 'woman's mission' (1992, pp. 73, 78). In comparison with Salt's frequent references to the distress caused by women being dragged from their homes to labour, the address of the Female Political Union did not comment on women's work outside the home, except to condemn their governors who 'make our FOOD DEAR and our LABOUR CHEAP'. In the reported discussions of the Union, as in its address, it was the experience of motherhood, rather than employment, that was seen as the strongest tie uniting working-class women across the nation, although motherhood was constructed as a form of labour, as well as a familial duty and a loving bond. Mrs Lapworth, the chairwoman of the Union, contrasted the expectations of rich and poor women, particularly in their experience as mothers, in order to confirm the members' understanding of social and political injustice and to stir their confidence to seek an improvement in their condition. Lapworth self-consciously appropriated and reworked pre-scriptive literature on the duties of motherhood. She opened one meeting by reading some verses 'expressive of maternal affection' in order to point out that the poor did not lack affection but just the means to indulge their children. Reflecting on her own suffering when she first became a mother, she asserted that:

> At that time she thought there must be something wrong on the part of those over them, or she would not have been in that condition, particularly when she knew that there were hundreds around her, of her own sex, who had never laboured, and did not know how to labour, and were enjoying all the comforts of life. Had she then known as much of the real cause of her distress, as she did at the present time, she would have sallied forth and forced on a combination of the working classes.

Rich ladies, Lapworth claimed, were not ignorant of, but rather 'insensible' to, the sufferings of the poor, and only talked of them in order 'to procure more labour for the least money'. Where Salt called on the Union to emulate the activities of the female abolitionists, Lapworth pointed out that certain ladies in the town who concerned themselves with the welfare of black slaves were blind to the mortality rates among infants in the Birmingham workhouse (*Birmingham Journal*, 29 September 1838, p. 3).

As Michelle de Larrabeiti notes, where middle-class abolitionist women could 'only speak of the experience of oppression and poverty in terms of the "other", the Chartist women inflect the rhetoric differently as they had not only personally experienced poverty and hardship but had been the *object* of similar rhetorical descriptions' (1988, p. 112). Chartist women's self-vindication as dutiful and loving homemakers contested the persistent denunciations of working-class women's domestic attainment and attachment. While referring to the exploitation of female labour, Lapworth concentrated on the cultural and emotional effects of deprivation and inequality, rather than analysing in detail the nature of the employment relationship itself. Poor women, she implied, had internalised their oppression, fearing criticism and pity from their friends as well as their superiors. Their newly acquired political analysis should empower the members of the Union to examine their individual experiences of poverty as part of their common condition:

> They must recollect that, however wealthy those above them might be, they were nothing more than their fellow women, and they must not be frightened of their displeasure. Above all things, they must not be ashamed of their poverty. She knew that often a blush of shame twinkled upon their cheeks, when a friend happened to walk into their houses and caught them eating an inferior or scanty meal. She knew they were accustomed to make apologies, and feel as if they had been caught in some bad act. She hoped ... they would openly acknowledge it, that they would make it known, and talk of it, and ask the cause of it ... the rich would say the poor were looking for equality. She denied it. They did not want to disturb the rich in their enjoyments; but the rich must not be surprised if the poor felt unhappy, when they could not get anything like a sufficient quantity of food or raiment for their labour. (*Birmingham Journal*, 29 September 1838, p. 3)

Lapworth's reminiscences allow a fleeting glimpse of the interiority of one Chartist subject, for the Chartist press rarely recorded the dialogue of individual Chartist women. Clearly, her recollections do not provide a transparent account of lived experience, for Lapworth gave dramatic shape to her 'experience' to gain the attention of her audience and to give force to her political analysis. Nevertheless, with its acknowledgement of personally and privately felt shame and anxiety, the emotional register of her speech is different from that of the stylised female addresses, with their high-blown, uplifting rhetoric of collective struggle.

Personal recollection could sanction more idiosyncratic, and hence in some ways more disruptive voices, than the formulaic political address, with its univocal and one-dimensional invocation of female experience. This is demonstrated by another member of the Female Political Union who challenged her critics by re-enacting Salt's vindication of the female politician. There are significant differences in the tone of this female speaker and that of her political mentor. To much applause, she recounted to the Union how she had rounded on some 'Tory acquaintances' who had 'violently attacked' her for meddling in politics:

> She replied, that she would not have done so, had she not suffered by politics; and had she not found that, by leaving politics entirely to the men, her condition, and that of her neighbours, was getting worse. She considered the women had a right to interfere for the purpose of procuring such changes as would improve their situation. The lords and ladies of the land enjoyed all the good things of creation, while those who procured them could not touch them. She had long given up the practice of repeating that part of the grace before meals which thanked the Almighty for his 'good creatures' because seldom or never did it happen that good creatures came to her humble table. (Hear! Hear!). (*Northern Star*, 1 September 1838, p. 6)

In place of melodrama, this Chartist woman used irony to mock bitterly the sanctimony and false piety of the wealthy. Through her use of black humour she constructed the members of the Union as a knowing community, sharing a joke at the expense of the wealthy and the hypocritical. Like Lapworth, by lambasting the high and mighty, she reduced them to size, and made them the targets of a just and righteous anger.

With their participation in political discussion, the members of the Female Political Union acknowledged their growing self-confidence. Mrs Lapworth attributed this assurance to the political education they were grateful to receive from the Council members; 'the women knew little of politics, but they were daily becoming better acquainted with them and ought to feel thankful to those gentlemen who took the trouble to instruct them.' Had their mothers and grandmothers studied politics, she added, the women would not be enduring such miserable conditions (*Birmingham Journal*, 1 September 1838, p. 7). The gracious acknowledgement that women paid to their male instructors for troubling to teach them was part of the stylised chivalric code that Chartists negotiated in mixed-sex political arenas. Chartists established their own culture of 'separate spheres', as when a gallery was set aside for the 'females' at a public meeting; but, nevertheless, the leadership role played by the committee-members of the FPU was publicly recognised by their allocation of seats alongside leading members of the Political Council (*Birmingham Journal*, 8 September 1838, p. 7). The importance of the FPU was further emphasised when it was granted two places on the Council. These positions were filled by Miss Mary Ann Groves and Mrs Birch, although there were no subsequent reports of their participation in that body (*Birmingham Journal*, 10 November 1838, p. 6; 22 December 1838, p. 6). The absence of such reports may be indicative of the marginal role permitted women within the movement as a whole. Few women were ever nominated or elected to Chartist delegate bodies (Schwarzkopf, 1991, p. 239).

The members were encouraged by the instant success of their organisation. By the end of September 1838 it had nearly 3000 members and had raised 13,000 signatures for a women's petition for the Charter (*Birmingham Journal*, 22 September 1838, p. 7; 29 September 1838, p. 3). Although men tended to lead the speeches at the Union, at least as they were reported by the *Birmingham Journal*, women took more and more responsibility for running the meetings and began to treat the men as their own delegates. The speeches delivered by Chartist men at the women's meetings were similar to those they gave at the BPU meetings, indicating that they saw themselves as equally accountable to the women as to the men of the movement. The women members asked Salt and Collins for information about their lecture tours and the progress of the movement but they also insisted that their own contribution to the cause was acknowledged. When Collins praised the 'men of Birmingham' for their 'glorious victory' in presenting the case for the Charter at an anti-Corn Law meeting, one woman called out, 'And by the women in the meeting, Mr Collins; for we were there' (*Birmingham Journal*, 2 February 1839, p. 6). As the women members gained in political experience and confidence, they increasingly questioned the policies of their leaders.

'Taking Part Publicly in Angry Political Discussions': Gender and the Construction of Political Authority

Though Salt had worried that some reformers might question the legitimacy of women 'meddling' in politics, his plan for the national organisation of women met with an overwhelmingly positive response in the Chartist press. The fate of Europe, even, the *Northern Star* proclaimed, depended on the determination of other British towns to cooperate with Salt and the women of Birmingham (5 May 1838, p. 4). 'I have seen a woman making buttons in Birmingham, who would have beaten three lords', declared Bronterre O'Brien; 'women are sturdier petitioners than men, – wherefore, encourage their Unions' (*Northern Star*, 8 September 1838, p. 4). Such recommendations of the strength of female influence and power encouraged women to make demands on the movement. Rather than simply expressing their support for the Charter they began to intervene in debates over how the Charter would be won. As Chartists debated the legitimacy of different methods of political pressure, including the use of force, the ritual gesturing towards 'female influence' acquired different meanings. In the course of heated debates over political tactics, Chartists increasingly used the rhetoric of sexual difference to vindicate and ridicule opposing positions and to validate particular conceptions of political authority.

Political differences between the Female Union and its male supporters surfaced at a meeting in December 1838 when Collins read the political address from the Nottingham Female Political Union 'To the Patriotic Women of England'. This was the first female Chartist address to be printed in the *Northern Star* and it initiated a wave of addresses from women's associations across the country. Salt had spoken at one of the first meetings of the NFPU, but the Nottingham address offered a much more militant model of the female politician than that permitted by Salt. Where Salt eulogised women's 'influence', the Nottingham address repeatedly invoked the 'power' of women, a term which, as we have seen, was also used in the address of the Birmingham Union. Women should demand that their husbands support the Charter, it declared. The address anticipated an imminent struggle between the forces of progress and reaction, and launched a blistering attack on the middle classes who 'are now beginning to manifest their doubts and fears' and 'must ever be considered in the light of false friends'. By calling on the people to identify themselves with or against reform, the Nottingham Union clearly associated itself with the physical-force wing of the movement, which asserted the right of reformers to defend themselves and take the Charter by force if necessary. Women would play an indispensable role in the impending battle and therefore should be 'of good cheer':

> the time must and will arrive when your aid and sympathies may be required in the field to fight, for be assured a great and deadly struggle must take place ere our tyrant oppressors yield to reason and justice. They mean to slay and fight the people; while ours and yours will be the solemn duty to aid the wounded to dress their wounds, and perhaps to afford the last sad solace of our affections in the hour of death. ''Tis better to die by the sword than by famine',

and we shall glory in seeing every working man of England selling his coat to buy a rifle to be prepared for the event. (*Northern Star*, 8 December 1838, p. 6)

In response to the enthusiasm of the Birmingham women who loudly applauded the address, Collins warned that the Nottingham women demonstrated 'an exuberance of the warmth of feelings' and that to persuade the people to use arms for political purposes was unconstitutional and could lead to imprisonment and transportation (*Birmingham Journal*, 15 December 1838, p. 3). In Nottingham the address shook the fragile cross-class alliance that had marked the first months of Chartist agitation in the town but it was also symptomatic of a conflict that was dividing Chartists across Britain (Rogers, 2000, pp. 101–6).

By October 1838 sharp differences of opinion were being expressed about the best means of pressing the case for the Charter and what reformers should do if parliament refused to pass its demands. A range of measures were debated: a run on the banks for gold; abstinence from taxed goods; exclusive dealing, or shopping only with those who supported the Charter. Such measures enabled Chartists to take direct action. The Birmingham Union advertised a list of traders who supported the Charter and its members were urged to abstain from buying excisable goods such as alcohol; Mrs Lapworth already boycotted beer because of the tax on malt (*Birmingham Journal*, 3 November 1838, p. 3a; 27 October 1838, p. 3). More disputed was the plan for a 'national holiday' when Chartists would withdraw from labour until their demands were met; but most contentious of all was the question of whether Chartists had the right to arm and to drill in public, either to present a show of force, to defend the people if their meetings were attacked, or to take their rights by force if they were denied by parliament. However, drilling and torch-lit processions were already taking place, especially in the northern manufacturing districts where Chartism had grown out of the anti-Poor Law movement, which employed an apocalyptic rhetoric of militant resistance to class legislation, as expressed by the Nottingham Union's address.

The middle-class leaders of the Birmingham Political Council were implacably opposed to the rhetoric as well as the practice of physical force. The town took the centre-stage in debates between 'moral-' and 'physical-force' Chartists which culminated in the summer of 1839 in a showdown between Chartist protesters and the local council which attempted to ban Chartist meetings in the Bull Ring. These disputes have been at the heart of historical accounts of the fragmentation of the class alliance of the early Chartist movement. What has not been considered are the ways in which conceptions of 'moral-' and 'physical-force' were themselves framed by ideas about sexual difference, although recently Clark has examined how 'moral-' and 'physical-forcers' embodied competing models of radical masculinity (1995, pp. 224–7). In the first weeks of female organisation, the presence of women within the movement was generally welcomed by all Chartists as a sign of the moral authority and legitimacy of the movement. The debate over what constituted 'moral-force' lent alternative and fiercely contested meanings to the idea of 'female influence', while the meanings of sexual difference began to shape wider conceptions of political authority and legitimacy.

Most of the town's delegates to the Convention, including Salt, were leaders of the BPU Council and they formed one of the most vocal moral-force lobbies in the country, denounced by many physical-forcers as the 'foolish old women' of Birmingham (*Birmingham Journal*, 17, 24 November 1838). As the BPU leaders began to repudiate physical force, others pointed out that the same men had used the threat of force with great success in the prelude to the Reform Bill. In 1832, Attwood and other prominent reformers had threatened to lead an army of 500,000 men on parliament to demand the implementation of the Reform Bill (*Northern Star*, 25 August 1839, p. 4). The vindication of the right to self-defence enabled radicals to claim that they acted within the framework of the constitution, but at the same time to declare their unwavering support for popular rights and willingness to make the ultimate sacrifice. Here they could also point to recent claims by BPU leaders. Salt had argued in 1837 that 'if ever government violated the law, physical resistance would become a duty' (*Birmingham Journal*, 22 April 1837). Thus in October 1838 Mrs Lapworth defended, to much applause, the constitutionalist approach of the BPU while at the same time invoking the militant and heroic rhetoric of struggle popularised by the anti-Poor Law agitators:

> Some persons had said that they should have to fight for their rights and liberties, but she was of a contrary opinion. The members of the Political Union were determined not to be the aggressors; and the government knew their own interest too well to attack the people. If they should do so, the men would not have to stand alone to meet them – the women would be at their sides – the volley that laid the man on the floor lifeless, should lay his wife and children there too. (*Birmingham Journal*, 27 October 1838, p. 3)

This was the language imitated by the address of the Nottingham Female Political Union, with its gendered portrayal of physical resistance.

Where they had earlier accepted the local leadership's line on the use of physical force, members of the Women's Union, along with other rank and file Chartists in Birmingham, became increasingly frustrated with the cautious approach of the BPU leadership. At a meeting of the Men's Union Douglas of the *Birmingham Journal* castigated the language of the anti-Poor Law agitators, claimed that individuals should not arm for political purposes and warned that it might take years to achieve reform (*Birmingham Journal*, 3 November 1838, p. 3). In response, Lapworth told the Women's Union that women could ill afford to be patient: 'they had had years enough of misery: they [the women] would have settled affairs in a few months ... They were suffering too much, and would again suffer too much in the next winter to wait for *years*.' The radicals had been sowing the 'seed' of reform for years, Lapworth noted, and the 'harvest' must surely come soon. Mrs Oxford added she hoped it would take less than a year. Given the movement's validation of female suffering and endurance, Lapworth and Oxford were able to invoke the authority of their experience as women to vindicate their impatience. The desperation as well as the drama of the anti-Poor Law rhetoric corresponded with the women's own sense of frustration and determined resistance. The moderate John Collins had difficulty convincing them of the impropriety of physical-force rhetoric and the merits of caution. His recommendation that the women lay aside food in case of rising prices during the coming winter failed to allay their fears: 'That is impossible. We can barely subsist at present', called one voice (*Birmingham Journal*, 10 November 1838, p. 6).

The disputes over the relative merits of moral and physical force overlaid disagreements about the accountability of the local and national leadership, and the determination of Chartist policy (Tholfsen, 1958; Behagg, 1990, pp. 184–222). In mid-November two working-class radicals, Henry Watson and Thomas Baker, proposed the formation of district bodies to raise money more efficiently for the National Rent. The Union's Council rejected the plan, prompting Watson to condemn its anti-democratic leadership: 'If the propelling wheel to the resolution had been some wealthy man, there would not have been any objection raised to it. There was rather a tendency to aristocratic feeling amongst them, and when a wealthy man moved, they generally carried those resolutions' (*Birmingham Journal*, 17 November 1838). Regardless of the council's disapproval, working-class radicals in Birmingham formed a National Rent Committee. The Women's Union cooperated, appointing a ladies' committee to attend collection tables in different parts of the town (*Birmingham Journal*, 22 December 1838, p. 6c).

Political leaders in the town clearly worried about the effects of these debates on women's sense of political self-hood and some pleaded with the women to stick to their supportive, organisational role. 'By their good conduct they had won everybody to the cause of female unions', Salt reminded the WPU, 'and by a continuance of the same conduct, and the force of moral power, they would gain all they required' (*Birmingham Journal*, 12 January 1839, p. 3). In a similarly patronising vein, Collins urged women: '[D]on't bother your heads about physical force. If there comes a necessity for it the Convention will not shrink from it' (*Birmingham Journal*, 16 March 1839, p. 5). A member of the Working Men's Committee begged the women to use their 'influence' to restrain the men from indulging in 'strong language' (*Birmingham Journal*, 9 March 1839, p. 3). Women seem to have warmed more to Bronterre O'Brien who, to applause, exhorted them to 'urge and advise their husbands to come forward – aye, even drive them to physical force if they could not succeed without'. They should employ the same 'gentle influence' that the women of Paris in 1789 had used on their husbands to overthrow the feudal system, 'for there was not a single measure of Reform then accomplished, except what was accomplished by the women'. As well as invoking women's historic contribution to Reform, O'Brien anticipated a future where women would exercise political authority in their own name. They should be able to advise their husbands on their choice of elected representative 'and it was strange if they should not even be fit to elect one themselves' (*Northern Star*, 1 June 1839, p. 5). Paradoxically, in order to maintain the enthusiasm, confidence and goodwill of the Women's Union, even self-proclaimed moral-forcers invoked heroic images of women's bravery and fervour in struggle. At the Union's tea party at the Town Hall, attended by 1000 people, Joshua Scholefield MP, also eulogised the women who had pulled down the Bastille and wished that if men ever used arms to defend their country, women would be in the front ranks (*Birmingham Journal*, 12 January 1839, p. 3). Such endorsements of female power seem to have confirmed rather than undermined the women's commitment to militancy. Lapworth observed at the following meeting of the Union 'that as they drew near the time of war, their spirit increased' (*Birmingham Journal*, 26 January 1839, p. 3).

Men were not alone in exploiting the language of sexual difference for political effect. At the end of March 1839, four of the six Birmingham delegates to the Chartist National Convention, including Salt and Douglas, resigned over the continued use of physical-force language at the Convention. By the end of the following month, the BPU had been suspended and, with the exception of Collins, all the Birmingham delegates to the Convention had resigned. Lapworth declared herself 'bitterly disappointed' by Salt's resignation, especially since he had raised women's expectations of victory: 'In the first instant Mr. Salt placarded the town, and called the women to come forward and join the great and noble cause, which they imagined they had almost won.' Where once Salt had courted the loyalty of the women of Birmingham, Lapworth took his resignation from the Convention as an act of political, personal and even romantic betrayal. She expressed her political dissatisfaction by questioning his masculinity; although she believed he was a 'good man' she found him 'more timid and fainthearted than many of the women' and 'she would never renew her faith in a man who had once deceived her'. Lapworth defended the Convention as far surpassing the Houses of Parliament and chided Salt for failing to account to the Women's Union for his actions (*Birmingham Journal*, 13 April 1839, p. 3). Lapworth's frustration seems to have been shared by other members who were unwilling to listen to pleas not to judge Salt too hastily. He was given a polite reception at the two following meetings of the Women's Union, when he replied to Lapworth's criticisms and returned the Union's bank book, but in June the secretary, Miss Groves, had to persuade the meeting that, as the founder of their Union, Salt deserved a hearing, though like Lapworth she held him to be a weak and timid man (*Birmingham Journal*, 13 April 1839, p. 3; 20 April, 1839, p. 7; *Northern Star*, 8 June 1839, p. 5).

There is some evidence that the female Chartists were radicalised by the desertion of their former allies. With the collapse of the BPU, the *Birmingham Journal* ceased its weekly reports of the Women's Union which found itself without a promoter or a meeting place. A former Council member, who had resigned from the Chartist Convention, was one of the magistrates who banned the use of the Bull Ring for public meetings when the Convention moved to Birmingham in May 1839 (Behagg, 1982, p. 79). In defiance of this prohibition, the Chartists held nightly meetings at the Bull Ring. On one procession to the Bull Ring, Feargus O'Connor, publisher of the *Northern Star*, and other national leaders, stopped *en route* at the women's meeting where they listened enthusiastically to Lapworth regretting how quickly men's opinions of female politicians could change once women expressed their political independence. 'For the first time', she complained, 'women are obliged to sue for countenance to men, and our great trumpet the *Journal*, no longer sound[s] the note of female fame, but laughs at female virtue and female politicians. (Hear, hear.) It is only by supplication, that our views can now find favour in the eyes of our former friend.' Lapworth rejected the deferential role accorded to women by Salt and others. Women should act as politicians, speaking for themselves rather than pleading for guidance and approval. She advised the Union to ally with the O'Connorite Chartists; 'but ladies, we have a substitute, and a good one, in our own *Northern Star*. (Cheers.) We look upon Mr O'Connor, as the leader of public opinion.' In future, she implied, women would not submit passively to any leader but play an assertive and self-reliant role:

we have been obliged to practice the art of speaking for ourselves, for no man's mouth was open on our behalf, during the absence of our friends. (Hear.) Ladies, I am quite sure that whatever may be the strength of the female mind elsewhere, that in Birmingham we have resolved to brave all danger and defy all opposition for the acquirement of woman's title to freedom. (*Northern Star*, 6 July 1839, p. 8)

Despite O'Connor's effusive endorsement of the Women's Meeting, the *Northern Star* headed its coverage of the procession with a eulogy to the '*Indomitable courage and manly conduct of the men of Birmingham who carried the Reform Bill*' (*Northern Star*, 6 July 1839, p. 8).

There are no extant reports that the Women's Union had debated hitherto the question of the political rights and representation of women. Lapworth's advocacy of women's claim to freedom seems to have stemmed from the members' direct engagement in Chartist political activity and debate, and from their disappointment with their male allies, implicit in Lapworth's charge that 'no man's mouth was open on our behalf'. Encouraged by their political mentors to exert their influence as women, the Union had sought to expand its sphere of authority; yet with the rejection of the petition and the fragmentation of the movement, the Union found it easier to assert than to exert power. In November 1839 the FPU met in the Socialist chapel to consider how to support the families of John Collins and William Lovett after their arrest in connection with the Bull Ring demonstrations. Lapworth recalled that when Collins had prophesied his imprisonment, 'the women rose in a body, and exclaimed – "Then we will fetch you out!".' 'Where were those women now!', she remonstrated. Although she saw that many were still present, she called on the women to fulfil the more realisable task of supporting the prisoners' families, a role that had traditionally been adopted by female reformers (*Northern Star*, 9 November 1839, p. 3). Even these efforts went unnoted, for this was the last meeting held by the FPU to be extensively reported by the *Northern Star*, despite O'Connor's fervent pledge of support. The *Northern Star* devoted three pages to the release of Collins and Lovett from Warwick Gaol in August 1840. The Female Radical Association had prepared a 'splendid banner' to mark the occasion and members of the committee rode in the procession behind the carriages of the 'victims' and their families, and the Chartist delegates. '[W]ell dressed females occupied seats around the platform' at the public meeting to welcome Collins back to Birmingham, but no woman addressed the meeting or replied to the toast to the ladies at the end of the celebratory dinner. Despite his firm support for the FPU, and the fact that in gaol he had written a plan for a new form of Chartist organisation which included women's suffrage, Collins addressed his thanks to his 'Friends, fellow-townsmen and brother slaves' (Lovett and Collins, 1969, p. 61; *Northern Star*, 1 August 1840, pp. 7, 8, 1).

By the spring of 1840, over 500 Chartists were imprisoned and many more had emigrated (Epstein, 1982, p. 212). With the loss of local and national leaders, the Chartists were compelled to re-evaluate their organisational methods. Many argued that the movement needed a firmer, more unified base than that provided by the mass platform and demonstration. At a meeting in October 1839 on the arrest of Lovett and Collins, the London delegate Robert Hartwell urged the Birmingham Female Union not to be discouraged, for the recent 'check' to the cause had 'dispelled a great deal of delusion which some parties had practised on the people and taught them that while speech-making and action were very well in their way, an effective organisation was the thing wanted to accomplish their object'. A firm supporter of female union, Hartwell linked the building of an effective movement to the organisation of women, describing the establishment of Female Radical Associations in London (*The Charter*, 6 October 1839, p. 590). For others, by contrast, effective organisation was signalled by a specifically masculine model of association. One national leader, Peter McDouall, complained that:

Our associations were hastily got up, composed of prodigious numbers, a false idea of strength was imparted, and enthusiasm was wrought up to the highest pitch, thence originated a sense of security, which subsequent events proved to be false, and why? because no real union existed at the bottom ... we never would have sustained the slightest check in the movement, *if we had begun to unite like men, and to organise like a number of brothers.* (*McDouall's Chartist and Republican Journal*, 3 April 1841, pp. 1–2; my emphasis)

Dorothy Thompson indicates that some Chartists were particularly critical of O'Connor's flattery of the crowd, of the cost and showiness of processions and soirées and the excessive excitement created by the torchlit marches. The manhood of the Chartists was often derided by their opponents who portrayed the movement as being in the hands of reckless women and youths. Vulnerable to such attacks, some Chartists criticised the politics of mass demonstration as infantile, dis-organised, lacking seriousness, and like McDouall associated organisation and purposefulness with manliness. Thompson may be right that the formalisation of Chartist organisation also involved a masculinisation of politics, both in its style and composition. Although significant numbers of women continued to join the National Charter Association and the Chartist Land scheme, subscription-based membership may have discouraged the participation of women, as well as the unskilled and low-paid working classes, who lacked the resources and time for regular meetings (Thompson, 1984, pp. 129–30, 121–3; D. Jones, 1983).

The desire for permanent and formal structures of organisation was met by two national bodies: the National Charter Association, led by O'Connor and his supporters; and the National Association for Promoting Political and Social Improvement – the moral-force 'New-Move' initiated partly from Birmingham by Collins and Arthur O'Neill. Both movements found support from 'the ladies' whose contribution had changed little in style. The ladies organised a tea party in support of O'Neill's Chartist Church and presented him with a velvet waistcoat (*Northern Star*, 20 February 1841, p. 1). The original committee of the Female Union appears to have backed the O'Connorite NCA, for several members were honoured guests at an NCA dinner. Lapworth responded 'with great feeling and elegance, which did honour to her sex' to a toast which suggested 'that if one lady were fit to rule, another is fit to vote'. Her reply echoed the demands of the early female Chartist societies that women withdraw their affections from men who failed to support the Charter: 'If the females were advised by her, she would make the men do their duty; not a smile would greet them, not a button should be sewn on their clothes, nor an atom of comfort should they enjoy, until the Charter was passed into law' (*Northern Star*, 13 March 1841, p. 1). Her admonition received loud cheers but did not intimate any new campaigning methods that could be exercised by women.

Conclusion

Although most reformers in Birmingham and elsewhere enthusiastically welcomed the support of women and often continued to do so throughout the Chartist decade, it certainly seems to be the case that, intentionally or not, Chartist men failed to provide women with the organisational structures, resources and recognition that would enable them to sustain regular political activity. In a hostile political environment, even those men who advocated the female suffrage and female organisation in principle often neglected in practice to take measures that would make women's active participation possible. The collapse of the BPU, and with it the loss of sympathetic coverage from the *Birmingham Journal*, removed a major channel of communication between the Female Union and the women of the city, and it is consequently impossible to trace the history of its demise. The *Northern Star* would continue to publish letters and addresses from female Chartists but while it welcomed the eloquent though often formulaic political addresses, like many Chartists it clearly did not want women to take part in the political disputes that must surely be a condition for full democratic participation (Rogers, 2001). 'We must not have the women "quarrelling": the men make "mess" enough', the editor warned when the Nottingham Female Charter Association sought to challenge the secretary of the London FCA (15 July 1843, p. 4). But although Chartist men could have done much more to assist their political sisters, this does not mean that they actively wanted to subordinate them, either in the political arena or the home.

In what sense might language itself have set limits on female participation? Clearly understandings of political capacity and authority were shot through with ideas about sexual difference. Though the ideal of 'woman's mission' structured the development of women's participation within a whole range of voluntary, religious and political organisations, it did so in different ways and with very different outcomes. The Birmingham Female Society for the Relief of the Negro Slaves mobilised the discourse of woman's mission to persuade the national anti-slavery movement to adopt the radical demand for immediate emancipation, as stated in the first political address on the topic by their secretary Elizabeth Heyrick, *Immediate, not Gradual Abolition* (London, 1824). As Christian women, they claimed, they must do everything in their power, and not rest a moment, in their duty to relieve the suffering of their fellow human beings (Midgley, 1992, pp. 75–6). Many female anti-slavers would also begin to assert their right to take part in public debate, and even demand their own political representation, despite reservations and even censure from male abolitionists. The Female Political Union would adopt many of the campaigning measures employed by the female anti-slavery societies: petitioning, exclusive dealing, fund-raising, political addresses, tea parties. The Chartists appealed to their fellow countrywomen on the basis of their shared suffering; they could no longer resist the cries of their children and must take to the political arena. Is it possible that by privileging women's experience and knowledge of suffering, the movement, including the female Chartists, encouraged women to adopt an uncompromising position and that, for many, impatience may have led to disappointment, followed by resignation or despair? After all the 'influence' and 'force' asserted by the Chartist men and women was answered by the excessive force of the state which actively sought to break the movement in 1839 and 1840. But if Chartist rhetoric and practice failed to prepare women for the long haul of political struggle, surely it was also the case that labouring women like Mrs Lapworth simply did not have the time, the financial resources, the space, or the physical energy available to the middle-class ladies who successfully ran the abolitionist campaign? Political effectiveness is contingent on the social organisation of material power as well as on the availability of political discourse.

Bibliography

Alexander, S. 'Women, Class and Sexual Differences in the 1830s and 1840s: Some Reflections on the Writing of a Feminist History', *History Workshop Journal* 17 (1984), pp. 125–49.

Behagg, C. 'An Alliance with the Middle Class: The Birmingham Political Union and Early Chartism', in J. Epstein and D. Thompson (eds), *The Chartist Experience: Studies in Working-class Radicalism and Culture, 1830–60* (Basingstoke: Macmillan, 1982), pp. 59–86.

— *Politics and Production in the Early Nineteenth Century* (Routledge, 1990).

Belchem, J. 'Republicanism, Popular Constitutionalism and the Radical Platform in Early Nineteenth-century England', *Social History* 6 (1981), pp. 1–35.

The Birmingham Journal.

Briggs, A. (ed.) *Chartist Studies* (Macmillan, 1959).

Brooks, P. *The Melodramatic Imagination: Balzac, Henry James, Melodrama and the Mode of Excess* (New Haven: Yale University Press, 1976).

Butler, J. *Gender Trouble: Feminism and the Subversion of Identity* (Routledge, 1990).

Clark, A. 'The Rhetoric of Chartist Domesticity: Gender, Language and Class in the 1830s and 1840s', *Journal of British Studies* 31 (1992), pp. 62–88.

— *The Struggle for the Breeches: Gender and the Making of the British Working Class* (Berkeley: University of California Press, 1995).

— 'Manhood, Womanhood, and the Politics of Class in Britain, 1790–1845', in L. de Frader and S. Rose (eds) *Gender and Class in Modern Europe* (Ithaca: Cornell, 1996a), pp. 263–79.

— 'Gender, Class and the Constitution: Franchise Reform in England, 1832–1928', in J. Vernon (ed.) *Re-reading the Constitution: New Narratives in the Political History of England's Long Nineteenth Century* (Cambridge: Cambridge University Press, 1996b), pp. 239–53.

Davidoff, L. and C. Hall *Family Fortunes: Men and Women of the English Middle Class* (Hutchinson, 1987).

Epstein, J. *The Lion of Freedom: Feargus O'Connor and the Chartist Movement, 1832–1842* (Croom Helm, 1982).

— *Radical Expression: Political Language, Ritual and Symbolism in England, 1790–1850* (Oxford: Oxford University Press, 1994).

Flick, C. *The Birmingham Political Union and the Movements for Reform in Britain, 1830–1839* (Folkestone: Archon Books, 1978).

Frow, R. and E. (eds) *Political Women, 1800–1850* (Pluto Press, 1989).

Gammage, R.G. *History of the Chartist Movement, 1837–1854* (New York: Augustus M. Kelly, 1969).

The Gauntlet (London).

Hall, C. *White, Male and Middle-class: Explorations in Feminism and History* (Oxford: Polity, 1992).

Hamilton, S. 'The Construction of Women by the Royal Commissions of the 1830s and 1840s', in Yeo (1998), pp. 79–105.

Heyrick, Elizabeth *Immediate, Not Gradual Abolition; or, an inquiry into the shortest, safest, and most effectual means of getting rid of West-Indian slavery* (1824).

Holyoake, G. J. *Sixty Years of an Agitator's Life* (T. Fisher Unwin, 1906).

Hovell, M. *The Chartist Movement* (Manchester: Manchester University Press, 1925).

John, A. *By the Sweat of their Brow: Women Workers at Victorian Coal Mines* (Routledge and Kegan Paul, 1984).

Jones, D. 'Women and Chartism', *History* 68 (1983), pp. 1–21.

Joyce, P. *Visions of the People: Industrial England and the Question of Class, 1840–1914* (Cambridge: Cambridge University Press, 1991).

— *Democratic Subjects: The Self and the Social in Nineteenth-century England* (Cambridge: Cambridge University Press, 1994).

Larrabeiti, M. de 'Conspicuous Before the World: The Political Rhetoric of Chartist Women', in Yeo (1998), pp. 106–26.

Lopatin, N. *Political Unions, Popular Politics and the Great Reform Act of 1832* (Basingstoke: Macmillan, 1999).

Lovett, W. *Life and Times of William Lovett in His Pursuit of Bread, Knowledge and Freedom* (G. Bell and Sons, 1920).

Lovett, W. and J. Collins *Chartism: A New Organisation of the People* (Leicester: Leicester University Press, 1969).

Lowe, J. 'Women in the Chartist Movement, 1830–1852' (MA thesis, Birmingham University, 1985).

McCalman, I. 'Females, Feminism and Free Love in an Early Nineteenth-century Radical Movement', *Labour History* (Canberra), 38 (1980), pp. 1–25.

McDouall's Chartist and Republican Journal (Manchester).

Midgley, C. *Women against Slavery: The British Campaigns, 1780–1870* (Routledge, 1992).

The Northern Star (Leeds).

Pinchbeck, I. *Women Workers and the Industrial Revolution, 1750–1850* (Virago, 1985).

The Pioneer (Birmingham).

Rogers, H. *Women and the People: Authority, Authorship and the English Radical Tradition in the Nineteenth Century* (Aldershot: Ashgate, 2000).

— 'Any Questions? The Gendered Dimensions of the Political Platform', *Nineteenth-century Prose* (forthcoming, 2001).

Rose, S. *Limited Livelihoods: Class and Gender in Nineteenth-century England* (Berkeley: University of California Press, 1993).

Salt, T.C. 'Evidence to Select Committee on Manufactures, Commerce and Shipping', vol. 2 (1833), pp. 273–86; repr. British Parliamentary Papers, *Industrial Revolution: Trade 2* (Shannon: Irish University Press).

Schwarzkopf, J. *Women in the Chartist Movement* (Basingstoke: Macmillan, 1991).

Scott, J. *Gender and the Politics of History* (New York: Columbia Press, 1998).

Stedman Jones, G. 'Rethinking Chartism', in his *Languages of Class: Studies in English Working-class History, 1832–1982* (Cambridge: Cambridge University Press, 1983), pp. 90–178.

Taylor, B. *Eve and the New Jerusalem: Socialism and Feminism in the Nineteenth Century* (Virago, 1983).

Tholfsen, T. 'The Chartist Crisis in Birmingham', *International Review of Social History* 3 (1958), pp. 461–80.

Thomis, M. and J. Grimmet *Women in Protest 1800–1850* (Croom Helm, 1992).

Thompson, D. 'Women and Nineteenth-century Radical Politics: A Lost Dimension', in A. Oakley and J. Mitchell (eds) *The Rights and Wrongs of Women* (Harmondsworth: Penguin, 1983), pp. 112–38.

— *The Chartists: Popular Politics in the Industrial Revolution* (New York: Pantheon Books, 1984).

Thompson, E.P. *The Making of the English Working Class* (Harmondsworth: Pelican, 1982).

Vernon, J. *Politics and the People: A Study in English Political Culture, 1815–1867* (Cambridge: Cambridge University Press, 1993).

Yeo, E. (ed.) *Radical Femininity: Women's Self-Representation in the Public Sphere* (Manchester: Manchester University Press, 1998).

3 'A secret conviction that nothing can be changed', or 'Abolishing a part of yourself'?: George Orwell's *The Road to Wigan Pier* (1937)

T.G. Ashplant

George Orwell's *The Road to Wigan Pier* (1937), continuously in print since its first publication, has attained something akin to iconic status with regard to both its author and its society. If *Animal Farm* and *Nineteen Eighty-Four* represent Orwell the political novelist, then *Wigan Pier* represents Orwell the social critic and political polemicist. Similarly, *Wigan Pier* acts as a shorthand for representations of Britain during the Depression of the 1930s.[1] Yet, like much of Orwell's work, its meaning and value have been fiercely debated by both contemporaries and later critics (as recently by Pearce, 1997). This chapter will sketch different critical approaches to *Wigan Pier* in terms of its production, signification and reception, examining some of them in greater depth to show how a cultural history approach can illuminate the text as a source of meaning. It will begin by locating the production of the text in its historical context, and its author in his biographical trajectory.

Historical Context

The Wall Street Crash of 1929 helped precipitate a major economic depression in the industrialised nations, hitting Europe in the summer of 1931. Its impact in Britain exacerbated an existing situation where, following a brief postwar boom in 1919 and 1920, the nation had experienced mass unemployment from the winter of 1920/1. Until the outbreak of the Second World War in 1939, there were never fewer than 1 million unemployed; the onset of the depression pushed this to a peak of 2.7 million in 1932. The impact of the depression in

101

Britain was very uneven socially and geographically. The working class was hit much more severely than the lower-middle or middle classes. The prewar staple industries of the British economy, geared to export markets – cotton, coal, iron and steel making, and shipbuilding – were worst hit; they were concentrated especially in south Wales, the north of England and central Scotland. The newer industries, aimed at the domestic market – car manufacture, light electrical goods, house building – were less severely hit; they were located especially in a great arc stretching south from Birmingham and Coventry to Oxford, and then eastward to greater London. A deep division, in opportunities for work and all that that meant (income, welfare and morale), opened up between north and south (Stevenson and Cook, 1994, chs 1–3; Thorpe, 1992, chs 3–4).

In Britain the minority (second) Labour Government, elected in 1929, collapsed in the autumn of 1931, the Cabinet having split over a demand to cut the level of unemployment relief. It was replaced by a coalition, calling itself the National Government, which swiftly called a general election. Its resultant landslide majority comprised an overwhelming majority of Conservatives together with most of the small number of Liberal MPs, joined by a very few breakaway National Labour MPs. Re-elected with a smaller but still very large majority in 1935, the National Government remained in office until 1940 (Stevenson and Cook, 1994, chs 6, 13; Thorpe, 1992, ch. 2; Pugh, 1993, ch. 13). The dominance of this impregnable, right-of-centre government throughout the decade meant the exclusion from both political power and influence on policy of both left-wing and centrist ('middle') opinion (Marwick, 1964). The supporters of Labour and socialism were in some disarray. Following the failure of the 1929–31 Labour Government (elected on a promise to deal with unemployment, which had then doubled), left and right in the Labour Party struggled to find new policies (Pimlott, 1977; Thorpe, 1997, chs 3–4). Its co-founder and long-term affiliate, the Independent Labour Party (ILP), a source of internal left-wing opposition since the mid-1920s, severed its links and broke away in 1932; but it failed to prosper, and was soon reduced to a small if committed group trying to find an elusive revolutionary political space between Labour and communism (Dowse, 1966).

Outside the parliamentary arena, the trade unions had been seriously weakened both numerically by continuing high unemployment (though there was some recovery towards the end of the decade), and politically by the defeat of the General Strike in 1926 (Pelling, 1971, ch. 10). On the far left was the Communist Party of Great Britain (CP), committed to revolutionary change on the model of the Russian Revolution of 1917. Small in numbers, it was influential both in the trade unions and among intellectuals. Affiliated to the Communist International, its policy in all key respects was controlled in fact, though not in theory, by Moscow (Branson, 1985; Morgan, 1989; Thompson, 1992, ch. 2). It played a major role in organising the unemployed, via the National Unemployed Workers Movement (NUWM), founded in 1921 and led with dedication by the communist Wal Hannington (Stevenson and Cook, 1994, ch. 9; Croucher, 1987; Kingsford, 1982). On the far right was the British Union of Fascists (BUF), founded by Sir Oswald Mosley in October 1932 in imitation of Mussolini's Italian fascists. After initially attracting some support from the 'respectable' right, the BUF began to lose such backing after the much-publicised violence of its stewards at the Olympia rally in June 1934; by 1936, it was turning explicitly to anti-semitism to gain support (Stevenson and Cook, 1994, ch. 11; Lunn and Thurlow, 1980; Thurlow, 1987).

By the mid-1930s, then, Britain was a country suffering – unevenly – the social effects of long-term unemployment, ruled by an effectively Conservative government with an unchallengeable majority. While liberal and moderate left-wing opinion struggled to find effective alternative strategies and policies, a small but active minority looked towards a revolutionary challenge to the existing order. It is this situation that is addressed by *Wigan Pier*. Part I seeks, by its harsh delineation of grinding work, poverty and deprivation, to compel readers to attend to the crisis; while Part II probes the apparent failure of socialists, those who should be offering an alternative vision and a sense of how to achieve it, to make a political impact.

Authorship

The author of *Wigan Pier* was born Eric Arthur Blair in 1903, into what he very precisely termed the 'lower-upper-middle-class' (113); his father was a Sub-deputy Opium Agent in the Bengal Civil Service.[2] He was '*upper*-middle' because his was a professional family, but '*lower*-upper-middle' because his father – a relatively low-ranking colonial officer – belonged to a less-well-off stratum of that class. Blair attended a (private) preparatory school, St Cyprian's, and then Eton between 1911 and 1921. His family's relatively insecure economic status is betrayed by the fact that St Cyprian's took him on reduced fees, and at Eton he was a scholarship boy. Intellectually able but apparently uninterested in extending his formal education, Blair followed his father's path into colonial service, joining the Imperial Indian Police in Burma where he served from 1922–7.

It was his experiences there which first edged Blair towards political dissent and led eventually to a revolt against imperialism. On his return home for the standard sabbatical leave, he left the police. He was to reflect on this experience in his first novel *Burmese Days* (1934), and also in the essays 'A Hanging' (1931) and 'Shooting an Elephant' (1936). He now set out to become a writer (of essays and novels). In search of experience of life at the bottom of society, he went on the tramp in and around London. This was both before and after the 18 months he spent in Paris in 1928–9, latterly in some poverty, writing his first novel and short stories (all unpublished), and publishing his first journalism in French left-wing papers (Davison, 1996, pp. 24–30). This experience of hardship led to his first book, *Down and Out in Paris and London*, published in 1933 at the age of 30. It was the first work to appear under the pseudonym, newly adopted to spare his family embarrassment, of 'George Orwell'. This was to be the name by which he increasingly became known to new acquaintances, and the name under which he was to achieve fame as a writer (Crick, 1992, pp. 233–4). While trying to develop his embryonic literary career, he scraped a living in traditional fashion via private teaching and work as a bookseller's assistant.

Orwell's politics before 1936 remain difficult to track precisely, since both the literary and biographical evidence is slender and somewhat contradictory. In Paris in 1928–9 he had mixed with acquaintances on the left, and was remembered as supporting communism (Newsinger, 1999, p. 21). His first published writings, in French, include three essays in a small leftist periodical on the condition of the English working class, which offer forceful, if simplistic, socialist sentiments (Davison, 1996, pp. 25, 28).[3] After his return to England, however, both his anti-imperialism and his putative socialism disappear. Nothing he published from 1931–6 carried any clear political message; his early writings in English Alex Zwerdling (1974, pp. 65–7) describes as those of a reformist liberal, who knows what he hates but has little idea why it exists or what to do about it.[4] Most of his friends recalled him as hardly socialist in these years; Zwerdling (1974, pp. 62–5) sees him as an unwilling socialist, an apolitical man eventually forced by the times to be political, and a pessimist in an optimistic creed. His pessimism, which came out of his sense of personal failure, dominates his first three novels – *Burmese Days*, *A Clergyman's Daughter* (1935), and *Keep the Aspidistra Flying* (1936) – all of which recount failed rebellions. Yet he was in contact with socialists of the non-CP left. The great majority of his journalism from 1930–5 was published in the *Adelphi*, which had become the unofficial theoretical journal of the ILP; and politics were certainly discussed among his friends in 1934–5 (Newsinger, 1999, pp. 22–3, 26–7, 30). The political crisis of the 1930s was to push many further to the left: liberals towards socialism, reformist socialists towards communism (Zwerdling, 1974, pp. 68–70). But for Orwell himself this shift does not seem to occur fully until 1936–7.

In January 1936 Orwell finished his third novel, *Keep the Aspidistra Flying*. Victor Gollancz, his publisher, now commissioned him to write a book about the conditions of the unemployed in the industrial north. He had great faith in Orwell as a novelist; but wanted him to write something like *Down and Out*, only now about the mass experience of poverty and unemployment (Crick, pp. 277–9). Orwell thereupon gave up his job in a bookshop and set off. He was in the north of England for two months, from 31 January to 30 March; mostly in Wigan, Sheffield and Barnsley, with a few days in Liverpool and a week spent with his sister in Leeds. He came openly as a writer, not disguising himself as he had done earlier while on the tramp. He had letters of introduction from Richard Rees (a literary editor), Middleton Murry (proprietor of the *Adelphi*), and from London ILP members; these political contacts led him to the working-class political activists who were to be his crucial links to northern working-class life (Crick, 1992, pp. 279–90). He spent four days with Frank Meade, a trade union official and *Adelphi* contact, on a Manchester council estate. Meade suggested a study of Wigan, which was suffering high unemployment through pit and factory closures and short-time working; and gave him the address of Joe ('Jerry') Kennan, an electrician, ILPer and NUWM activist. Orwell stayed at 'clean and decent' lodgings (so the Kennans described it) for a week; and then moved to the famous tripe-shop for two weeks. He moved to Sheffield on 2 March, staying with a miner's family; there he did much work on housing, being taken round by William Brown, an unemployed communist. On 13 March he went to Barnsley, where he stayed for two weeks. Here, Tommy Degnan (another communist) was his guide; he made more trips down the pit, and further visits to houses (Crick, 1992, pp. 280–93).

During his time in the north, Orwell wrote a chronological account, the text of which has since been published as 'The Road to Wigan Pier Diary' (hereafter referred to as the 'Diary'). He spent the rest of 1936 re-working this material, plus research notes and relevant publications he had accumulated, into the final text of *Wigan Pier*, which avoids any such chronological structuring.[5] During the period of writing, he attended both an ILP and an Adelphi Centre (non-sectarian socialist) summer school; the ILP was now the political organisation he was closest to. His experiences in the north clearly contributed to a more explicit political engagement; Orwell was now ready to declare himself a socialist. But he was still unclear over two major questions (an uncertainty reflected in *Wigan Pier*): how socialism was to happen; and what was the relationship between socialism and industrialisation (which he hated) (Crick, 1992, pp. 294–5).

In Spain, a civil war had broken out in July 1936 when the military, with extreme nationalist and fascist backing, rose against the republican government. With Hitler and Mussolini intervening to support the rising, and then the USSR starting to aid the republican government, the Spanish conflict rapidly became also a proxy struggle between international fascism and communism. Sympathisers for both sides, but especially the republicans, came from across Europe and North America to fight as volunteers, the anti-fascists seeing this as the last hope of preventing another European-wide war. Orwell delivered his manuscript to Gollancz in December 1936, secured credentials from the ILP, and departed immediately for Spain, leaving his wife power to negotiate with the publisher. He fought for the republicans in Spain for the first five months of 1937 as part of the militia of the POUM (an independent Marxist party). Seriously wounded, he returned to England in June 1937.

His experience in Spain had crucial effects on Orwell. It enabled him to separate the questions of socialism and industrialisation (since most of Spain was non-industrialised, and much of the support for the government came from anarchist-led peasants and agricultural labourers); it also convinced him, as he powerfully recorded in *Homage to Catalonia* (1938), that a classless society could work. From Spain he wrote that at last 'I really believe in socialism, which I never did before' (1970, p. 301). However, his experience of the communist persecution of the anarchists and then the POUM (in the interests, as they saw it, of ensuring unity during a military conflict) made him implacably suspicious, and openly critical, of communist manipulation of other socialists and sympathisers. Despite his links with and sympathy for the ILP, Orwell actually joined it only in 1938 (1970, pp. 373–5). But he left it once the Second World War broke out because it continued its prewar anti-militarist line, whereas he switched stance to support British resistance to Hitler. He then worked with *Tribune*, which represented the left wing of the Labour Party (Crick, 1992, pp. 365–6, 376–80; Zwerdling, 1974, pp. 70–1).

Many of the meanings that have been located in *Wigan Pier* derive from the history of its author. In part, this is via its open espousal of autobiography. It draws on its author's contemporary labours as novelist and allotment holder for vivid illuminations of the miners' toil, while its arguments about class invoke and wrestle with profound social divisions inculcated during his childhood socialisation. Its imagery of horror is rooted in Orwell's past schooling as well as his present lodging. Its polemic with socialism is shaped by the author's (real but limited) engagement with socialist organisations. However, in part the links between authorial history and text remained concealed. Male gender claims, rooted in upbringing and career, permeate the text, but only 50 years later would they come fully into focus as structuring assumptions.

The meanings that can be attached to *Wigan Pier* arise not only from the experiences of its author in his historical context, but also from the systems of signification which structure it as a text – one which, by its form and subject-matter, invokes a range of intertextual references. Like much of Orwell's writing, it is generically mixed. Part I is predominantly a social investigation, Part II a political polemic; while running through both parts, claiming to validate and authenticate them, is a fragmentary autobiographical narrative (Fowler, 1995, p. 62). It will be examined here from the perspective of four modes of signification at work in the text – as social investigation, literary documentary, political polemic, and autobiography – genres with their own history and characteristic forms, each with its specific inflections in the 1930s.

Social Investigation

Wigan Pier is a work of social investigation conducted via personal enquiry. The 1930s was a decade of considerable social tension, comparable to the 'hungry' 1840s, or the 1880s with its linked crises of urban unemployment and poverty. Each of these decades had produced a flood of social investigations into the 'condition of England', most famously by Henry Mayhew in the 1840s and Charles Booth in the 1880s (Bulmer, Bales and Sklar, 1991; Englander and O'Day, 1995). In similar fashion, the 1930s saw a large number of social enquiries, employing various styles of investigation. Some were social scientific, developing a tradition stretching back to the social science societies of the mid-nineteenth century (such as B.S. Rowntree's *Poverty and Progress* (1941), or the Pilgrim Trust's *Men Without Work* (1938)); others, like Orwell, offered a narrative of personal enquiry (J.B. Priestley's *English Journey* (1934)); others again were works of polemic (Wal Hannington's fiercely political *The Problem of the Distressed Areas* (1937)).

Such social investigations have their generic conventions too, just as much as novels or autobiographies; and *Wigan Pier* shares fully in these. As in other sociological surveys, coal mining is taken as the archetypal proletarian industry (chs 2–3); so *Wigan Pier* does not mention cotton, although it too was an important industry in the town. Its central concern is poverty and its relationship to unemployment (chs 4–6), which had been at the heart of sociological enquiry since the work of Booth and Rowntree in the late nineteenth century. Comparison with a work in the social science tradition helps reveal the specific characteristics of Orwell's text. In *Poverty and Progress*, Rowntree's analysis of housing conditions (1941, pp. 223–80) shows its social scientific commitments most obviously in its detailed categorisation and quantification (especially of types and quality of housing) and in its comparative perspective (different categories of working-class housing in York are compared, and York housing conditions in 1936–9 are contrasted with other similar towns, with the overall British picture, and with its own past). *Wigan Pier* differs in both perspective and aim. Orwell lacked Rowntree's detailed knowledge of change over a generation (Pearce, 1997, pp. 425–6), but more importantly his primary focus was not on what had been achieved but on what remained to be done. The bulk of Chapter 4 concentrates on the conditions of Wigan's worst slums (46–52), and on the caravan dwellings which he deemed the worst effect of the housing shortage (56–9; cf. Rowntree, 1941, pp. 253–5). Where Orwell differs markedly from Rowntree is in his awareness of the problem of representation. Having given examples from his notes on individual houses, and described what a row of back-to-back houses is like to live in, he adds: 'But mere notes like these are only valuable as reminders to myself' (52). The following pages (53–4) try to make more vivid for the reader what such conditions imply for those living in them. Though Rowntree ends his chapter with a reminder of the 'heavy task' still to be accomplished in slum clearance and upgrading of marginal housing stock, his main emphasis is on the substantial improvement since 1900 (1941, pp. 223, 234, 276). Orwell's conclusion is markedly more guarded: 'On balance, the Corporation estates are better than the slums, but only by a small margin' (67).

Wigan Pier is also shot through with a contrast of north versus south (ch. 7) – a division especially marked in the 1930s, and deployed to powerful effect both by Priestley (1934, pp. 397–409) and in several photo-journalist spreads in *Picture Post* (Taylor, 1983). It could be argued that Orwell's implied reader is precisely the middle-class southerner who needs to be informed about the living conditions of the northern working class; at several points in his account of the coal mine the experiences of such a reader are taken as a point of contrast (21–2, 39; cf. Williams, 1997, p. 169).

As its full title indicates, *The Road to Wigan Pier* is an account of a journey; as such, it shares generically in two traditions. The first is diachronic: the journey was a long-established frame for narratives of personal enquiry into social problems, where the middle-class explorer ventures into the unknown world of the working class and reports back on conditions there. It was used by both liberal reformers and socialists (Keating, 1976). One of the most famous examples was William Booth's *In Darkest England, and the Way Out* (1890); and Orwell was acquainted with the forays into the East End that Jack London had made when writing *The People of the Abyss* (1905). Dodd traces how Orwell distances himself from the easy knowingness and superiority to which this tradition often lent itself. In Chapter 1 Orwell takes pains to establish himself as doubly different, both a traveller and a southerner. In Chapter 2 he plays on the trope of travelling to establish his difference from, even inferiority to, the miners, emphasising the strenuous unpaid labour which their 'travelling' (to the coalface) involves, and which he can barely manage (Dodd, 1982, pp. 131–2). The second tradition is synchronic: in the 1930s the trope of the journey became more generally prominent. Dodd suggests that travel writing was arguably the most important literary form of the decade, very appropriate for those restless with inherited beliefs, and eager to explore and discover new allegiances (1982, p. 128).

Documentary and Realism

The form of *Wigan Pier* was also influenced by contemporary literary developments. A powerful new cultural influence in the 1930s was the documentary movement. The term originated in film, with John Grierson (Swann, 1989; Aitken, 1990); and was then taken up in photography – Humphrey Spender (1982; Frizzell, 1997), *Picture Post* (Hopkinson, 1970; Hall, 1972); literature – Storm Jameson (1937), John Sommerfield (1936; Laing, 1980); and social inquiry – Mass-Observation (Chaney and Pickering, 1986; Baxendale and Pawling, 1996, pp. 17–45). In *Wigan Pier* some specific documentary elements are evident: in the account of the trip to the coal face (ch. 2), in the quotation of actual documents in the text (pay-stop, 37, 39; UAB scales, 71), and in the use of photographs to reinforce the depiction of living and working conditions. Yet these factual elements remain relatively superficial, not indicative of any wholesale commitment to a documentary ethic or aesthetic.[6] A more fruitful connection with documentary is suggested by Keith Williams's situating of *Wigan Pier* within the framework of what he terms 'new reportage'. This recognised film as the key medium for documentary, and sought to emulate it in written form; while also re-directing modernism's concern with self-analysis so as to lay bare the devices by which the documentarist tried to reproduce reality authentically (Williams, 1997, pp. 164–6). Both these concerns are present at the opening of *Wigan Pier*. Chapter 1 foregrounds the authorial persona as mediator for understanding the world to which the reader is being introduced. Chapter 2 uses literary montage to produce a 'biography of things', closing the distance between production and consumption of coal so as to reveal its omnipresent underpinning of cultural and political activity (Williams, 1997, pp. 167–70).

But the text also draws on older, more conventional literary devices, as can be seen by examining the opening and closing chapters of Part I. Roger Fowler (1995, pp. 63–4) distinguishes three overlapping styles of realism in Orwell's writing. Descriptive realism focuses on particularity: physical details and material facts. This style is closest to social scientific writing, and deploys the devices of documentary. It can shade into what Fowler terms naturalism (or sordid realism), where facts are used to evoke physical squalor, mental suffering and extreme emotions (often of disgust or revulsion). This style dominates the famous account of the lodging house. Since this is the opening scene of the book, it acts as a frame, shaping the reader's responses to all that follows (Fowler, 1995, pp. 81–4). As Fowler notes, there are also examples of micro-framing throughout Part I (for example 45, the opening of the chapter on housing), so that the reader is primed to read passages of neutral descriptive realism within the context of a wider authorial judgement already made (Fowler, 1995, pp. 82–3). The third variant Fowler terms surrealism (or hyperrealism), a more metaphoric style which intensifies the reader's unease by hinting at an alien or fictional world behind the visible, and intensely described, reality. When Orwell, at the start of Chapter 7, recapitulates his journey north to the 'real ugliness of industrialisation' (97), he depicts the landscapes in surreal and other-worldly terms: the slag heap like a flock mattress, the lunar landscape of Wigan, and the hellish night-sky of Sheffield (97–9).

The use of both older conventions of realism, and emergent devices of documentary, suggests the more densely literary quality that distinguishes *Wigan Pier* from writing in the social scientific tradition. The subordination of literal accuracy to wider aims can be seen by contrasting the published text with the 'Diary' (Pearce, 1997, pp. 426–9) . Comparison of the closing pages of Chapter 1 (14–17) with the 'Diary' entries for 15 February and 2 March (1970, pp. 203, 216) reveals much about Orwell's intentions and methods. In his initial account, the famous encounter with a young woman kneeling to clear a blocked drain occurred as he walked up an alley in Wigan. In the published text, this vision occurs as he is on the train leaving the town. This has the effect of doubly distancing the narrator (and hence also the reader), sitting in a warm carriage and being carried safely away from the bleak urban landscape.[7] The scene of birds copulating in a snow-covered landscape (actually seen a fortnight later in Sheffield) is shifted to the train journey so that it can represent the transition from urban squalor to rural beauty.

Political Polemic

In addition to reporting on the condition of England, *Wigan Pier* also conducts a political argument: Part II offers itself as a critique of aspects of socialism from within the left (160–1). Two linked themes are central to this polemic: class relations, and the character of socialism and socialists. As has been noted, Orwell had relatively little interest in, or even knowledge of, socialist politics before 1936. His main connection had been via his ILP friends in London over recent years; and this continued during the writing of *Wigan Pier*, with his attendance at the socialist summer schools – directly reflected in *Wigan Pier* in his notorious attacks on ILP-style socialists (161–2) (Rai, 1988, pp. 52–3; Crick, 1992, pp. 254–5). In the political argument he now developed, suggests Alok Rai, Orwell neither returned to the callow socialism of his Paris years nor took over that of any of his possible mentors (Gollancz, the *Adelphi*, or the ILP); instead he set about reinventing socialism, rejecting the stock responses of both the middle class and the left (1988, pp. 69–72). He showed a sense, if blurred, of class as *economic* injustice; but he was much more sensitive to class as a *social* category.

All the critical literature on Orwell both testifies to, and itself enacts, the contradictoriness in his political writing. At its simplest, this refers to his overall political stance, what Rai terms 'the strenuously divided and tense, polemical form of his political attitudes' (Rai, 1988, p. 67). Despite his own repeated assertions of being a socialist from 1936 onwards, he has been claimed by some on the right as having finally seen through that illusion, and denounced by others on the left as either a renegade, or one who was never a true socialist. This contradictoriness is also evident within the text of *Wigan Pier*. It cannot be usefully described as 'ambiguity', since one of the characteristics of Orwell's style is its robust declarative assertiveness. 'Ambivalence' comes a little closer, since there is a sense of a tension or struggle between different stances or viewpoints; but it is a veiled conflict which appears to be acted out without the author's full awareness. Two related aspects of this conflict, and the ways they are manifested textually, will be considered here: his attitudes towards working people's understanding of their situation in society, and towards their capacity for political action.

As regards the first of these aspects, what I have termed the 'veiled' nature of the conflict becomes evident in the diversity of critical response, with different readers offering plausible but diametrically opposed readings. This can be explored by looking at what is arguably the single most discussed passage in *Wigan Pier*, Orwell's encounter with a woman kneeling to clear a blocked drain (15). It is a passage that can be read thematically in terms of both class and gender. Philip Dodd (1982, 132–5) offers a subtle close reading which emphasises Orwell's scrupulousness in the recognition of ineffaceable distance. Having used in the 'Diary' (1970, p. 203) his common trope of epiphanic encounter, which involves direct engagement with another ('she looked up and caught my eye'), in the published version Orwell modified this to 'She looked up ... and I was almost near enough to catch her eye.'[8] The relocation of the encounter, from a street where both are on the same level to a glimpse from the window of a train, represents, Dodd argues, 'at once a rejection of the stance of identification of *Down and Out* and an expression of his conviction that identification of the middle-class individual with the working class is not possible, and that he is irremediably a "passenger" – "a passer by or through", according to the *OED* – in his relation to that class' (1982, p. 135). This intertextual analysis serves to ground Dodd's argument that Orwell is here refusing to pretend that he 'has access to what this young northern woman, from a different class from his own, believes, thinks and feels'. He only *saw* her, can offer only a *reading* of her thoughts based on minimal evidence (Dodd, 1982, p. 134).

This interpretation rests on detailed attention to the text, and clearly responds to Orwell's overt intention: to emphasise to his comfortable, southern, middle-class readership that this was not the 'ignorant suffering of an animal' but the circumstance of one who knew 'how dreadful a destiny it was' (15). Yet Dodd himself, in a shift that mimics Orwell's own contradictoriness, is subliminally aware that this is not the whole story. His very next paragraph opens: 'The germ of Orwell's stance, or at least *that part of it which admits ignorance rather than pretends intimacy ...*' (Dodd, 1982, p. 135–6; my emphasis). What Dodd's reading pushes, somewhat awkwardly, to the margins, Janet Montefiore brings back to the centre. She notes how commonly, in socialist writing of the decade, a woman's body is used as a signifier of class. Wealthy women personify the privileges of the upper classes, while their converse is 'the figure of the oppressed working-class woman doomed to drudgery, who often appears in "realist" prose, her bodily degradation representing the dumb misery of her whole class' (Montefiore, 1996, pp. 94, 99; ch. 3 *passim*). She draws attention to two realist short stories, published in the 'Writing in Revolt' issue of *Fact* (July 1937), in which such women *signify* misery without *understanding* it (a capacity reserved for the reader) (Montefiore, 1996, pp. 99–103).[9] By contrast Orwell concedes to his kneeling figure complete consciousness of her situation; but it is a consciousness that can nevertheless only be articulated by the mediating figure of the middle-class observer (Montefiore, 1996, p. 100). Furthermore, it is in fact an *ascribed* consciousness, that of a passive, suffering victim; it gives no voice to the woman herself, and rests on the suppression of actual working-class voices, female and male, which Orwell had heard.[10]

The counterpart to Orwell's ascribing an aware but passive consciousness to his symbolic slum-dweller is his repression of the active communist politics he encountered. This is evident from comparison of *Wigan Pier* with the 'Diary'. In the latter, he records meetings with various working-class communists, individually and *en masse*, about whom he forms diverse verdicts. At a NUMW meeting in Wigan addressed by Hannington he was 'surprised by the amount of communist feeling here'; but a fund-raising social for an international communist defence fund was contemptuously dismissed.[11] Among the speakers at a meeting in Barnsley, Tommy Degnan, a local miner, was singled out as 'effective', whereas the men in the crowd were dismissed as 'gaping with entirely expressionless faces' (Orwell, 1970, 241–2).[12] In Liverpool, he was 'very greatly impressed' by George Garrett, a local seaman and writer who had published in the *Adelphi*, and urged him to write his autobiography (1970, pp. 213–14). Brown, the embittered communist who guided him around Sheffield, Orwell described as helpful and generous; and sketched in the 'Diary' a sympathetic analysis of how his political anger might be linked to his physical and emotional difficulties (1970, pp. 217, 221–2). As Gloversmith (1980, pp. 117–19) comments sharply, all this specificity disappears from the published text, where it would interfere with the overall polemical thrust.[13] Instead, a contrast is set up between the 'professional communist' who speaks the 'usual bookish stuff' and 'jargon', and the ordinary working-class communist who (like the socialist) is not 'orthodox' or logically consistent in his political beliefs, and does not grasp the deeper implications of socialism (163–4). The creed of communism 'is never found in its pure form in a genuine proletarian' (166). This view is necessary to sustain Orwell's claim that working-class intellectuals divide into two groups: those who remain working class, improve their education, and are active politically – 'one of the finest types of man we have'; and those who climb into the middle class, whether via the literary intelligentsia or the labour movement – 'less admirable' (151–3).[14]

This way of representing working-class communists (and socialists) might be compared with J.B. Priestley's account of Bob, whom he met in Newcastle (1934, pp. 297–301). Priestley sets out to engage the reader's sympathy for Bob – hard-working, a proud father, 'something of a natural leader' who in a more fluid society would rise through his merits. He devotes most of his leisure to the unemployed settlement, or the People's Theatre; and even does 'a little careful water-colour sketching ... very creditable to an untrained man' (1934, p. 298). For Bob's political views, however, Priestley has less time. His one great effort 'to jump clear of this beer and betting jungle, this brutal fatalistic acceptance of the miserable muddle of our present society' is seen to have exhausted Bob's mental abilities. Quite sternly realistic in relation to his own workmates or neighbours, he is quite unrealistic both about 'the workers' as a whole (whom he idealises) and about employers or managers (who are seen as 'sneering cunning tyrants'). 'The world he lives in is not the sad muddle that most of us have begun to recognise, but is a mysterious and melodramatic place of vast sinister conspiracies, in which capitalists and bosses and officials plot together to trick him and his mates' (1934, p. 299). His communism is no rational alternative to a society in crisis, but a utopian escape. 'Nevertheless', Priestley concludes, 'I thought Bob himself a grand chap' (1934, p. 300). In one sense, Priestley's portrait of Bob could be taken to cast doubt on Orwell's claim that no actual worker is an orthodox communist. But in another sense, the two texts reinforce one another. Running through both Orwell's and Priestley's accounts, in the former case generalised, in the latter embodied in a representative figure, is a division between the shrewd wisdom of the worker in his familiar world, and the dangers he faces when he leaves it – whether actually through social mobility or theoretically through adoption of a political creed.

The different emphases of Dodd's and Montefiore's readings surely respond to a real conflict within Orwell's politics. Certainly he wished to break through the crudest of class stereotyping and assert the humanity of the Wigan working class, whether miners or slum dwellers. Yet he was unable to allow that humanity to speak for itself in whatever ways it chose. Instead he continued to speak on its behalf, ventriloquising his own views through various tableaux in the text, and suppressing voices which did not fit. It is not that Orwell could not hear the voices of the working class; the 'Diary' duly records them. But various factors – his predetermined sense of what was truly working class, his hostility to intellectuals of all classes, his somewhat patronising attitude to women – combined to exclude them from his finished text. To admit those voices, even more to attend to their contemporary struggles, would have disrupted his dominant vision of that class as passive, suffering victim.[15]

Rai (1988, pp. 72–80) offers an ambitious psychological exploration of why this might be so. He draws attention to a passage in *Wigan Pier* where Orwell is discussing his time as a policeman. 'It was the first time that I had ever been really aware of the working class, and to begin with *it was only because they supplied an analogy.* They were the *symbolic victims* of injustice, *playing the same part* in England as the Burmese played in Burma' (p. 138; Rai's emphases). The implication of the highlighted phrases, suggests Rai, is that the real social victims were also simultaneously symbols in some hidden personal drama of Orwell's. Underlying this, he posits a complex relationship between Orwell's perceptions of the external political world, and the internal psychological mechanisms through which he approaches and interprets that world:

it is impossible to say whether the 'adversarial' mental and emotional set so characteristic of him, the split within his own consciousness between 'victimisers' and symbolic 'victims', was *produced* by the situations to which Orwell was exposed, both as an anti-imperialist policeman and as a bourgeois socialist, or whether it was merely *precipitated* by them. There is the further possibility that the author's mind, taut with its symbolic tensions, actually *sought out* situations, real as well as imaginary, which reproduced or reflected ... its own 'adversarial' structure. (Rai, 1988, p. 73)

Such is the power of this adversarial structure that 'it appears that Orwell's sense of his own identity as a "socialist" is constituted by the tensions between the two terms of the symbolic conflict ... between "victims" and "victimisers", and so is, crucially, dependent upon their *continued, antagonistic, coexistence*' (Rai, 1988, p. 74). Orwell's symbolic drama would then centre on *becoming* (rather than simply being) a socialist, on a *process* of seceding from an imperialist and capitalist society, since it was there that 'the tension of the act of secession, of resistance, could be repeatedly re-enacted'. Its structure would be most easily stabilised if Orwell were to be found siding with a class locked in the position of resistant but permanent victim, rather than one actively transforming its situation.[16]

A parallel unresolved tension is present in Orwell's depiction of the contradictions of being a middle-class socialist (145–51). It demanded, he believed, the impossible: that you reject the culture of the class into which you were born. This meant giving up habits and mores rooted deeply in middle-class daily life – tastes, customs, accent, bodily deportment – which were in fact fundamental to identity (Rai, 1988, pp. 69–72). Orwell believed middle-class socialists negotiated this contradiction by harbouring 'a secret conviction that nothing can be changed' (146); were this not so, they would be forced to confront the reality that 'to abolish class distinctions means abolishing a part of yourself' (149). Though he attributed this impossible dilemma variously to revolutionaries and intellectuals, Orwell is here also exploring a personal conflict, one whose continued holding-in-suspension matches that of the permanent victim.

Autobiography

A further strand of the text, interwoven with both social investigation and political polemic, is autobiography. Orwell draws explicitly on his own experience both to validate the harshness of mining labour and to dramatise the depth of class separation. Autobiography was a crucial literary form in the 1930s and one to which Orwell was repeatedly drawn (Alldritt, 1969, pp. 63–84). Montefiore notes that autobiographical writing in the decade often took oblique forms, surfacing in plays, novels, poetry and travel writing as well as in recent literary history or documentary. In particular, she notes the frequency of 'the short memoir of childhood and schooldays, citing the writer's own experience as an exemplary "case-study"'. Her analysis of the structure of these case-studies delineates a pattern in which *Wigan Pier* clearly shares: a brief glimpse of Eden leading to the oppressive shades of the educational prison-house, an ironic double vision in which the writer's ominous awareness of contemporary historical crisis illuminates earlier youthful illusions. Such writings 'describe the writer's social construction in order both to explain where his ideas come from and to show a practical example of history's effect on a (comparatively) innocent subject' (Montefiore, 1996, pp. 44–6; chs 1, 6 *passim*).

Alldritt (1969, pp. 66, 69–74) reads the significance of the autobiographical element in the opposite direction. In contrast to *Down and Out* and *Homage*, accounts of times when Orwell 'managed to enter into fruitful relationships with the world beyond himself', he regards *Wigan Pier* as a more introspective text. Orwell's picture of English society, he suggests, is in some ways more compelling as a metaphor for his own life than as an account of contemporary social/political developments. Part I is framed by the contrast of the 1936 present (the Brookers' revolting lodging house in chapter 1) set against the past of Orwell's childhood (the 'mythical' warm, proletarian home of Chapter 7).[17] The text reports his exclusion – through his middle-class upbringing – from a rich experience of childhood (represented by his working-class friends/pursuits, 117–18); and especially from physicality and the body. This interpenetration of self and society, so that the representation of each can be read as a metaphor for the other, is consonant with Rai's analysis of Orwell's politics above.

Contemporary Reception

Its particular mode of publication affected both the circulation of *Wigan Pier*, and the nature of its immediate reception. In March 1936 Gollancz had founded the Left Book Club (LBC). It was always difficult for political books to reach a wide audience; he had the pioneering idea of adopting the book club format, whereby a large membership and guaranteed sales would allow prices to be kept low. In the intense political climate of the late 1930s, with both the domestic and international situations in crisis, the club was hugely successful. The three editors were Gollancz himself, together with John Strachey (who was close to the CP) and Harold Laski (a senior member of the Labour Party). Books cost 2s 6d per month; the monthly book was always taken from Gollancz's list, and was often written specially for the club. The club also published a monthly *Left (Book) News*, with a review of the month's choice, and political and club news. Supplementary book schemes were later added (Morgan, 1989, pp. 254–76; Lewis, 1970; Reid, 1979; Samuels, 1966; Dudley Edwards, 1987). Orwell's had been an independent commission, before the club was founded. When he sent the manuscript to his agent in December 1936, he suggested its chances of being chosen for the LBC were small 'as it is too fragmentary and, on the surface, not very left-wing' (1970, p. 288). In fact, the publisher contacted him almost by return, and opened negotiations. Aware of the hostility the book's political attacks would arouse among the left, Gollancz suggested offering Part I alone in an LBC edition, while issuing the whole text only in a small trade edition. This was resisted, and Gollancz instead resolved his political dilemma by writing a critical Foreword (1937) to the text. Hence *Wigan Pier* was published simultaneously with its first critical reception (Crick, 1992, pp. 309–10). Publication in the LBC helped it achieve major circulation. The club edition was published on 8 March 1937 with a simultaneous higher-priced trade edition; in May Part I was issued separately by the LBC as a supplementary volume for 'propaganda purposes'. The *News Chronicle* also published a short section in June 1937 in a series on young writers. By November 1939 a total of 47,000 copies had been sold (Davison, 1989, p. xiii; Crick, 1992, pp. 311, 340).

Gollancz's Foreword already signalled *Wigan Pier* as a controversial work even within the political circles it was aimed at (Crick, 1992: pp. 342–6; Rodden, 1989: pp. 42–3, 104–7; Meyers (ed.), 1975: pp. 99–113). Among the non-communist left, it provoked measured criticism, as well as praise.[18] Among the CP and its fellow-travellers, it provoked considerable hostility. The *Daily Worker* strongly denounced both the book and Orwell himself; while Laski in *Left News* endorsed the Foreword and added his own criticisms.[19] Later evaluations of Gollancz's Foreword have been shaped in large part by the subsequent reputations of the two men and the political courses they took (Crick, 1992; pp. 309–10; Rodden, 1989; pp. 107–9). Gollancz was, for three years, a prime example of a fellow-traveller, to a considerable extent a knowing one. He was deeply embarrassed by the text's criticisms of the left and especially its jibes at communism. However, his response to Orwell should not be read simply in the light of their divergent attitudes to the Soviet Union, both in 1937 and later. First, Orwell's attack in *Wigan Pier* was on the left as a whole, the pacifist ILPers as much as communist fellow-travellers. Secondly, his attacks on communism were directed not at, for example, the mass killings during the collectivisation of agriculture, nor at the injustices of the Moscow trials; but first at what he saw as the 'fashionable' affiliation to the communist movement of leftist intellectuals, and secondly at the commitment of the Soviet Union, endorsed by many others on the left, to ever-increasing industrialisation. It was only after his experiences in Spain that Orwell would focus explicitly on the duplicity of communist political practice. Here he offers merely a glancing, though acute, description of Bolshevik commissars as 'half-gramophone, half-gangster' (201) – a phrase which indeed caused Gollancz embarrassment. A proper evaluation of the Foreword, and the political issues at stake, would require resituating it within the synchronic context of the Left Book Club and the intense political atmosphere of the later 1930s. Gollancz and his fellow LBC selectors had been driven to support the struggle for a Popular Front, and consequently suppress their doubts about both communist and Soviet policy, by their overmastering fear of the advance of fascism, and the apparent unwillingness of the British government to take any steps to resist (Thomas, 1973; Dudley Edwards, 1987; Newman, 1989; 1993; Kramnick and Sheerman, 1993). Orwell too was not exempt from these dilemmas, as he struggled to formulate adequate political responses within a complex international situation; this is visible in his own shifts of position for and against pacifism in 1938–9.

Through its widespread sales, and the political controversy it provoked, *Wigan Pier* was the book that first brought Orwell to the attention of a wide readership, and introduced him as a political commentator. John Rodden, in his comprehensive study of the development of Orwell's literary reputation, sees *Wigan Pier*, together with the publication in the following year of an account of Orwell by his school friend and fellow writer Cyril Connolly in *Enemies of Promise*, as contributing substantially to one of his key images – that of 'Rebel' (Rodden, 1989, pp. 105–6). While elements of this image were already in place through Orwell's earlier writing and reviewing, 'the major change with *Wigan Pier* was its big audience and the fact that Orwell was starting to see himself not just as an Establishment outcast in solidarity with the poor but as a rebel *of* and *against* the left, a man of the left impatient with radical jargon and Marxist theory' (Rodden, 1989, p. 106).

Later Interpretations

There has been a wide and often conflicting range of appropriations of Orwell's work in general and *Wigan Pier* in particular (Rodden, 1989, pp. 39–50). In the 30 years after his death in 1950 the predominant approaches were literary critical and political. Literary critics stressed the generic indeterminacy (sometimes taken as confusion) of his work as a whole, and especially the works of essay/polemic/memoir; and gave much attention to conflicts over language, which was a theme of these writings, and of his last two, generally taken as his greatest, novels. Much more contentious was the political debate around Orwell. With the publication of *Animal Farm* (1945) and *Nineteen Eighty-Four* (1949), he rapidly became appropriated (despite his avowed adherence to democratic socialism) within a very powerful Cold War frame of reference. Orwell was held up as a man who had seen through the pretensions of socialism to its inevitable failure as a revolutionary cause (*Animal Farm*), and to its thinly concealed lust for power for its own sake (*Nineteen Eighty-Four*). Critics from the left responded sharply to this, most famously in Edward Thompson's anti-Cold War essay 'Outside the Whale' (1960). Orwell's relation to socialism was problematised or even questioned; his attacks on socialism and socialists in *Wigan Pier* were used as evidence for the doubtful nature of his political affiliations. This debate over Orwell's relationship to the left continued long after the most embattled phase of the Cold War; it was tackled by a new generation in Christopher Norris's collection *Inside the Myth* (1984).

In last 20 years, while these themes have continued to be debated, new lines of enquiry have emerged. Here, I shall look at feminist readings of the text as profoundly gendered; and relatedly, at how literary readings in terms of voice and persona, shaped by reception theory, help reveal how its textual qualities underpin its political force.

Women in *Wigan Pier*

In one significant development, Orwell's writing has come under the critical gaze of feminist scholars. Where previous debate had largely addressed issues that were the explicit subject of *Wigan Pier* itself – class and socialism, attention was now turned to what had been a barely noticed sub-text – gender. Rodden has taken this as a case study which 'exemplifies what happens to an author when he is interpreted, out of his own time, by a relatively new perspective' (Rodden, 1989, p. 213). Deirdre Beddoe (1984) and Beatrix Campbell (1984) have addressed the treatment of women in *Wigan Pier* and linked it to wider literary and political themes in Orwell's work. They argue that his representation of working-class women remains silent about their roles in employment and politics, while imbuing their domestic roles with pathos or romantic myth. In *Wigan Pier* he omits all mention of women in the cotton industry; and, while recording that women once worked underground in the pit (30), locates this in the past and remains silent about those still employed at the pit-brow.[20] Daphne Patai adds to the indictment his treatment of unemployment as an exclusively male problem and his failure to examine how it pressed harder on women, whether they were unemployed themselves or the wives of unemployed men (1984, pp. 71–3). Responding to this critique, Peter Davison has pointed out that few contemporary social investigators, even women, focused on the problems of working women (1996, pp. 74–5). Though one might cite counter-examples (Priestley, 1934, pp. 279–81; Pilgrim Trust, 1938, pp. 31–2, 82–4, 235–43), it is clear that here again Orwell was working within existing generic conventions, and that his neglect of working women's specific circumstances was certainly not unique.[21]

However, it is not simply a matter of Orwell failing to notice working-class women's circumstances. Not only does he also say nothing of their strong history of trade union and political activism in Lancashire over the preceding generation, as Beddoe notes (1984, pp. 148–53); but when he does encounter evidence of such activity or awareness it is suppressed or denigrated. This suppression can be seen by considering some passages in the 'Diary' that do not reach the published text. In Sheffield he stayed with the Searles, of whom he gives a long description notable for the warmth and friendliness towards them which he clearly felt. He comments: 'I was surprised by Mrs S's grasp of the economic situation and also of abstract ideas – quite unlike most working-class women in this, though she is I think not far from illiterate' (1970, p. 220). He records the following incident: 'We had an argument one evening in the Searles' house because I helped Mrs S with the washing-up. Both of the men disapproved of this, of course. Mrs S seemed doubtful. She said that in the North working-class men never offered any courtesies to women ... and she took this state of things for granted, but did not see why it should not be changed' (1970, p. 222). Orwell notes that this is particularly anomalous now that so many men are out of work but adds: 'Yet I think it is instinctively felt by both sexes that the man would lose his manhood if, merely because he was out of work, he became a "Mary Ann".' This last comment alone appears in *Wigan Pier* (75), thereby sealing a loophole of actual debate and discussion that might have disturbed the pattern Orwell wishes to depict. Again, in the 'Diary' he records attending an NUWM fund-raising social; his anger at what he sees as the lack of revolutionary spirit is vented specifically upon the women present (1970, pp. 206–7).[22] These omissions and denigrations are in line with Campbell's analysis of Orwell's wider attitude to the working class – a class which can suffer, which can organise, but which cannot think, struggle or win (Campbell, 1984, pp. 127–9). Any thinkers it does produce he detaches from the class, just as he does Mrs Searle from other working-class women.

Where the working woman does feature is as housewife – current victim of appalling housing conditions (15, 53–5, 58); or member of the idyllic remembered household (108). Yet each of these portrayals is shot through with contradiction. While Orwell invites sympathy for the women struggling to bring up families in dirty and demoralising slum dwellings, and recognises the impact that a large family has (55), he adds birth controllers to his litany of contemptible fanatics (129, 150) (Beddoe, 1984, pp. 149–50, 153). His contrast of the working-class family, united around the domestic hearth (107–8), with the middle-class family, unable to take part in a strike because riven by gender conflict (106–7; cf. 75), rests – Campbell points out – on ignorance of the ways in which industrial action may strain cross-gender working-class loyalties (1984, pp. 130–1).[23]

Rodden has offered a defence of Orwell against aspects of these feminist criticisms, arguing the need to distinguish between 'contextualizing to understand and historicizing to whitewash'.[24] To expect of Orwell, writing in the 1930s and '40s, that he should anticipate the values of the 1980s, is ahistorical. Rodden's primary claim is that, judged by contemporary standards, Orwell's 'attitudes towards femininity and social roles were conventional for his time, among socialists as well as non-socialists' (Rodden, 1989, p. 218).[25] He notes that in the 1930s the feminist movement was at a low point, and even many women on the left felt there were more important causes to fight. While conceding that the characterisation of the birth control movement as a whole as 'fanatics' is 'totally unfair', he points out that one of its most prominent leaders, Marie Stopes, was a member of the eugenics movement and had 'proposed sterilization for the poor, the feeble-minded, and half-castes' (Rodden, 1989, pp. 219–20).

There is considerable value in Rodden's general interpretative stance here and in some of his specific defences of Orwell. At times, however, he accepts too easily what is in effect Orwell's own characterisation of those he criticised. In particular, to view the birth control movement only through the prism of Stopes's eugenicist demands was to ignore the wider case that could be and was made for it by socialist feminists at the time (Rowbotham, 1977; cf. Pearce, 1997, p. 413 n. 17). Rodden also comments, of the parallel disparagement of homosexuals and vegetarians, that it 'stemmed not only from Orwell's sometime intolerance of others' idiosyncrasies but also from a genuine (and not unjust) belief that they were crackpot special interest groups' (1989, pp. 220–1). This defence itself betrays inadequate contextualisation. The tradition in English socialism which argued that sexual and (what might today be termed) ecological questions must be an integral part of any socialist transformation stretched back to the 1880s (Rowbotham and Weeks, 1977).[26] The relevance and importance of these issues was asserted accurately and forcefully by Gollancz in his Foreword (1937, pp. 94–5). Rodden concedes, over birth control, that Orwell 'never argued his case in his work' (1989,

p. 220). What he did, rather, was to *assert* it forcefully and by casual abuse. It is this failure to be aware of and address, rather than dismiss, alternative perspectives within the socialist movement which might be central to a historically sensitive criticism of Orwell's treatment not just of feminists but of other socialists during his supposed critique from within.

Voice and Persona

One of the most distinctive features of Orwell's writing, especially in his non-fictional work, is the narrative voice. That voice has been the focus of significant critical attention recently. A close technical analysis of its construction has been made by Fowler. He has described Orwell's idiolect as aiming at a spoken, demotic or colloquial, quality, thereby aiding the characterisation of the narrator as an on-the-scene, down-to-earth observer very ready to pronounce blunt judgements (Fowler, 1995, p. 9). Various linguistic devices are used to establish that claim to authority, drawing especially on the tradition of the personal, opinionated essay or pamphlet (Pomeroy, 1987). A confident subjectivity is indicated by sweeping generalisations, which allow subjective impressions to be presented as statements of fact. Another frequent characteristic is a hyperbolic negativism, in which stereotyped targets are attacked via simplified caricatures. Fowler identifies some of the characteristic devices used here: images evoking smell and dirt; animal imagery; and frequent paratactic lists which reduce all their (diverse) components to a single (hated) quality (Fowler, 1995, pp. 49–50, 53–9). Many passages in the political polemic of Part II are narrated in that hyperbolic voice (for example 161, 169). Fowler has also analysed what he terms Orwell's dialogic attitude. 'the voice implied by the writing is directed towards an imaginary, but apparently specific, addressee; everything which is said takes its tone from a dramatic stance towards an assumed reader' (Fowler, 1995, p. 45). This voice summons up and addresses a 'you' in terms that 'suggest an energetic interrogator who is putting great pressure on the reader to agree with [its] interpretation'.

Already in the 1980s, with a political acuteness deriving respectively from a postcolonial critique of liberal social democracy and from feminism, Alok Rai and Daphne Patai had each identified, and argued against, the pressure of this confident voice. Rai urged that the apparent transparency of Orwell's prose must be resisted. His political writings *appear* to be immediately available, not needing literary analysis. We as readers must insist on the need for such analysis to make space in which we can look at Orwell's work against the swamping pressure of historical immediacy (Rai, 1988, pp. 3–5).[27] That work is essentially polemical, so we need to suspend belief, refuse the experience of *plausibility*, and focus attention instead on the authorial consciousness which mediates reality in this, disarmingly transparent, way (Rai, 1988, pp. 7–9).[28] Patai analysed some of the characteristics of that polemical voice. One of its favourite rhetorical strategies is the blanket generalisation ('No ...', 'All ...'), which brushes aside all reservations by its force and confidence. She notes two preferred narrative postures: the 'voice-of-the-people', who identifies himself with all who are decent/honest/thinking, thereby excluding from these virtues those who disagree; and the 'voice-in-the-wilderness', who alone has the courage to tell the unpopular truth (Patai, 1984, p. 10).[29] The latter stance seems to contradict the former, but in fact complements it; together they flatter the reader, especially one who feels threatened by working-class, socialist or anti-fascist politics, by telling a 'truth' about the left which is both reassuringly commonsense and boldly transgressive (Patai, 1984, pp. 9–11).[30]

Growing critical attention has also been given to the process of the historical reception of literary texts, and the ways in which this reception in turn shapes later readers' responses. This has led to a more questioning attention to both the construction and later reinterpretation of Orwell's persona. The image of the *author* (Eric Arthur Blair become George Orwell), and the *narrative voice* in the text, between them and through their reception help form the literary *persona* of this writer (what is evoked when a text is described as 'Orwellian'). In the years immediately before and after his death a powerful persona was constructed around Orwell; particularly influential in this was the critic V.S. Pritchett, who described Orwell in 1946 as 'the most honest writer of our time' and in an obituary as 'the wintry conscience of a generation', 'a kind of saint' who 'prided himself on seeing through the rackets, and on conveying the impression of living without the solace or even the need of a single illusion' (Patai, 1984, p. 2; Rodden, 1989, pp. 109–13, 123–4, 324–5). This verdict, obviously in part a product of taking Orwell at his own estimation, was later adopted, with variations, by many other writers on Orwell. The establishment, reworking and effects of this persona have been traced in great detail by Rodden (1989; cf. Patai, 1984, pp. 2–14). First, the persona of 'Orwell' can be and is claimed by different political factions, by means of selective readings of Orwell's works; Rodden offers an exhaustive account of the development of a whole panoply of 'Orwells', during his lifetime and subsequently. Secondly, this persona has proved impervious to correction by biographical research (such as that by Crick); in other words, it has a life separate from and independent of the actual life and writings of Orwell. Thirdly, through the operation of the author-function (Foucault, 1986), this persona shapes how we read the texts of Orwell.

Both Rai and Patai have traced (part of) the origins of Orwell's persona to certain features of his narrative voice. They have stressed how acceptance of/submission to that voice has contributed to establishing and embellishing his persona; and Patai has paid tribute to the power of that persona in shaping readings of Orwell texts, by reflecting on her own experience of writing about them (Patai, 1984, pp. ix–x). Each then goes on to argue that there are deep ideological roots of Orwell's contradictions, and of the voice which both enacts and masks them. For Rai, they lie in the contradictions within the project of democratic socialism; and in particular those – which Orwell himself emphasised – between the interests of the British working class and of exploited colonised peoples, and between his own class of origin (to which he deeply attached for his identity and values) and his rejection of the economic and political privileges of that class (Rai, 1988, pp. 63–4, 67, 108–11, 163–4).

Androcentrism

For Patai, the roots of Orwell's contradictions lie in what she terms his *androcentrism*. His texts address, even create, a specifically masculine reader. At the heart of his writing, damaging if not undermining his avowed standards of justice, is a commitment to an embattled masculinity. This underlies not just his covert and overt misogyny (his neglect/dismissal of women, as seen by Campbell and Beddoe), and his homophobia in the narrow sense (his disparaging of all forms of political opponents, *especially* those on the left, as unmanned, 'nancy'), but also his clinging to a paradigm of gender relations that locates a certain form of hypertrophied masculinity as central (Patai, 1984, pp. 14–17).

Patai's analysis in terms of androcentrism allows her to bring into a single focus apparently disparate elements of *Wigan Pier*. Part I idealised the male worker as manly. This is most vivid in Orwell's admiring account of the near-naked bodies of the coal miners, in the face of whose strength and skill he feels himself humbled (20, 29) (Patai, 1984, pp. 75–7).[31] But equally crucial is the matching picture of the patriarchal household, with the father firmly in charge (107–8) (Patai, 1984, pp. 77–81).[32] However, Orwell's relationship to these workers is highly ambivalent. They are both desired and feared, idealised and denigrated. The desire/fear couplet may be approached via the famous dispute over Orwell's supposed claim that the working class smell. In the immediate aftermath of publication, Orwell fiercely repudiated making any such statement (Crick, 1992, pp. 344–5). But as Patai has shown in her analysis of the relevant passage (119–20; cf. 133–4), the narrative repeatedly shifts between the claim that the middle class (are brought up to) believe the working class smell – the claim which Orwell publicly stood by – and an apparent statement of the fact that they do smell (Patai, 1984, pp. 80–1).[33] Patai points out that his revulsion from smell, and from any intimate physical contact, which purports to be a matter of class, is in fact also gendered – it is a revulsion from working-class *men*. Orwell explicitly notes that he felt no such revulsion with women (122).[34] She argues that his revulsion from working men is the negative of his fascination with their bodies; Orwell is reassuring himself and his readers that this fascination is in the context of a fundamental commitment to heterosexuality (Patai, 1984, pp. 82–4). The idealisation/denigration couplet is revealed in Orwell's portrayal of the working class as properly suspicious of, indeed hostile to, education (107). The idealised worker is the one who labours, skilfully and uncomplainingly, with his body; the denigrated worker is the one who educates himself out of his class (151–3, 164). Orwell's working-class man, as Campbell emphasised in his depiction of working women, works, suffers, but does not think.[35] I would suggest that this ambivalence towards workers is simultaneously one of class and gender. The miner, as Orwell powerfully shows, is an Atlas who holds the pyramid of class exploitation on his stooped shoulders. He is also an archetypal figure of that tough masculinity which Orwell repeatedly celebrated and claimed for himself (Patai, 1984, pp. 7–8, 15–16). Well might he then feel a complex of emotions towards such a man – guilt, admiration, desire, envy. The working-class male, unlike women, was a proximate figure of both desire and threat.

This ambivalence towards the working class in Part I may be linked with Patai's analysis of Orwell's anxiety about socialists and socialism in Part II. She suggests that homophobia can be defined more widely than simply hatred of homosexuals. Rather, it is characterised by fear of *any* change in sex roles; as such, it exerts a constant pressure on *all* men. So Orwell is to be found showing revulsion not only from homosexuals, but from any 'unmanly' men – hence the splenetic passage of abuse against the socialists on the bus, against vegetarians and pacifists (161–2) (Patai, 1984, pp. 84–5). She links his embattled attitude to his fellow socialists with his opposition to industrialisation. Orwell argues in the closing chapters of *Wigan Pier* that the machine is bad because it undermines qualities we (i.e. *men*, adds Patai) admire (i.e. *in men*) – physical courage and strength. The underlying logic of his argument, she suggests, runs as follows: 'difficulty equals hardness equals opposite of softness equals masculine'. Hence it is unsurprising that for Orwell, just as socialist 'cranks' are precisely those who challenge traditional gender roles, so socialism itself is suspect for the threat it poses to the necessary conditions for true manliness (Patai, 1984, pp. 87–94).

Again, Rodden (1989, pp. 221–3) comes to the defence; but because his commentary is focused primarily on the vicissitudes of Orwell's reputation, rather than on the substantive interpretative issues, he arguably fails to register the full force of Patai's case. His response oscillates between criticism of her global characterisation of Orwell (as misogynist), and acknowledgement (though not integration) of key elements of her analysis. He sets Patai's work in two contexts: that of 1970s and '80s feminist criticism; and that of a disappointed admirer of Orwell. First, drawing on debates in those decades between feminist critics themselves, he suggests that in certain cases:

> feminist ideology, which enabled original insights by feminist Left critics into Orwell's dismaying *machismo* and regressive gender politics, also blinds many of them to the complexity of his *oeuvre* and of his historical situation. Their *own* obsession with gender politics ... has prevented them from appreciating legitimate concerns other than gender (e.g. class, race, nation) which Orwell did express explicitly and effectively. (Rodden, 1989, p. 222)

Again, the general point is well made; but it fails to recognise, I believe, the way in which Patai's analysis of the workings of gender in Orwell's writing shows it to be imbricated with, rather than separate from, those other concerns. Orwell's androcentrism, for Patai, issues not simply in dismissive treatment of women in general, or feminists in particular, but also in constructions of class, race and nation which are shaped by that gender commitment. Patai's argument here joins with Campbell's critique considered earlier, which connected the removal of agency and of the power to think from women with Orwell's parallel depiction of workers.

Rodden's second contextualisation has more force. He suggests that Patai and other feminists in the 1980s have 'expected more of Orwell than of his contemporaries'. Hence, like many other critics of Orwell (especially on the left), they come to feel an embittered disappointment when he does not live up to their (unfair) expectations (Rodden, 1989, p. 224). For Rodden, such an outcome is structural to the analysis of 'the politics of literary reputation' which his study offers. Significant literary (as well as other) figures, he argues, can become models of transference and identification. 'The receiver accents his model's strengths and downplays or rationalizes his shortcomings – and does the reverse with his cautionary anti-model.' While much of the time people may work with a composite model to form their ideal selves, for certain individuals in certain circumstances their identification with a single such figure as model may be 'sweeping, direct, and passionate' (Rodden, 1989, pp. 84–6). Examined over time, such an identification may mutate in the features of the model which it values, or shift sharply from admiration to rejection.[36] The situation is particularly complex when a historic shift of values takes place, as with the emergence of second-wave feminism. This shift, suggests Rodden, shows:

> how history can overtake an author, so that he becomes judged by standards he could not have anticipated in his own day. He must ... not merely be a man of his time if he is to remain a figure; subsequent generations of readers must be able to project *their* bedrock values as *his*. When a figure can no longer accommodate his readers' idealized self-images, his status is in jeopardy. (Rodden, 1989, p. 224)

In this light, Rodden suggests that disillusion may underlie some of the more sweeping negative remarks on Orwell which Patai (like other left feminist critics) offers. Of the fact of this disappointment there can be no doubt, since Patai herself describes the process of her own disillusionment vividly at the start of her book (1984, pp. ix–x). Nevertheless, Rodden's own arguments may concede more to Patai than he explicitly accepts. His analysis of literary models recognises that the figure 'invites a certain kind of identification, or limits it, by his behavior. By assuming a certain rhetorical stance or tone, the writer as model takes on a certain role – and "pressures" or "guides" his readers into roles of his choosing' (Rodden, 1989, p. 85). It is precisely that rhetorical stance, and the resulting pressure on the reader, that Patai (like Rai) analyses and (angrily) rejects. Rodden notes that before the rise of feminist literary criticism from the 1970s 'Orwell had no distinctive reputation among women'. In considering reasons for this, he points out:

> Most critic-readers who have cast Orwell as an intellectual model and have played major roles in the making of his reputation have been men. And these facts of Orwell's reception history suggest, in turn, much about how writers become figures – i.e. not just because they stand as political or generational exemplars, but for unstated, less visible reasons too, e.g. because they are also inspirational gender models. (Rodden, 1989, pp. 211–12 and 212n)

He goes on to note that:

> the gender gap is there. Many women cannot 'read themselves into' Orwell very easily. They come to him with the expectation that he

speaks to 'the common reader', only to find the dialogue virtually
closed. His reader seems to be the common *male* reader, and the
disappointment is keen. (Rodden, 1989, p. 225)

He acknowledges that the Orwell cult is in part a cult of masculinity,
and one which has had a specific appeal to male intellectuals.[37]

It is striking that, in defiance of dominant literary critical trends of
the last two decades, much discussion of Orwell continues to read his
texts biographically.[38] Thus in criticising and defending Orwell, Patai
and Rodden move back and forth between life and works. In part, this
response is invited by Orwell himself. *Wigan Pier* is autobiographical
in two senses: it relates in substantial (if selective) detail both the
recent and more distant history of its author; and it advances that
personal history as a warrant for the authenticity of its reportage and
argument. But it is also invited by the critical focus on persona. As
Rodden shows in exhaustive detail, the reception of Orwell's work,
and the reputation it has acquired, are constructed in part through
the evaluations of authoritative voices, some of whom knew Orwell
personally, others of whom created him as a model on the basis of
biographical report as well as textual reading.[39] In attempting to go
beyond readings which simply conform to that persona ('Orwell the
truth-teller'), the slippage from analysis of narrative voice (which both
Rai and Patai undertake) to critique of biography is very easy. It is
evident in Patai's closing remarks on *Wigan Pier*.

There *is* a certain transparency in Orwell's writing – not, however,
that usually assumed ... a prose so clear that it lets us 'see through'
to the object described. Orwell's writing ... displays quite a different
kind of transparency, that of prose so emotionally laden, full of
associations of such obviously personal significance, that it lets us
see clearly not the purported object of this prose but the man who
composed it. (Patai, 1984, p. 94)

The bringing together of these diverse critical approaches to *Wigan
Pier* demonstrates the complexity of a cultural history reading, and
the ways it can help to break down binary analytical divisions
(individual/society, text/context). A biographical focus on Blair/Orwell
reveals him to be an individual who is (as he himself insisted) socially
produced – whether this is viewed diachronically (his upbringing and
career creating a man profoundly marked by class, gender and racial
ways of understanding and engaging with the world) or synchronically
(his involvement in the socialist politics of the late 1930s embroiling
him in the same dilemmas and self-contradictions as those whom he
so sharply criticised). Textual analysis alone cannot determine the
meaning of *Wigan Pier*, as is shown by commentators' subtle but

opposed readings of two of its most famous passages (the woman clearing the drain, the belief that the working classes smell). The contradictions thus revealed lead outside the text once again, to the class-, gender- and racially-divided world which produced it. Meaning is generated also by the positioning of readers; hence a major shift in gender politics can uncover a dimension of the text invisible both to the author and the contemporary readers he addressed, so much was it part of their taken-for-granted perceptual frame.

Notes

All emphases in quotations are in the original except where otherwise stated.

1. This chapter refers to the Penguin Twentieth Century Classics edition of 1989; page references are given in brackets in the text.
2. Biographical details about Orwell not specifically referenced are taken from Crick (1992).
3. Rai (1988, p. 53) describes them as 'characterised by a kind of brash and uncomplicated socialism which is not normally associated with Orwell'; he suggests they are 'trying out a somewhat unfamiliar rhetoric'. However, the texts survive only in their French translations, which may not record precisely Orwell's own terminology. Re-translations into English are included in Orwell (1998, pp. 122–7, 128–38).
4. *Down and Out*, addressed like *Wigan Pier* to a middle-class readership, advocates only very limited reforms. Rai (1988, p. 53) notes: 'It is ... with a slight sense of shock that one realises how *little* there is of politics in Orwell's writings of the years 1930–5.' He discusses (pp. 53–7) the absent, or muted, sense of political context in these writings.
5. Pearce, 1997, pp. 414–15, offers a detailed and convincing argument that the 'Diary' was written 'soon after the events it describes' (p. 416). Davison (in Orwell, 1998, p. 417) suggests the surviving typescript is a copy (probably made after the trip) of 'entries handwritten at the time of the events described'. Crick (1992, pp. 280 and 628 n. 8) had argued it was not a contemporaneous diary, but a first draft for the book. Orwell's research notes are reprinted in 1998, pp. 538–84. His letters written during the researching and writing of *Wigan Pier* are in 1968, 243–8, 250–4, 257–9, 262–3, 288.
6. This can also be seen in the role of the photographs in the book. Taken from agency pictures, and drawn from other parts of the country, they are neither specific illustrations of the text, nor a carefully structured photo essay (Davison, 1989, p. xiv). There

is a marked contrast with Hannington (1937), where photographs and captions are closely integrated with the political argument of the text.

7. Cf. Williams (1997, pp. 170–1). For further discussion of this passage, see pp. 111–12 below.

8. Dodd (1982, pp. 133–4) cites as parallels both the meeting with the southerner in Chapter 1, and the opening and closing encounters of *Homage*.

9. One of the stories is by the working-class writer James Hanley. Strikingly, Montefiore notes that Storm Jameson's famous essay on documentary (1937), published in that same issue of *Fact*, likewise assumes that it is male writers who will record this suffering.

10. Cf. Pearce (1997, p. 420). Montefiore (1996, p. 102) notes also the contradictory testimony of working-class women's autobiographies, which record 'vigour, intelligence and courage against the odds'. C. McNelly Kearns (1987, pp. 102–4, 108–11) draws a parallel with Orwell's analysis of the (supposed) thoughts of a black Senegalese soldier – once again, the product of authorial ascription – in his 1939 essay 'Marrakech' (1970, pp. 426–32).

11. Hannington was a 'poor speaker, using all the padding and clichés of the Socialist orator'; but the audience, though very rough and unemployed, 'very attentive' (1970, p. 201). Of the social he wrote: 'I suppose these people represented a fair cross-section of the more revolutionary element in Wigan. If so, God help us. Exactly the same sheep-like crowd – gaping girls and shapeless middle-aged women dozing over their knitting – that you see everywhere else. There is no *turbulence* left in England' (1970, pp. 206–7).

12. Orwell had earlier visited Degnan, who had been thrown out of a BUF meeting for heckling, and got some information about mining conditions from him (1970, pp. 232–3).

13. In Part I praise is given to the efforts of the NUWM (77), and more briefly the *Daily Worker* (80).

14. The former may be represented in the Diary by Jerry Kennan, socialist electrician, and Paddy Grady, unemployed miner (1970, pp. 198–9); the latter by Meade (p. 198), Wilde, the Yorkshire secretary of the Club & Institute Union (pp. 226, 228–9), and Hannington himself, 'with the wrong kind of Cockney accent (once again, though a Communist entirely a bourgeois)' (p. 201).

15. Klaus (1985, pp. 155–7) contrasts Montagu Slater's *Stay Down Miner* (1936), reporting the recent successful pit occupations that had driven out non-union labour in South Wales. Cf. Newsinger (1999, pp. 34–5). Orwell's dominant vision was to be partially disrupted and displaced by his experiences in Spain. But defeat,

and disillusionment with the behaviour of the left, drove him back to something near his original perspective in *Animal Farm* and *Nineteen Eighty-Four*.

16. *Animal Farm*, with its cyclical movement from exploitation via revolution to restoration, and *Nineteen Eighty-Four*, with its stasis of permanent warfare, could then be read as dramatising the impossibility of ever moving beyond the act of (defeated) rebellion.

17. Cf. Pearce (1997, 425–6) on *Wigan Pier* 90–1. For similar reference to the Edwardian past as better, see Priestley (1934, pp. 156–73, 189–204).

18. See Ethel Mannin, quoted in Crick (1992, p. 343). Walter Greenwood in *Tribune* and Arthur Calder-Marshall in *Time and Tide* (Meyers, 1975, pp. 99–100, 101–3) both took issue with aspects of Part II. Hamish Miles in *New Statesman* (Meyers, 1975, pp. 110–13) was less critical.

19. For CP criticisms, and Orwell's attempt to draw Gollancz to his defence, see Crick (1992, pp. 343–5). Laski's review in Meyers (1975, pp. 104–7). Crick (1992, p. 311) cites an LBC speaker quoted in *Left News* who claimed 'this book has exercised our wits .... we sit up and sharpen our brains so as to refute his erroneous notions'.

20. There is only a passing allusion to mill girls in the opening sentence (3). In the 'Diary' he locates women working underground some 60 years earlier (1970, p. 234). Pit-brow women: Beddoe (1984, p. 152); Campbell (1984, p. 129).

21. Patai (1984, pp. 73 and 284 n. 53) notes his parallel silence on the differential impact of poverty on working women, even though he was aware of 'the routine sacrifice of women's interests to those of men' among the middle class; cf. Beddoe (1984, pp. 144–6).

22. In a perhaps not dissimilar way, although both the Brookers are given a hostile presentation, Orwell chooses to comment of the wife: 'I suspect that her only real trouble was over-eating' (5), whereas in the 'Diary' (1970, p. 203) she is described as 'ill with a weak heart'.

23. Middle-class women feature in the text in their own right only fleetingly, as cartoon representatives of capitalist oppression or middle-class prejudice (52, 34). These portrayals of women are not specific to *Wigan Pier*: Campbell (1984, pp. 130–2); Patai (1984, pp. 74–5) citing parallel examples from later writings. Beddoe (1984, pp. 140–8) shows how Orwell's neglect there of both the fact and the structural role of working women's employment is paralleled by the way his accounts of middle-class women (which are almost entirely confined to his novels) largely ignore the importance of their paid work.

24. Rodden (1989, pp. 211–26, quoted at p. 224); elsewhere he expresses this as the difference between 'judging him by the present or trying to understand him in his own historical moment' (p. 217).

25. Rodden also cites a range of biographical testimony to deflect the charge that Orwell was personally misogynistic, or hostile to women (1989, pp. 212, 215, 218, 220–1). Cf. Davison (1996, pp. 142–3).

26. Rodden is aware of other long-lasting components of the socialist lineage; hence his (appropriate) locating of Orwell in the tradition of Robert Blatchford (1989, p. 438 n. 139).

27. Rai urges a strategy that will 'insist on maintaining the critical distance which the urgent contemporaneity, the flaunted topicality, of the work seems determined to obliterate'. For 'despite the foregrounded historical markers, there is ... a mediating, shaping, consciousness at work' (1988, p. 5).

28. Rai defines this suspension of belief by contrast with the suspension of disbelief necessary to engage with a fictional work (1988, p. 8).

29. Patai cites the following examples of the former from *Wigan Pier*: 'no-one capable of thinking and feeling' (178); 'every intelligent person' (187–8); 'Everyone ... knows' (198); 'so many normal decent people are repelled' (202).

30. In sharp contrast to these readings, which identify a single narrative voice with the views of Orwell the author, Lynette Hunter (1984, pp. 45–69) refutes any such identification. She argues instead that there is a shifting and developing voice, which gradually bifurcates into an 'aware and learning narrator', and a middle-class 'type' (p. 61) with a set of stock responses to what it sees of working-class life. This split voice challenges its readers in increasingly complex ways to question their automatic prejudices. Hunter notes that most contemporary and later readers have not interpreted the text in this way, and concedes that what she conceives as Orwell's narrative strategy has failed (pp. 68–9). The elusive nature of this aspect of *Wigan Pier* is markedly revealed in conflicting interpretations of his account of the working-class woman he sees in Wigan; see above, p. 111.

31. For the way in which Orwell's picture focuses on individual miners, at the expense of the structures in which they work, see Patai (1984, pp. 75, 286–7 nn. 58–9).

32. For the omissions central to this nostalgic image, see Patai (1984, pp. 79–80).

33. Patai comments (1984, p. 80) that the narrative 'generates a good deal of ambiguity', and cites (pp. 287–8 n. 67) several critics who have taken Orwell as sharing that belief. It might be

possible to rescue the coherence of the text here by arguing that it enacts the shift from being taught that workers smell, to internalising that belief and so experiencing them as smelling. However, there is an emotional charge to Orwell's writing on this theme which suggests he is not in such conscious control of his argument. Davison (1996, pp. 72–3), defending Orwell, shares precisely the same slippage.

34. Nor did Orwell experience such revulsion from Burmans, towards whom he felt 'almost as I felt with a woman' (132–3). On this transformation of Burmese males into social females, see Patai (1984, pp. 24–6, 38, 83).
35. Cf. above, p. 120.
36. For an example of the former, see Rodden's account of Irving Howe (1989, pp. 336–53, 360–1); of the latter, his account of Raymond Williams (pp. 188–200).
37. Rodden (1989, p. 225); cf. his recognition of Orwell's 'tough guy posturing in some of his work' (p. 214). Patai (1984, pp. 15–18, 89), discusses Orwell's address to a specifically masculine reader.
38. Hunter (1984) is a major exception here.
39. Prichett is an example of the former; Lionel Trilling (Rodden, 1989, pp. 73–84) of the latter.

Bibliography

Aitken, I. *Film and Reform: John Grierson and the Documentary Film Movement* (Routledge, 1990).

Alldritt, K. *The Making of George Orwell: An Essay in Literary History* (Edward Arnold, 1969).

Baxendale, J. and C. Pawling *Representing the Thirties: A Decade in the Making, 1930 to the Present* (Basingstoke: Macmillan, 1996).

Beddoe, D. 'Hindrances and Help-meets: Women in the Writings of George Orwell', in Norris (ed.) (1984), pp. 139–54.

Booth, C. *Life and Labour of the People in London* (Macmillan, 1902).

Branson, N. *History of the Communist Party of Great Britain, 1927–41* (Lawrence & Wishart, 1985).

Bulmer, M., K. Bales and K.K. Sklar (eds) *The Social Survey in Historical Perspective 1880–1940* (Cambridge: Cambridge University Press, 1991).

Campbell, B. 'Orwell – Paterfamilias or Big Brother?', in Norris (ed.) (1984), pp. 126–38.

Chaney, D. and M. Pickering 'Authorship in Documentary: Sociology as an Art Form in Mass-Observation', in J. Corner (ed.) *Documentary and the Mass Media* (Edward Arnold, 1986), pp. 29–46.

Crick, B. *George Orwell: A Life* (1980; new edn., Harmondsworth: Penguin, 1992).

Croucher, R. *We Refuse to Starve in Silence: A History of the National Unemployed Workers Movement, 1920–46* (Lawrence & Wishart, 1987).

Davison, P. 'A Note on the Text' (1989), in Orwell (1937), pp. xiii–xv.

— *George Orwell: A Literary Life* (Basingstoke: Macmillan, 1996).

Dodd, P. 'The Views of Travellers: Travel Writing in the 1930s', *Prose Studies* 5.1 (1982), pp. 127–38.

Dowse, R.E. *Left in the Centre: The ILP 1893–1940* (Longman, 1966).

Dudley Edwards, R. *Victor Gollancz: A Biography* (Gollancz, 1987).

Englander, D. and R. O'Day (eds) *Retrieved Riches: Social Investigation in Britain 1840–1914* (Aldershot: Scolar Press, 1995).

Foucault, M. 'What is an Author', in P. Rabinow (ed.) *The Foucault Reader: an Introduction to Foucault's Thought* (Harmondsworth: Penguin, 1986), pp. 101–20.

Fowler, R. *The Language of George Orwell* (Basingstoke: Macmillan, 1995).

Frizzell, D. *Humphrey Spender's Humanist Landscapes: Photo-Documents, 1932–1942* (New Haven, CT: Yale University Press, 1997).

Gloversmith, F. 'Changing Things: Orwell and Auden', in F. Gloversmith (ed.) *Class, Culture and Social Change: A New View of the 1930s* (Brighton: Harvester, 1980), pp. 101–41.

Gollancz, V. 'Foreword' (1937), in Meyers (ed.) (1975), pp. 91–9.

Hall, S. 'The Social Eye of *Picture Post*', in Birmingham Centre for Contemporary Cultural Studies, *Working Papers in Cultural Studies* no. 3 (Autumn 1972), pp. 71–120.

Hannington, W. *The Problem of the Distressed Areas* (Gollancz, 1937).

Hodges, S. *Gollancz: The Story of a Publishing House 1928–1978* (Gollancz, 1978).

Hopkinson, T. (ed.) *Picture Post 1938–50* (Harmondsworth: Penguin, 1970).

Hunter, L. *George Orwell: The Search for a Voice* (Milton Keynes: Open University Press, 1984).

Jameson, S. 'Documents', *Fact* 4 (July 1937), pp. 9–17; repr. in P. Deane (ed.), *History in Our Hands: A Critical Anthology of Writings on Literature, Culture and Politics from the 1930s* (Leicester: Leicester University Press, 1998), pp. 312–18.

Kearns, C.M. 'On Not Teaching Orwell', in H. Bloom (ed.) *George Orwell* (New York: Chelsea House, 1987), pp. 97–112.

Keating, P. *Into Unknown England 1866–1913: Selections from the Social Explorers* (Fontana, 1976).

Kingsford, P. *The Hunger Marches in Britain 1920–40* (Lawrence & Wishart, 1982).

Klaus, H.G. *The Literature of Labour: Two Hundred Years of Working-class Writing* (Brighton: Harvester, 1985), pp. 128–76.

Kramnick, I. and B. Sheerman *Harold Laski: A Life on the Left* (Hamish Hamilton, 1993).

Laing, S. 'Presenting "Things as They Are": John Sommerfield's *May Day* and Mass Observation', in F. Gloversmith (ed.) *Class, Culture and Social Change: A New View of the 1930s* (Brighton: Harvester, 1980), pp. 142–60.

Lewis, J. *The Left Book Club: An Historical Record* (Gollancz, 1970).

Lunn, K. and R. Thurlow (eds) *British Fascism* (Croom Helm, 1980).

Marwick, A. 'Middle Opinion in the Thirties: Planning, Progress and Political Agreement', *English Historical Review* 79 (1964), pp. 285–98.

Meyers, J. (ed.) *George Orwell: The Critical Heritage* (Routledge, 1975).

Montefiore, J. *Men and Women Writers of the 1930s: The Dangerous Flood of History* (Routledge, 1996).

Morgan, K. *Against Fascism and War: Ruptures and Continuities in British Communist Politics, 1935–41* (Manchester: Manchester University Press, 1989).

Mowat, C.L. *Britain between the Wars 1918–40* (Methuen, 1956).

Newman, M. *John Strachey* (Manchester: Manchester University Press, 1989).

— *Harold Laski: A Political Biography* (Basingstoke: Macmillan, 1993).

Newsinger, J. *Orwell's Politics* (Basingstoke: Macmillan, 1999).

Norris, C. (ed.) *Inside the Myth: Orwell: Views from the Left* (Lawrence & Wishart, 1984).

Orwell, G. 'A Hanging' (1931), in Orwell (1970), pp. 66–71.

— *Down and Out in Paris and London* (1933; Harmondsworth: Penguin, 1989).

— *Burmese Days* (1934; Harmondsworth: Penguin, 1989).

— *A Clergyman's Daughter* (1935; Harmondsworth: Penguin, 1989).

— *Keep the Aspidistra Flying* (1936; Harmondsworth: Penguin, 1989).

— 'Shooting an Elephant' (1936), in Orwell (1970), pp. 265–72.

— 'The Road to Wigan Pier Diary' (1936), in Orwell (1970), pp. 194–243.

— *The Road to Wigan Pier* (1937; Harmondsworth: Penguin, 1989).

— *Homage to Catalonia* (1938; Harmondsworth: Penguin, 1989).

— *Animal Farm* (1945; Harmondsworth: Penguin, 1989).

— *Nineteen Eighty-Four* (1949; Harmondsworth: Penguin, 1989).

— *The Collected Essays, Journalism and Letters of George Orwell, vol. 1: An Age Like This 1920–1940* eds S. Orwell and I. Angus (Harmondsworth: Penguin, 1970).

— *The Complete Works of George Orwell, vol. 10: A Kind of Compulsion, 1903–1936*, eds P. Davison with I. Angus and S. Davison (Secker & Warburg, 1998).

Patai, D. *The Orwell Mystique: A Study in Male Ideology* (Amherst: University of Massachusetts Press, 1984).

Pearce, R. 'Revisiting Orwell's *Wigan Pier*', *History* 82 no. 267 (July 1997), pp. 410–28.

Pelling, H. *A History of British Trade Unionism* (2nd edn., Harmondsworth: Penguin, 1971).

Pilgrim Trust *Men without Work* (Cambridge: Cambridge University Press, 1938).

Pimlott, B. *Labour and the Left in the 1930s* (Allen & Unwin, 1977).

Pomeroy, R.S. '"To Push the World": Orwell and the Rhetoric of Pamphleteering', *Rhetoric Society Quarterly* 17.4 (1987), pp. 365–412.

Priestley, J.B. *English Journey* (Heinemann, 1934).

Pugh, M. *The Making of Modern British Politics, 1867–1939* (2nd edn., Oxford: Blackwell, 1993).

Rai, A. *Orwell and the Politics of Despair: A Critical Study of the Writings of George Orwell* (Cambridge: Cambridge University Press, 1988).

Ramsden, J. *The Age of Balfour and Baldwin 1902–1940* (Longman, 1978).

Reid, B. 'The Left Book Club in the Thirties', in J. Clark *et al.* (eds) *Culture and Crisis in Britain in the 30s* (Lawrence & Wishart, 1979), pp. 193–207.

Rodden, J. *The Politics of Literary Reputation* (New York: Oxford University Press, 1989).

Rowbotham, S. *A New World for Women: Stella Browne, Socialist Feminist* (Pluto Press, 1977).

Rowbotham, S. and J. Weeks *Socialism and the New Life: The Personal and Sexual Politics of Edward Carpenter and Havelock Ellis* (Pluto Press, 1977).

Rowntree, B.S. *Poverty: A Study of Town Life* (Macmillan, 1901).

— *Poverty and Progress: A Second Social Survey of York* (Longmans, Green, 1941).

Samuels, S. 'The Left Book Club', *Journal of Contemporary History* 1 (1966), pp. 65–86.

Shelden, M. *Orwell: The Authorised Biography* (Heinemann, 1991).

Sommerfield, J. *May Day* (1936; Lawrence & Wishart, 1984).

Spender, H. *Worktown People: Photographs from Northern England 1937–8* (Bristol: Falling Wall Press, 1982).

Stevenson, J. and C. Cook *Britain in the Depression: Society and Politics, 1929–39* (Harlow: Addison Wesley Longman, 1994).

Swann, P. *The British Documentary Film Movement, 1926–46* (Cambridge: Cambridge University Press, 1989).

Taylor, J. 'Picturing the Past: Documentary Realism in the 30s', *Ten.8* no. 11 (1983), pp. 15–31.

Thompson, E.P. 'Outside the Whale' (1960), in his *The Poverty of Theory and Other Essays* (Merlin, 1978), pp. 1–33.

Thompson, W. *The Good Old Cause: British Communism 1920–1991* (Pluto Press, 1992).

Thorpe, A. *Britain in the 1930s: The Deceptive Decade* (Oxford: Blackwell, 1992).

— *History of the British Labour Party* (Basingstoke: Macmillan, 1997).

Thurlow, R. *Fascism in Britain: A History, 1918–1985* (Oxford: Blackwell, 1987).

Williams, K. 'Post/Modern Documentary: Orwell, Agee and the New Reportage', in K. Williams and S. Matthews (eds) *Rewriting the Thirties: Modernism and After* (Harlow: Addison Wesley Longman, 1997), pp. 163–81.

Zwerdling, A. *Orwell and the Left* (New Haven: Yale University Press, 1974).

4 'A black gash of shame', or 'The wings of an abstract bird'?: The Vietnam Veterans Memorial (1982)

Joanna Price

On 13 November 1982 the Vietnam Veterans Memorial in Washington DC (hereafter the VVM) was formally dedicated, seven years after American 'advisers' were finally withdrawn from Saigon. The idea of the memorial had been conceived as a private initiative by a Vietnam veteran, and although it was eventually built on a site of national prominence, its construction was privately funded. The design of the memorial generated an intense controversy, which resonated with still unresolved feelings surrounding America's involvement in the Vietnam War.

A public memorial is traditionally required to justify, through its symbolism, the losses that a nation has sustained in the war. However, various elements of the United States' involvement in the Vietnam War rendered it subsequently difficult for Americans to construct narratives that either satisfactorily resolved the ethical and political questions raised by their participation or enabled them to bring their mourning for losses sustained in the war to closure. America's initial involvement in the conflict had been covert: there had been no official American declaration of war. In 1954 President Eisenhower articulated what later became known as 'the domino theory' to justify the American military presence in Vietnam: if Indo-China fell to the communists, the other countries of Southeast Asia would quickly follow. In 1961 President John F. Kennedy began sending thousands of armed troops, who were authorised to fire upon the enemy, as 'advisers' to South Vietnam. The commitment of troops was escalated by Johnson until the late 1960s. Nixon began a gradual withdrawal of troops from Vietnam but it was not until the collapse of the South Vietnamese government in April 1975 that Ford finally evacuated remaining Americans from Saigon. The official justification of America's increasing commitment of troops to the conflict as an

The Vietnam Veterans Memorial, Veterans' Day, 11 November 1991
(c) Patrick Hagopian.

attempt to protect 'democracy' and 'freedom' against the communist
threat in Southeast Asia, manifested by North Vietnamese insurgency
in South Vietnam, had been strongly opposed by a large number of
Americans. This opposition was fuelled by widespread media
coverage of the war, showing atrocities committed by both sides,
which led many people to question the conduct of American troops.
Perhaps most significantly in terms of the ability of Americans to come
to terms with the effects of the war, America was defeated (Neal,
1988, pp. 129–32).

   Despite the initial controversy over the design of the memorial to
commemorate the American dead of this war, the memorial has been
widely embraced by the American public since its dedication. Here,
Americans' attempts to work through their mourning for losses
sustained in the war, and to participate in the production of memories
about the war around individuals who lost their lives in it, are publicly
enacted and witnessed. In this chapter I will explore the ways in which
the struggle between diverse individuals and groups of Americans over
the meaning of these memories has been played out through the
various stages of the production of the memorial, from the initial
proposal of a memorial in a climate of official forgetting of the
Vietnam War, through the controversy which raged over the design of
the memorial, and in the subsequent stages of its reception by the
American people and government.

The properties of the VVM as a cultural artefact, and the response of the American people to it, have been the subject of extensive popular and scholarly literature. Analyses of the memorial have been produced from a variety of disciplines, including sociology, anthropology, communications studies and history, and have crossed the boundaries between these disciplines. Focusing on specific formal elements of the memorial, and accounts of the public's response to them and to the memorial as a whole, I will draw upon these studies to show how the negotiation over meaning which has marked the production, signification and reception of the memorial is also part of a dialogue over the construction of, and relation between, public memory, History, histories, cultural memory and personal memories. Debate about the signification of the memorial has shaped each phase of its production, from its design, through the compromises that were reached about its construction.

The Conception

The scene of the conception of the VVM has become legendary in the history of the memorial. One night in 1979 Jan Scruggs, a Vietnam veteran, was moved by watching the Hollywood film *The Deer Hunter* to ask who remembered the names of the Americans who had died in Vietnam (Buckley, 1985, p. 64). As a working-class 18-year-old Scruggs had volunteered to serve in Vietnam where, between 1969 and 1970, half of his company were either killed or, like Scruggs himself, wounded. After his year in the war zone Scruggs returned to the States and eventually married, gained a college education during which he completed a graduate study of 'the psychological adjustments facing Vietnam veterans' (Hess, 1987, p. 264), and was employed by the Labor Department. Scruggs's adjustment to civilian life in post-Vietnam America was by no means typical of all Vietnam veterans.

The difficulties confronting Vietnam veterans in adjusting to civilian life after the traumatising experiences of war were compounded by their reception by a country that wanted to forget the war. President Ford set the tone of what was to be the official American response to the war during the immediate postwar years, in a speech he made to Tulane University students on 23 April 1975, seven days before American troops withdrew from Saigon. Ford stated that:

Today America can again regain the sense of pride that existed before Vietnam. But it cannot be achieved by refighting a war that is finished – as far as America is concerned. The time has come to look forward to an agenda for the future, to unity, to binding up the nation's wounds and restoring it to health and optimistic self-confidence. (Ehrenraus, 1989, p. 102)

Ford's appeal to Americans to reconcile their differences by looking to the future rather than the past was an injunction to forget which required the erasure of many histories, including most notably that of the Vietnamese victims of the war, but also that of internal dissent about America's participation in the war. More unusually, American veterans were to be denied both official and popular recognition of their contribution to the war. No public honours were conferred upon them through ceremonies such as homecoming parades. The main attempt during this period to secure the government's acknowledgement of the veterans' participation in the war focused upon the need to rehabilitate the veterans to social normalcy. In 1978 the Vietnam-Era Caucus, a group of US representatives and senators who had served in the military during the Vietnam war, proposed a 'Vietnam Veterans Week' to Congress. In the discussions of this proposal they drew attention to the large numbers of Vietnam veterans who were divorced, serving prison sentences, and who needed treatment for drug and alcohol abuse (Wagner-Pacifici and Schwartz, 1991, p. 387).

In the late 1970s a high proportion of the veterans were indeed suffering from the conditions caused by the trauma of the war, such as survivor guilt and disturbing memories. Their isolation was compounded by the lack of popular and government recognition of their contribution to the war or the effects of the war upon them (Neal, 1988, pp. 139–43). These problems contributed to the popular perception of the 'deviancy' of the veterans (Wagner-Pacifici and Schwartz, 1991, p. 387), in addition to the identification of the veterans with the mistakenness of the cause for which America had claimed to be fighting in Vietnam, atrocities committed during the war, and the American defeat. Peter Ehrenraus has commented: 'Those who were killed and those who returned were the embodiment of a national moral character in crisis; regardless of how one defined those failures, they were its personification. How could Americans celebrate that which they abhorred and disdained in themselves?' (1989, p. 100).

This was the context in which former infantryman Scruggs watched *The Deer Hunter*, and was inspired by its portrayal of the 'healing' of a working-class Pennsylvania community which had been 'shattered by the war' with the idea of building a memorial to the Americans who had died in Vietnam (Hass, 1998, p. 10). Pursuing this vision, Scruggs incorporated the Vietnam Veterans Memorial Fund (VVMF) in April 1979. The core of the VVMF was composed mainly of white veterans and it drew support from both those who had believed in and those who had opposed the war. Organisers of the VVMF decided that the Memorial would be funded entirely by private donations, as the veterans did not want to be perceived as asking for government handouts, and because they believed that 'building it with private contributions would also prove that a larger American public wanted to remember' (Hass, 1998, p. 11). Members of the public who wrote letters to the VVMF in support of its project frequently 'claimed to be motivated ... by empathy for the soldiers who suffered and died', rather than by 'patriotism' or a concern for national 'unity' (Bodnar, 1992, p. 4).

In November 1979 legislation was introduced to secure a site of national prominence for the Memorial. Scruggs's attempt to rally support for the bill amongst members of the US Senate and the House of Representatives was assisted by his use of rhetoric that would enable politicians to accommodate the memorial as a symbol which would defend the nation and 'foster national unity and patriotism' (Bodnar, 1994, p. 75). The emphasis placed by Scruggs and other members of the VVMF on commemorating the soldiers who had died in the war could be appropriated by politicians as a strategic separation of the soldiers from the controversial 'cause' for which they had fought (Wagner-Pacifici and Schwartz, 1991, p. 388). This separation was reinforced by the request of members of the VVMF for a veterans' memorial, not a war memorial. Scruggs's representation of the memorial as a symbol of national reconciliation also proved politically astute (Scruggs and Swerdlow, 1985, p. 36), anticipating President Carter's own rhetoric when he signed the bill into law on 1 July 1980.[1] This law authorised a site for the VVM in the Washington Mall's Constitution Gardens, an area whose existing edifices consecrated the ideals of nationhood: the Lincoln Memorial is situated to the west, the Capitol to the east, the White House to the north and the Jefferson Memorial to the south.

Members of the VVMF decided that the design for the Memorial would be selected through an open national competition. The jury for the competition comprised eight male experts in the fields of architecture and sculpture. The VVMF stipulated that in their selection of the winning design the jury must adhere to specific criteria. The Memorial was intended to be reflective and contemplative in character; harmonise with its surroundings; contain the names of those who had died in the conflict or who were still missing; and make no political statement about the war (Fish, 1987b, p. 3). From among 1421 entries, the jury unanimously agreed to award the first prize to a design by Maya Ying Lin, a 21-year-old Chinese-American woman undergraduate student of architecture at Yale University. The design duly received the required approval of the National Capitol Planning Commission, the Fine Arts Commission and the Department of the Interior. However, it immediately became the subject of intense controversy.

The Controversy

The memorial designed by Lin consists of two walls, each nearly 250 feet long, of 70 panels, and made of highly-polished black granite. The walls meet at an angle of 125 degrees, forming a 'V' shape, which descends from ground level at its tips to a depth of ten feet below ground at its apex. 'The wall' is inscribed with the over 58,000 names of American casualties of the Vietnam War, in chronological order of loss, beginning where the east wall joins the apex with the name of the first American to have died in Vietnam in 1959, and ending where the west wall joins the apex with the last recorded loss in 1975. The eastern wall points to the nearby Washington Monument and the western wall to the Lincoln Memorial. In Lin's design no mention was made on the memorial of the Vietnam War. Besides conforming with the design criteria, in being 'contemplative' in character and 'harmonising' with its surroundings, the memorial expressed Lin's own interpretation of its function. She stated that her intention was that the memorial would confront the visitor with the stark fact of death:

> 'These [American troops in Vietnam] died. You have to accept that fact before you can really truly recognise and remember them. I just wanted to be honest with people. I didn't want to make something that would just simply say, "They've gone away for a while." I wanted something that would just simply say, "They can never come back. They should be remembered."' (Bee, 1989, pp. 198–9)

The controversy that Lin's design provoked highlights the issues surrounding the commemoration of the dead of a war whose interpretation remains contested. While many members of the VVMF supported Lin's design, opposition to the design was soon voiced by such powerful figures as H. Ross Perot, the Dallas billionaire and maverick intervener in political causes. Perot had provided the seed money for the design competition but he now mobilised opposition to the project, commissioning a poll of former Prisoners of War (POWs), 67 per cent of whom disliked Lin's design.[2] Opposition to the design from amongst the veterans was led by two professional military men, James Webb, a Naval Academy graduate and author of the Vietnam War novel *Fields of Fire*, and Tom Cahart, West Point graduate and recipient of several accolades for bravery in the war.

In the eyes of its critics the absence from Lin's design of the traditional iconography of war memorials translated into a countersymbolism that amounted to a critique of America's involvement in the war. As no reference was made to the Vietnam War on the memorial, it offered no textual justification of the cause for which the people whose names were inscribed on the wall had died. No framing inscription conferred honour on the dead. Cahart described the memorial as a 'black gash of shame and sorrow', commenting that 'in a city of soaring white monuments ... we get a black ditch in the ground' (Buckley, 1985, 66). Because the black of the granite was a departure from the 'ennobling' white of traditional war memorials, it was perceived by critics such as Cahart as the colour of shame. In addition, rather than rising gloriously into the sky, like the obelisk of the Washington Monument, for example, the memorial would be dug into the earth like 'a black ditch', as Cahart described it, or a 'mass grave', as Webb put it (Buckley, 1985, p. 66), or an 'enormous pit' as Tom Wolfe saw it (1982, p. B1). These sentiments were echoed in the conservative press: according to the *National Review*, 'the invisibility of the monument at ground level symbolises the "unmentionability" of the war' (1981, p. 1064), thereby compounding the point made by the absence of mention of the war on the memorial.

In a subsequently oft-cited contemporary rehearsal of the controversy, 'Art Disputes War: The Battle of the Vietnam Memorial' (1982), Tom Wolfe interpreted the debate as a battle over aesthetics, although Wolfe's polemic against the 'tribute to Jane Fonda'[3] reveals that in this case, as throughout the history of the memorial, aesthetics cannot be separated from politics. Wolfe inveighed against 'the Mullahs of modernism', the jurors who selected Lin's design,[4] whom he regarded as the product of the institutionalisation of European modernism and its 'peculiar mental atmosphere' in the States. Assuming that the jurors had been guided by the high modernist precept of art-for-art's-sake, Wolfe criticised the elitism of their choice of a work which, in being abstract, would therefore be irrelevant and inaccessible to the American public. Wolfe's criticisms were echoed by William Hubbard in his 1984 article 'A meaning for monuments'. In the two years that had elapsed between the commentaries of Wolfe and Hubbard the public's embrace of the memorial had become apparent. However, Hubbard regarded it as a flaw of the memorial's modernist abstraction that it did not harness the 'overwhelming' emotion which the names on the wall aroused. To Hubbard, unlike subsequent commentators who have noted the 'eloquence' of the memorial, the memorial 'does not speak' (1984, p. 21), and its silence is due to the modernist credo that 'artworks ... would not be *about* things in the world but would themselves *be* things in the world' (1984, p. 26). Hubbard argued that the emotion produced by the memorial is akin to the 'visceral "rush"' produced by the shock of the new with which abstract artworks confront the spectator. He concluded:

> Little wonder, then, that the sheer emotional impact of the Vietnam Veterans Memorial satisfies us. Not having the idea that artworks can provide guidance in human dilemmas, we do not sense the

absence of such guidance here. We take from the monument not a resolution of our conflicting emotions over the war, but an intensified, vivified version of those emotions. (1984, p. 27)[5]

The assumption underpinning Wolfe's and Hubbard's criticisms is that the proper role of public, specifically commemorative, art, is to use readily understandable symbolism to communicate 'common sociopolitical goals' and embody 'values and beliefs shared by its audience' (Beardsley, 1981, p. 43). Such commonality was hard to find in a post-Vietnam America divided not only by dissent about the legitimacy of American involvement in the war but also by issues about American democracy raised by the Civil Rights and Women's Liberation Movements. Given the absence of consensus in American society at the time, a public war memorial might be expected to serve the function of creating the illusion of consensus. James Young, in his study of Holocaust memorials *The Texture of Memory*, has explained that the representation of consensus by public memorials is founded upon the invocation of 'common memory':

> Rather than presuming a common set of ideals, the public monument attempts to create an architectonic ideal by which even competing memories may be figured. ... If part of the state's aim ... is to create a sense of shared values and ideals, then it will also be the state's aim to create the sense of common memory, a foundation for a unified polis. (1993, p. 6)

As Young suggests, the concept of 'a nation' depends upon its proponents' representation, to the people, of their being unified by 'a common memory'. People who are dispersed geographically, and who may be ideologically and culturally heterogeneous, are persuaded that they belong to 'an imagined political community', as Benedict Anderson has defined 'the nation' (1983, p. 6), by a narrative of temporal cohesion and purposiveness. This narrative, enshrined in 'public history', presents a continuity between past, present and future and, moreover, justifies troubling episodes, such as wars, in the past or present, as being necessary to the country's 'progress' into the future. Through its symbolism a war memorial would traditionally be required to bring closure to a difficult moment in a nation's past and to mourning for losses sustained in the name of the nation. Hence, it has been stated that 'the memorial act implies termination' (Lowenthal, quoted in Campbell and Kean, 1997, p. 259). As many commentators have noted, the commemorative act of closure generally requires a common forgetting, a denial of those elements of the past not assimilable to the narrative of a nation's progress, in order to revise representation of the past into a 'common memory' (Young,

1993, pp. 13–14; Campbell and Kean, 1997, p. 259; Huyssen, 1995, p. 250; Gillis, 1994, p. 7; Sturken, 1991, p. 137).

The problem with Maya Lin's design for the VVM, as its critics saw it, was that it would not bring about closure by endorsing the Vietnam War as necessary to the American nation's future. It contained no textual statements or traditional commemorative symbolism to resolve the ambiguity created by its 'abstract' formal elements. The 'V' shape of the memorial was variously interpreted, for example, as 'immortalizing' the 'V' sign made by anti-war protesters (*National Review*, 1981, p. 1064), and 'V for Vietnam, victim, victory, veteran, violate, and valor' (Sturken, 1991, p. 123). Maya Lin's own comments have suggested that she did indeed use her interpretation of the stipulation that the memorial 'harmonize with its surroundings' to offer a critique of imperialist ideology, specifically the relation between masculinity and conquest, which traditional war memorials may glorify. When asked, 'Do you think the memorial has a female sensibility?', Lin responded: 'In a world of phallic memorials that rise upwards, it certainly does. I didn't set out to conquer the earth, or overpower it, the way Western man usually does. I don't think I've made a passive piece, but neither is it a memorial to the idea of war' (Hess, 1987, p. 273). Insofar as the memorial is culturally encoded 'feminine', by virtue of the fact that its 'V' shape and its integration into the earth produce 'the image of engulfing, nurturing, and enfolding' (Foss, 1986, p. 333), it could be read as a critique of the dominant form of American masculinity and, by association, American men's participation in and conduct of the war.

Opponents of Lin's design, requiring that the memorial acknowledge the heroism of the Americans who died in the Vietnam War and the cause for which they died, demanded that a flag and appropriate inscription be added, the black walls changed to white and moved above ground (Buckley, 1985, p. 66). The request for a white memorial was retracted when a black general pointed out that 'black is not a color of shame'.[6] But James Watt, Reagan's Secretary of the Interior, refused to grant a construction permit for the memorial until an American flag and a 'more heroic, representational, figural memorial' was added to Lin's design (Hass, 1998, p. 18).

The Compromise

A compromise was reached through the addition to the memorial of inscriptions, a flag and a statue. These additions were required to recuperate the memorial to a nationalist narrative, thereby honouring the dead. The two inscriptions, which are at the apex of the memorial, allude to the Vietnam War, and pay tribute, on behalf of 'the nation', to the 'sacrifice' and 'devotion to duty' of 'its Vietnam veterans'.[7] The inscription on the base of the flagpole also refers to the war, and to 'the principles of freedom' for which the veterans fought in it.[8]

Frederick Hart, a realist sculptor, was commissioned by a panel of Vietnam veterans to make the statue. The resulting bronze piece depicts three young soldiers, one white, one black, and one of indeterminate ethnicity, possibly intended to be Hispanic. Hart's realism, informed by painstaking research, lies in the detail of his rendering of the soldiers' uniform, guns and ammunition. The addition of the statue, which was dedicated at a ceremony attended by President Reagan on 11 November 1984, appeased those who had criticised the anti-heroic and abstract nature of Lin's design, although it was derided by many of those who had embraced Lin's vision. The *New York Times*, for example, observed: 'To try to represent a period of anguish and complexity in our history with a simple statue of armed soldiers is to misunderstand all that has happened, and to suggest that no lessons have been learned at all from the experience of Vietnam' (Buckley, 1985, p. 62). However, the artistic merit or symbolic connotations of the statue itself have often been considered by subsequent critics to be subsidiary to the way in which the statue interacts with the VVM. The figures, positioned at the edge of a group of trees, are facing the memorial as though they are 'turning upon it almost as a vision', as Hart put it (Fish, 1987b, p. 13). The haunting quality of the soldiers' gaze has been attributed to the fact that they appear to be contemplating, in perpetuity, the names of the dead inscribed on the wall (Danto, 1985, p. 153; Griswold, 1986, p. 710; Gaspar, 1989, p. 22). Thus the figures interact with the memorial to emphasise the fact of death, rather than to glorify the sacrifices made in war.

The addition of the Hart statue, with the specificity of its representation of the ethnically differentiated male GIs, did fuel further debate, however, about who could lay claim to representation in public memory. The act of commemoration always presumes decisions about who will be remembered and who excluded from remembrance; whose version of memory or history will be represented and who, therefore, will gain ownership of the meaning signified by the act of commemoration; and which narrative of the past will be authorised by the commemoration (Yoneyama, 1995, pp. 501–2). The implications of such decisions were apparent to Americans who had been sensitised to the connection between power and historical representation by the oppositional political movements of the 1960s and '70s. Thus the inscription of the names of the American dead and missing on the wall caused attention to be drawn to various exclusions: some have questioned why the names of the Vietnamese victims of the war are not included there; others why American soldiers who died as a consequence of the war but not during it have not been recognised there; and yet others why anti-war protesters have not been written into the history commemorated by the wall. The names of only eight women appear on the VVM. However, the Vietnam Women's Memorial, which was added in 1993, recognises the contribution of the more than 10,000 American women who served in Vietnam during the war.

A Dialogic Space

Through the reception of the VVM by the public, commentators for the press and scholarly critics, the interpretation (and hence production) of its significance has continued to be negotiated. The complexity of the cultural and political significance of the memorial has become increasingly apparent as the often eulogistic commentaries contemporary with its initial reception by the public have been succeeded by a wealth of more mediated interpretations, which seek to locate the initial response within a broader political narrative or cultural critique.

The dedication of the VVM on Veterans Day 1982 was attended by over 150,000 people and it testified to the powerful emotional response that, from this point, the memorial would generate. An article entitled 'The Black Gash of Shame', which appeared in the *New York Times* in April 1985, reported the swiftness of popular acceptance of the memorial, given the controversy over Lin's design. The article concluded that: 'Vietnam gashed our history, but this memorial is no gash. Ten years after the war, America may not yet comprehend the loss of those 58,000 lives; but at least it has found a noble way to remember them' (p. 22). The memorial has subsequently become one of Washington's most visited tourist sites.

The dedication ceremony and the accompanying programme of events during the week of 7 November provided a forum for diverse organised and spontaneous articulations of people's responses to the war. The continuing plight of the veterans was central to these events and the discourses surrounding them. Various organisations sponsored panels on Agent Orange and post-traumatic stress disorder, and held an open house for families of those killed or missing in Vietnam (Oman, 1982, p. 55).[9] The veterans themselves adopted differing positions in relation to patriotic sentiment. During the veterans' march down Constitution Avenue to the memorial, before its dedication, some veterans carried American flags, others bore placards expressing contestatory views, such as 'No more wars. No more lies' (Bodnar, 1992, p. 7). After the dedication many of the veterans spontaneously embraced the memorial as providing a common locus for the expression of grief relating to memories of the war (Fish, 1987a, p. 82). Full official recognition of the VVM was withheld, however: it was not until 11 November 1984, a few days after the dedication of the Hart statue, that President Reagan attended ceremonies at the Mall to formally accept the memorial on behalf of the nation. In his acceptance speech Reagan alluded to the memorial as 'a symbol of both past and current sacrifice' and as a reflection of 'a hunger for healing', concluding that 'it's time we moved on, in unity and with resolve, with the resolve always to stand for freedom, as those who fought did, and to always try and preserve the peace' (Haines, 1986, p. 14).

It is apparent from the popular response to the memorial, and the many and various representations of the memorial in discourses relating to the Vietnam War, that it provides a 'dialogical' space (Young, 1993, p. xii) in which the meaning of the war and its effects can be negotiated. John Bodnar, for example, interprets the history of the VVM as exemplifying a contest over meaning between 'vernacular culture', composed of 'ordinary' people, mainly the veterans, and the proponents of 'official culture', who seek to use the symbol of the memorial to resolve conflicts about power in present society (1992, pp. 13–20; 1994, pp. 74–87). One might also conceptualise the memorial, after Pierre Nora, as a 'site of memory', a place where 'memory crystallizes and secretes itself'. According to Nora, such 'sites of memory' are formed 'at a particular historical moment, a turning point where consciousness of a break with the past is bound up with the sense that memory has been torn – but torn in such a way as to pose the problem of the embodiment of memory in certain sites where a historical continuity persists' (1989, p. 7). The VVM signifies a war that ruptured American public memory or history, in the sense that the metanarrative through which that history had been articulated, namely that it was America's manifest destiny to bring about historical progress through the defence of democracy, was now widely contested. At the same time, the memorial is located on a site whose other edifices, such as the Lincoln Memorial and Washington Monument, represent the continuity of the American nation through formative moments which are premised on 'sacrifice and martyrdom' (Haines, 1986, p. 6). The location of the memorial, therefore, combined with the ambiguity of its iconography and its function of commemorating the dead of a contested war, invite the visitor to reflect on the meaning of the war, as refracted through his or her personal memories. At the memorial, and through its representation in discourse, the 'production' and ascription of 'common meanings' to the memories of individuals occurs.[10] This constitutes 'cultural memory'.[11] The catalyst, for the visitor, of a connection between personal memory and shared memories in which the meaning of the war and the nation is being negotiated is frequently a name inscribed on the wall.

The Names

The *National Review* responded to Maya Lin's plan that all the names of the dead and missing be arranged on the wall in chronological order of loss with the criticism that: 'The mode of listing the names makes them individual deaths, not deaths in a cause: they might as well have been traffic accidents' (1981, p. 1064). Veterans who initially opposed the chronological ordering of the names, believing that it would be difficult for a visitor to locate a specific name, changed their mind when they saw that '600 Smiths', for example, were listed as Vietnam casualties. Jan Scruggs observed: 'Alphabetical listing would make the Memorial look like a telephone book engraved in granite, destroying the sense of profound, unique loss that each name carried' (Scruggs and Swerdlow, 1985, p. 79). The moving effect of the names on mourners became evident when, during the week of the dedication ceremony, the names were read aloud in a 56-hour candlelit vigil at the National Cathedral in Washington. This marked the creation, around the names, of 'a secular piety ... a people's religion'.[12] The sanctification of the names has gone hand-in-hand with a questioning of the significance of the deaths, however.

Critics have agreed that the powerful effect of the names is produced both by individual names in themselves and by the relation between individual names and the expanse of names which confronts visitors as they walk along the wall. The significance and ideological import of the listing of the names is elucidated by comparison with another Western form of commemorating war dead, the Tomb of the Unknown Soldier. Tombs of the Unknown Soldier were first dedicated in England, France and the US after the First World War, which had produced massive numbers of unidentifiable dead. At the same time, the dead who could be identified were marked by individual graves bearing their names. The deaths were legitimated by what George Mosse has called 'the Myth of War Experience' which turns upon 'the cult of the fallen'. According to Mosse, the 'cult of the fallen soldier' in Europe dates from the French Revolution and the German Wars of Liberation (1990, p. 35). During the French Revolution, the dead were 'commemorated individually' (p. 37), a recognition of the contribution of rank-and-file soldiers which was consonant with the principle of egalitarianism. At the same time, the deaths of individual soldiers served a symbolic function, as 'personal death became symbolic of martyred liberty' (p. 36). That is, through nationalisms informed by Protestant Christianity, deaths in war were sanctified as 'sacrifices' made to secure the continuity of the nation (p. 35).[13] In the United States, the practice of commemorating the deaths of common soldiers individually emerged during the Civil War (Hass, 1998, p. 38). The contemporaneity of the emergence of these two trends – marking *as* individual the deaths of soldiers, and invoking their deaths as symbolic of the ideology of the nation – draws attention to a contradiction which is particularly apparent in the American context, the contradiction, as Kristin Ann Hass has put it, 'of a nationalism predicated on individualism' (p. 38).

This contradiction has traditionally been obscured in the symbol of the Tomb of the Unknown Soldier. Through this symbol, the life, identity and name of the individual are erased, being subsumed to the representation of the nation as a whole and of all its peoples. As reported by the *London Times Armistice Supplement* on 12 November 1920, after the First World War this symbol was perceived as being consistent with the ideology of democracy, connoting that 'we are all equal, all members of one body ... one soul ... one desire that ... we may, indeed, all become members of one body politic and of one immortal soul' (Laqueur, 1994, p. 158). Successive American administrations' prevarications about establishing a Tomb of the Unknown Soldier of the Vietnam War have indicated a reluctance to invoke sacrifice to the now contested concept of the nation, however.

The construction of the Tomb in Arlington National Cemetery was authorised by Congress in 1973, the crypt completed in 1974 and a marble cover laid upon it in March 1975 (Arnheim, 1980, p. E4). However, the marble cover was removed (and subsequently the presence of the Tomb was effectively concealed by a red granite cover), seven days before the fall of Saigon, on the same day as President Ford made his speech at Tulane University enjoining his audience to forget the past. The concealment of the Tomb, in conjunction with Ford's speech, has been read as exemplifying 'a silence [about the war] that is politically strategic' (Ehrenraus, 1989, p. 100). The Pentagon, however, subsequently denied attempts to conceal the Tomb, explaining that due to advances in forensic science that had 'resulted in a high incidence of positive identification for those Americans whose remains had been recovered from Vietnam', it had not yet been possible to select an Unknown from the Vietnam War (Arnheim, 1980, p. E4).

In 1982, the year of the public's embrace of the VVM at its dedication, the Department of the Army placed a plaque at the site of the crypt of the Vietnam Unknown. The inscription on the plaque acknowledged that the Tomb was temporarily empty, but enjoined remembrance of 'the sacrifice of those who died for freedom in the Vietnam war' (Ehrenraus, 1989, p. 105). The government made further attempts to recuperate the Tomb of the Vietnam Unknown to its sanctified status in a nationalist narrative when, on Memorial Day 1984, at a ceremony attended by President Reagan, the remains of a soldier who had died in Vietnam were interred in the Tomb (Morrow, 1984, p. 27). The curious events surrounding the Tomb of the Unknown of the Vietnam War suggest that the sanctity of the symbolic function of the Tomb of the Unknown Soldier can no longer be assumed.[14] The events indicate the doubts of American administrations about whether the Tomb still naturalises the ideological justification of the deaths of individual soldiers as being for 'the nation'. This ideological premise is exposed to public deconstruction by the listing of the names on the VVM.

Robert Pogue Harrison has observed that the 'genius' of the Memorial 'lies in the way it particularizes the general at the same time as it reflects the general back upon the particular by simply listing the names of every man and woman who never made it back from Vietnam' (1997, p. 188). The memorial's 'particularization of the general' contrasts with the Tomb of the Unknown Soldier, where the particularity of the individual's identity is subsumed into representation of the whole. Consonant with the ideology of democracy, the particularisation of the names on the wall does not occur through any appended differentiation between the names, as for example, by military rank. The most striking intrinsic differentiation between the names, that of the diverse ethnicities which they connote, has been interpreted as suggesting the assimilation of those named into an American whole (Wagner-Pacifici and Schwartz, 1991, p. 401). The particularisation of the names that *does* occur is of a different order, relating to the memorial's production of the ascription of meaning to memory.

Harrison's insightful reading of the memorial relates it to articulations of the epic tradition by Homer, Virgil and Dante, a 'genealogy' which resonates with Maya Lin's statement that through the listing of the names in chronological rather than alphabetical order the wall would read 'like an epic Greek poem' (Sturken, 1991, p. 127). 'The epic's vocation', Harrison claims, 'as well as its burden, is to contain such excess [the excessive number of the dead] in its narrative, ideological drive towards synthesis' (1997, p. 188). However, he argues that 'the epic ambition to monumentalize the Vietnam War in the memorial wall comes to grief in the lyric singularity of each and every name' (p. 189). Each name invites the visitor to reflect on the death of an individual and, consequently, to recollect or imagine that individual's life. The 'lyric singularity' of each name is enhanced by the arrangement of the names: within the chronological frame, names are inscribed alphabetically within 'casualty days'. This arrangement invites the visitor to remember, or imagine, specific scenes of death. In *The Body in Pain: The Making and Unmaking of the World* Elaine Scarry argues that because the names on the wall demand that the visitor imagine the death in war of the individual, and then the lived life of that individual, each name is 'referentially unstable'. In other words, the imaginative process that witnessing the names necessarily demands of the viewer denaturalises the 'appended assertion' 'for my country', which is usually required to legitimate dying and killing in war (1985, pp. 121–3). Despite the inscriptions on the memorial, the diverse memories or imaginings produced by the names cannot be easily recuperated into a narrative of the sacrifice of individuals for the good of the whole. The names, and their interaction with the spatial organisation of the memorial, require that the visitor *participate* in the production of the meanings which are being ascribed to memory there.

The Journey

The spatial design of the memorial constructs the visitor's experience of time in a way that militates against situating the war in a linear narrative which has been brought to closure. Maya Lin has stated that: 'I didn't want a static object that people would just look at, but something they could relate to as on a journey, or passage, that would bring each to his own conclusions' (*National Geographic*, 1985, p. 557). The design of the memorial, and the organisation of the names, invites the visitor to undertake such a 'journey'. To begin the journey the visitor must use the directories to locate a particular name. Linear movement through time is evoked to the extent that the chronological ordering of the names reflects the pattern of American involvement in the war, with heaviest casualties in the late 1960s. However, the overall experience of the memorial is one of circularity. Maya Lin commented that through the chronological arrangement of the names, which begin and end at the apex of the memorial, 'the war's beginning and end meet; the war is "complete", coming full circle' (Ashabranner, 1988, p. 55). Yet the memorial's construction of the visitor's experience of time as circular arguably suggests ongoing repetition rather than completion. To trace the names chronologically, one must walk along the right-hand wall from the apex to its tip, then across to the tip of the left-hand wall, returning to the centre. At the centre, the names then begin again on the right-hand wall. This circular trajectory creates an impression of the eternal return of the war and of the American deaths in it. The impression that the war is ongoing is intensified both by the addition of new names to the wall, and by the symbols next to the names: each name

> is followed either by a diamond (indicating a death) or by a cross (indicating missing in action). When an individual MIA is confirmed to have been killed, the cross by that name is converted to a diamond. In the event that an individual listed as MIA is confirmed to have survived, a circle, as a symbol of life, will be inscribed around the cross. (Ezell, 1987, p. 149)

The symbolism of the diamonds and crosses, as well as the stand dedicated to the issue of POWs and MIAs which has been maintained by the Veterans' Vigil Society near the memorial since 1982, testifies to the belief, held by many Americans, that American soldiers remain against their will in Southeast Asia. Subscription to this belief both prevents the process of mourning for the loss of individuals from being completed, and allows the outcome of the war to be re-written in a revisionist fantasy of American empowerment (through the rescue of POWs by avenging Americans).[15]

The visitor's sense that she is undertaking a cyclical journey is intensified by the fact that she must walk down into the earth at the centre of the memorial, and then back out to ground level again. Lin has explained that this descent places the visitor at the 'interface' between life and death, 'between the sunny world and the quiet, dark world beyond, that we can't enter' (*National Geographic*, 1985, p. 557). The reflective surfaces of the black granite contribute to the impression that the wall forms a boundary or threshold between the living and the dead, for the visitor's image is reflected behind the names. According to one commentator, the reflections have the effect of making the living seem insubstantial: 'the living are in it [the memorial] only as appearances. Only the names of the dead, on the surface, are real' (Danto, 1985, p. 153).

Visitors frequently respond to individual names by touching or taking rubbings of them. These gestures have been attributed to the way the wall symbolises, through the materiality of the inscriptions in the granite, 'the encrypted presence of its dead' which seems 'at once given and denied' (Harrison, 1997, p. 187). The memorial has also generated another commemorative practice that, until recently, has been less common in the dominant WASP culture: the leaving of objects and letters at the wall.

The Offerings

Since its dedication visitors have left photographs, letters and a diverse assortment of other objects at the memorial. Some items left on one day, for example, included: 'dog tags, Smith R.L.; tobacco pouch with tobacco; baby picture from son Roy; cassette tape; Confederate ace of spades; bag of rice; note with check, "This check is to be used ... love, Mom"; picture of J.F.K. on prayer card attached to "Impeach Nixon" pin' (Hass, 1998, p. 87). From the outset, Park Service volunteers began to collect the objects and eventually the Vietnam Veterans Memorial Collection (VVMC) was established to house them. Since 1984 the collection has been stored and archived at the Museum and

Archaeological Regional Storage facility (MARS), a warehouse in Maryland.

In her groundbreaking work of cultural history *Carried to the Wall: American Memory and the Vietnam Veterans Memorial*, Kristin Ann Hass examines the practice of leaving objects at this 'living' memorial and constructs a methodological and contextual framework for interpreting the objects and their mnemonic significance. She contends that existing scholarship in 'material culture' tends either to dwell on the detail of the objects studied to the neglect of their cultural context, or to favour a semiotic approach which lacks detail as well as context (p. 31). Hass, therefore, sets out to 'build models for thinking about contexts and systems of signs together' (p. 32), offering her analysis of the objects left at the wall as 'an effort to think about the symbolic work that these things are doing and to figure out what this symbolic work, as a communication between the citizen and the nation, can teach us about how these Americans imagine the nation and their place in it' (p. 33). Hass achieves this interpretation by situating the VVM both within its own specific history and within the broader traditions of American war commemoration and private funerary practices. From her study of the latter, Hass concludes that the practice of remembering the dead by leaving personal tributes at graves may derive from ethnic American cultures, such as African, Mexican, Italian and Chinese, which share a belief in 'the active, ongoing relationship between the living and the dead' and the responsibility of the living to 'help the dead negotiate the liminal space between death and the afterlife' (p. 77).

Hass constructs a useful taxonomy of the objects, observing that they fall into five broad categories (with some of the objects belonging to more than one category): 'The great majority of objects mark specific individual memories, some speak to the problems of patriotism or community, some are negotiations between the living and the dead, some work to establish a community of veterans, and some make explicit political speech' (p. 95). Some items falling into the last group, objects relating to MIAs and POWs, such as POW/MIA bracelets, differ from the other objects in that their production and distribution is choreographed by groups with specific political agendas and an investment in a particular version of the war (p. 105). These objects contrast with the others, which attest to the 'anarchic' multiplicity and individuality of the memories being articulated through them.

Marita Sturken argues that the objects left at the wall are the source of two potentially different forms of ascribing meaning to memory. She interprets the leaving of the objects as being the expression of people's desire for 'testimony, transposed from personal to cultural artifacts, to bear witness to pain suffered', because the memorial speaks to a 'need to express in public the pain of this war, a desire to transfer private memories into a collective experience' (1991, p. 135). However, when they are archived in the VVMC, 'the objects are pulled from cultural memory – a discursive field in which they are presented to be shared and to participate in the memories of others – and made into aesthetic and historical objects'. Collected in the archive, the objects become available to co-optation to 'official history'. However, like Hass, Sturken believes that 'the narratives inscribed' in the objects and letters 'will continue to reassert strands of cultural memory that disrupt historical narratives' (p. 136), because embedded in each object is the personal history that motivated someone to leave it at the wall, and, further, because the archive differs from many in being unregulated – *everything* which is left is stored.

Making Memory

Many of the recent studies of the VVM participate in a critical debate about the potentially conflicting types of memory that are being formed there and through representations of the memorial in discourse. One axis of this debate, as Hass's and Sturken's analyses indicate, is the question of whether the memorial facilitates the creation of new forms and meanings of memory, which contest the narratives through which memory has formerly been shaped, or whether the memorial ultimately lends itself to recuperation by revisionist and nationalist narratives of the past.

An aspect of the production of memory at the memorial to which proponents of both sides of the debate have drawn attention is the fact that the practices adopted by visitors at the memorial are not simply spontaneous but are structured according to preconceptions about appropriate behaviour at the memorial and the nature of the experience one will undergo or witness there. Since the dedication of the memorial there has been much television and press coverage of people's responses to it and several 'keepsake' books have been published. These books comprise emotive accounts of the history of the memorial, such as Fish's *The Last Firebase* and Scruggs's and Swerdlow's *To Heal a Nation*, or collections of photographs of it, such as Ashabranner's *Always to Remember* and Ezell's *Reflections on the Wall*. Such 'reproductions' of the memorial contribute to the creation of its 'aura' as a sacred site, where the visitor can expect to undergo an intense and transformative experience of grief (Haines, 1986, pp. 7–8). Commemorative practices undertaken at the memorial, such as touching the names or leaving artefacts or letters there, have also been widely publicised, through articles in the press and testimonial books. For example, Thomas Allen's *Offerings at the Wall* (1995) comprises photographs of some of the objects; Laura Palmer's *Shrapnel in the Heart* (1988) is a collection of letters and poems which were left at the memorial; and Sal Lopes's *The Wall: Images and Offerings from the Vietnam Veterans Memorial* (1987) presents photographs of visitors' responses to the wall, interspersed with fragments of writing left there. One outcome of the reproduction of practices occurring at the memorial has been noted by the curators of the VVMC, who have expressed concern that two types of collection are emerging: the objects and letters that people have left as 'spontaneous, unmediated' communications of personal memory, and those which are 'inauthentic', having been prepared for preservation in the collection, for example, by being sealed or laminated, or with explanatory notes attached (Hawkins, 1993, p. 755; Berdahl, 1994, p. 106; Hass, 1998, pp. 24–6). The latter objects have been self-consciously framed to contribute to the formation of public history.

Since its inception, the memorial has been represented as an agent and locus of the 'healing' of both individual mourners and a bereft and divided nation. Central to the discourse of healing is the representation of the veterans: arriving at the wall psychologically, as well as often physically, wounded by their experiences of the war, they will be enabled to undergo a therapeutic or cathartic expression and purgation of their traumatic memories and grief. This process is in part the result of the veterans' experience, at the memorial, of a transition from prior isolation to the sharing of memories with a community or 'brotherhood' of veterans. Some critics have contended that visiting the memorial does indeed have a therapeutic effect: Sonja K. Foss, for example, argues that the memorial both arouses grief, because its iconography does not offer closure, and offers a protective space within which grief can be expressed, through its integration into the earth and its 'V' shape, which Maya Lin referred to as 'no more threatening than two open hands' (Foss, 1986, p. 333). Daphne Berdahl suggests that the memorial has created a 'physically framed space' in which 'veterans and their families could tell their stories', and that the public forum in which this story-telling takes place renders them 'performative' and therefore 'transformative (1994, pp. 94, 99). In her novel *In Country* (1985) Bobbie Ann Mason offers a fictional interpretation of the memorial's therapeutic effect. The novel's protagonists, the adolescent Samantha (Sam) Hughes, whose father died in the Vietnam war, before her birth, and her uncle Emmett, a veteran who is traumatised by his memories of the war, undertake a journey to the VVM. The ambiguous iconography of the memorial puzzles Sam: it oscillates between connoting immanence and transcendence, seeming variously 'a black gash in the hillside', 'like a giant grave' and 'like the wings of an abstract bird'. But, the narrative suggests, the memorial also facilitates for Sam and Emmett the culmination of a therapeutic process of confronting the past.

Several critics have pointed out, however, that the focus on the therapeutic healing of the individual in discourses about the memorial lends itself to historical revisionism. Both Berdahl and Sturken argue that this focus displaces attention from divisive questions about the war and enables a forgetting of 'the war's other victims, the Vietnamese' (Berdahl, 1994, p. 110; Sturken, 1991, p. 137). According to Harry Haines the discourse of healing is amenable to the manipulation and homogenisation of the meaning of the memorial by proponents of official culture. Haines cites Reagan's 1984 speech of formal acceptance of the memorial as marking the emergence of 'the administrative version of Vietnam memory': in the speech, Reagan invoked 'healing' as the process that would enable the people to accept the 'sacrifices' made in their name, an acceptance which would unite them and prepare them to support any future wars in defence of 'the peace' (1986, p. 14). In Haines's reading, representation of the therapeutic healing experienced by the veteran at the memorial fuels this revisionism, as it requires veterans to undertake a 'revision of memory to coincide with administrative power's version of consensus' (p. 15). Donald E. Pease argues, further, that the meaning of the VVM has been recuperated to serve an imperialist version of American history. Pease suggests that the memorial has been called upon to provide a 'symbolic resolution' to the 'constitutive instability' created not only by the Vietnam war but also by the breakdown of a Cold War consensus based upon the projection of internal divisions onto a national 'other' (the USSR) (1993, p. 558). According to Pease, the 'activation' of the VVM as 'the official national memory of the Vietnam era' followed upon Reagan's nomination of America's 'unwillingness to intervene in the Third World [as] a national pathology, the "Vietnam syndrome"' (pp. 574, 558). Through Reagan's rhetoric the memorial was associated with the recovery of national pride and a renewed belief in American exceptionalism.

Revisionist representations of the war are disseminated through popular culture by the 'Vietnam war nostalgia industry', which transforms the war 'into spectacle and commodity' (Sturken, 1991, p. 134) and erases any troubling questions about the war. The veterans in particular have become both the object of representation and a targeted consumer group for memorabilia associated with the war and its commemoration. Joshua Hammer has described how, for example, travel agencies are successfully promoting tours for Americans, including veterans, to Vietnam (thereby capitalising on the notion that confronting the scene of past trauma will facilitate therapeutic healing); and the hawkish *Vietnam* magazine intersperses amongst revisionist accounts of the war advertisements for such products as T-shirts depicting American icons of the war and 'Remembrance' sculptures of a veteran kneeling before the VVM. Plastic replicas and other 'spin-offs' of the Hart statue are generating substantial annual royalties (Hammer, 1989, pp. 31–2).

According to critics such as Haines and Pease, revisionist appropriations of the significance of the VVM predominate in discourses about the memorial. However, others such as Hass and Sturken, focusing on the production of memory *at* the memorial, suggest that the process of dialogue between different formations of memory takes precedence over the coagulation of the past into any one particular narrative. Proponents of both interpretations concur that the memorial is being invoked to represent the formation of 'community'. Different views about what type of community is being forged at the memorial, or through the representation of it, are central to whether critics regard the memory being shaped around the memorial as predominantly revisionist or interrogative.

Hass's contention that visitors' practices at the memorial (specifically, leaving objects there) 'seem to speak to a sense of loss of community, or, at the very least, the desire to forge a community' (1998, p. 123), can be aligned with a critical consensus that visitors to the memorial seek to participate in private mourning in a public space and through this act to belong, albeit temporarily, to a 'collectivity'. This proposition raises the question of how the 'collective' of people who are gathered at the memorial at any one time, or across time, can be taken as a paradigm of any form of community other than what it literally is: a disparate group of people temporarily in one place, unified by their mourning for losses sustained in the war, or by their desire to witness this process. Critics agree that the practices enacted by the people who visit the memorial articulate the desire to confer meaning upon their memories through socially unifying concepts such as that of the nation, but they differ as to the implications of this desire and the interpretations of 'the nation' which are being formed at the memorial.

Terrance M. Fox, for example, has described the VVM as 'a "sacred document" of "the new collectivism"' (1989, p. 218). Fox, a Vietnam veteran and of long-standing affiliation to the military, recounts how the VVM has occasioned him to reassess the ideological position that has shaped his response to it. He recalls how, in a 1983 article, he judged the design of the VVM to be 'inconsistent with American values', due to the 'internalised concept of military service' to which he then subscribed. In retrospect, Fox recognises his allegiance to 'the heroic military model' which valued 'individual creativity'. However, since the Second World War, Fox reflects, this model of military service has been replaced by the 'institutional military model', which relies on technological, bureaucratic and managerial control. Fox argues that this shift in military paradigms, which 'was accelerated by the Vietnam War', mirrored changes in American society, namely that 'a collectivist tendency was gathering momentum' (p. 213). Fox terms this 'tendency' the 'new collectivism', which he describes as 'an ideological movement, albeit one without central direction and control' (p. 218). He does not specify how the new collectivism operates as 'a movement'. However, he contends that in an increasingly pluralist post-Vietnam period, which has been characterised by the breakdown of consensus about such 'ethical' issues as abortion and homosexual rights, the new collectivism is unified by a 'moral appeal' for increased government intervention in 'private' life to redistribute economic resources across society. Fox regards the construction of the Vietnam veteran as victim as indicative of the 'new moralism'. He now interprets the VVM as symbolic of the 'collectivist' ideology, which he attempts to accommodate. According to this reading, the lack of hierarchical differentiation between the names on the wall betokens the 'suppression' of individualism, and the memorial draws attention to the connectedness of all Americans, in that the visitor must recognise that 'almost every American was touched in some way by the Vietnam War' (p. 218).

Charles Griswold takes an unambivalent view of the 'community' that he perceives being formed around the memorial. For Griswold the emblem of this community is the veteran who regains a 'sense of wholeness' through the therapeutic function of the memorial, which enables him to reconcile his doubts about the war with the belief that his 'service was honorable'. Whilst remaining neutral about the war, the memorial achieves its 'goal of rekindling love of country and its ideals, as well as reconciliation with one's fellow citizens' (1986, p. 713). The memorial enables Americans to renew their faith in the 'American principles' that unify them, at the same time as it allows interrogation of America's participation in the Vietnam War through its overarching dialogue with the symbols of nationhood that are in close proximity to it, such as the Washington Monument and Lincoln and Jefferson Memorials.

Susan Jeffords criticises Griswold's reading, however, based as it is on the relationship of the memorial to 'the entire Mall', arguing that: 'It is only through these abstracted godlike viewpoints and not those of the individual that the ideology of collectivity can be proposed and identified' (1989, p. 81). Moreover, Jeffords contends that Griswold's interpretation is an articulation of 'the masculine point of view', which she has earlier defined as the 'disembodied voice of [patriarchal] masculinity' (p. xiii). This construction of gender is premised upon Jeffords's equation of the masculine with the abstract and transcendent and the feminine with the 'experiential and immediate'. Jeffords continues:

> Only from the masculine point of view can such collectiveness be narrated, collectivities that finish, not simply with the integration of Vietnam, but with the regeneration of the belief that 'America remains fundamentally good,' revealing the extent to which the current regeneration of an American 'good' is intimately linked to and dependent on the regeneration of the American masculine. (p. 82)

This claim forms part of Jeffords's thesis that since the 1960s American men have felt themselves 'emasculated' by such occurrences as the conduct and loss of the war in Vietnam and the challenges made to normative white masculinity by the Women's and Civil Rights Movements. The scorned and wounded veteran was symbolic of this emasculation. Jeffords argues that from the 1980s pervasive popular cultural representations of the empowered avenging veteran (Rambo is a prime example), have been central to the 'remasculinisation' of American men and American culture. Following this line of argument, the 'brotherhood' of veterans at the VVM represents the re-formation of a sense of community around an ideology of nationalist masculinity. The changing formations of masculinity identified by Jeffords can be inserted into the broader cultural matrix delineated by Hass: that is, that the invocation of 'collectivity' at the memorial speaks to a mourning not only for the loss of individual soldiers but also for 'unnamed losses' such as those of 'masculinity, patriotism, working-class idealism and pride' (1998, p. 5).

The production of memory at the VVM clearly relates specifically to losses sustained in the Vietnam War and, as this chapter has shown, critics have argued persuasively that it also relates to the loss of various certitudes about national, social and personal identities which resulted from the war and other challenges posed to consensus during the decades of and after the war. Recent critical enquiry suggests that the American people's response to the memorial might also be interpreted within a more general context. Such enquiry addresses the significance of popular and scholarly responses to the VVM in relation to a broad set of debates about the function of memory in postmodern, or late capitalist consumer, societies. Several historians and cultural theorists have noted that in advanced consumer capitalist societies, including the United States, two apparently contradictory trends have emerged: on the one hand, it has been widely lamented that such societies are suffering from an historical or cultural amnesia; on the other hand, that there is a prevailing 'fascination, even obsession, with historical memory' (Davis and Starn, 1989, p. 1; Huyssen, 1995, p. 5;

Rosenzweig and Thelen, 1998, p. 3). Historical 'amnesia' is in some cases directly attributable to the desire for public forgetting of specific events, such as the Holocaust of the Jews, or the Vietnam War. But critics have also argued that amnesia is the inevitable product of consumer culture and its disseminators, the mass media, which seek to generate perpetual innovation and change (Huyssen, 1995, p. 254); attempt to 'weaken and transform' memories tied to heterogeneous regions or cultures in order to 'gain loyalty to products' (Bodnar, 1992, p. 252); and saturate the subject with fragments of evanescent and decontextualised information which resist organisation into historical knowledge (Huyssen, 1995, p. 5).[16] At the same time, and apparently paradoxically, it has been suggested that in contemporary consumer societies, 'a memorial or museal sensibility ... occupies ever larger chunks of everyday culture and experience' (Huyssen, 1995, p. 253). This 'sensibility' has been attributed to the way in which profit-driven consumer societies both produce and capitalise on a fascination with the past through the commodification of historical events, as is exemplified, for example, by 'museum attendance, historically oriented tourism, participation in festivals, and ... the media-driven excesses of nostalgia and commemoration of recent historical periods' (Michael Frisch, quoted in Rosenzweig and Thelen, 1998, p. 3). However, Andreas Huyssen attributes the current widespread fascination with memory and history to people's need for 'temporal anchoring' and 'to live in extended structures of temporality' (1995, pp. 7, 9), a need against which consumer culture, based on perpetual change, militates. Similarly John Gillis argues that the current preoccupation with memory attests to people's desire to preserve the traces of their everyday identities and those of their forebears, in a constantly changing culture which seeks to erase those traces (1994, pp. 13–16). According to Pierre Nora, it is precisely because 'we no longer live in a world suffused with memory or fully committed to overarching ideological narratives', such as the progress of the nation, that 'sites of memory' are sought where, through memory, 'relationships between past, present and future' can be defined (Davis and Starn, 1989, p. 3). The Vietnam Veterans Memorial provides a material and symbolic space where this work of memory can be collectively undertaken.

Notes

1. Carter stated: 'A long and painful process has brought us to this moment today ... Our nation was divided by this war. For too long we have tried to put that division behind us by forgetting the Vietnam War, and, in the process, we ignored those who

bravely answered their nation's call ... We are ready at last to acknowledge more deeply and also more publicly the debt which we can never fully pay to those who served' (quoted in Scruggs and Swerdlow, 1985, p. 42).

2. Hess recounts how the memorial's supporters argued that the poll was unrepresentative as 'POWs are more conservative than the average veteran' (1987, pp. 266–7). Perot also instigated an investigation of the VVMF's accounts, claiming that the fund had been mismanaged, but this claim was proved to be false, as Buckley explains (1985, pp. 68–72).

3. Jane Fonda gained notoriety amongst supporters of the war and many veterans by visiting Hanoi and posing on an enemy missile to protest against American involvement in the war.

4. The jury comprised landscape architects Hideo Sasaki and Garrett Eckbo; architects Harry Weese and Pitero Belluschi; sculptors Costantino Nivola, James Rosati, and Richard H. Hunt; and Grady Clay, editor of *Landscape Architecture* (Hess, 1987, p. 264).

5. Marita Sturken (1991, p. 121) refutes the claim that the memorial *is* a work of pure modernist abstraction: firstly, the names inscribed on the wall are referential, and secondly, whereas modernism in sculpture favours 'sitelessness', part of the effect of the VVM is produced by the 'site specificity' of its dialogue with national symbols, the Lincoln Memorial and Washington Monument, which are situated nearby on the Mall.

6. General George Price, quoted in Scruggs and Swerdlow (1985, p. 100).

7. These inscriptions read: 'In honor of the men and women of the armed forces of the United States who served in the Vietnam War. The names of those who gave their lives and those who remain missing are inscribed in the order they were taken from us'; and 'Our nation honors the courage, sacrifice and devotion to duty and country of its Vietnam veterans. This memorial was built with private contributions from the American people. November 11, 1982' (Fish, 1987b, p. 23).

8. The inscription reads: 'This flag represents the service rendered to our country by the veterans of the Vietnam War. The flag affirms the principles of freedom for which they fought and their pride in having served under difficult circumstances' (Fish, 1987b, p. 11).

9. Agent Orange was a herbicide used by US Armed Forces to defoliate the jungle and woodland that gave cover to the Viet Cong in South Vietnam. It is believed to have caused diseases such as cancer amongst survivors of the war and genetic disorders which are manifesting themselves in their children.

10. Young (1993, pp. xi–xii) contests the idea of 'collective memory', arguing that 'a society's memory' is an 'aggregate collection' of the memories of individuals, which derive from 'the individual's unique relation to a lived life' and are 'hers alone'. However, social institutions and rituals contribute to the creation of *forms* of memory, and the production of common *meanings* which are ascribed to memories and passed from one generation to the next through traditions, rituals and institutions.

11. I follow Sturken's definition of cultural memory as representing 'the many shifting histories and shared memories that exist between a sanctioned narrative of history and personal memory' (1991, p. 119).

12. Peter S. Hawkins likens the effect of the names on the VVM to that of the names on the AIDS Quilt (1993, p. 762).

13. Benedict Anderson argues that the rise of nationalism coincided with the decline of 'religious modes of thought', and so the symbolic significance conferred upon the dead by Christianity needed to be reformulated by nationalism in order to effect 'a secular transformation of fatality into continuity, contingency into meaning' (1983, p. 11).

14. The sanctity of the Tomb has subsequently been further contested. In 1998 DNA testing identified the remains of the 'unknown' soldier as those of Michael J. Blassie, an Air Force Lieutenant whose aeroplane was shot down in South Vietnam in 1972. The debate that unfolded in the *New York Times* as it reported this episode revealed the conflict between nationalism and individualism which surrounded it. Whilst some contributors argued that the anonymity of the remains needed to be preserved to protect the sanctity of the Tomb and 'the nation' which it represented (21 February 1998), others argued that the rights of the individual should be respected (27 April 1998), as manifested in this case by Blassie's mother's wish to have her son's remains 'brought home' (15 February 1998), so that he could be 'buried under a tombstone with his own name' (21 February 1998).

15. H. Bruce Franklin (1991; 1992) observes that since 1982 successive American governments have 'operated on the assumption that at least some Americans are still held captive' in Southeast Asia, and it has been a condition of America's re-opening trade relations with Vietnam, Laos and Cambodia that they provide 'the fullest possible accounting' for American MIAs. Franklin argues that it is extremely unlikely that Americans are still alive in these countries. Nevertheless, the widely held fantasy that they are has been fuelled by popular culture, in films such as *The Deer Hunter*, *Uncommon Valor* and the *Rambo* sequence.

According to these representations, the existence of the MIAs and POWs 'proves undeniably the cruelty and inhumanity of the Asian communists ... and the nobility of the cause for which the United States fought in Indochina' (1991, p. 46), and the fantasy of Americans returning to Vietnam to rescue the prisoners allows a rewriting of the Vietnam War, whereby the Americans are both 'victims' of the barbaric Vietnamese and heroic saviours of their countrymen.

16. For a seminal discussion of the contemporary subject's experience of temporality, see Jameson, 1991, pp. 1–54.

Bibliography

Anderson, B. *Imagined Communities: Reflections on the Origin and Spread of Nationalism* (New York: Verso, 1983).

Arnheim, W. 'The Hidden Tomb of the Vietnam Unknown', *Washington Post* (13 July 1980), p. E4.

Ashabranner, B. *Always to Remember: The Story of the Vietnam Veterans Memorial* (New York: Scholastic, 1988).

Beardsley, J. 'Personal Sensibilities in Public Places', *Artforum* (Summer 1981), pp. 43–5.

Bee, J.D. 'Eros and Thanatos: An Analysis of the Vietnam Memorial', in Walsh and Aulich (1989), pp. 196–204.

Berdahl, D. 'Voices at the Wall: Discourses of Self, History and National Identity at the Vietnam Veterans Memorial', *History and Memory: Studies in Representation of the Past* 6:2 (Fall–Winter 1994), pp. 88–124.

Bodnar, J. *Remaking America: Public Memory, Commemoration, and Patriotism in the Twentieth Century* (Princeton, N.J.: Princeton University Press, 1992).

— 'Public Memory in an American City: Commemoration in Cleveland', in Gillis (1994), pp. 74–89.

Buckley, C. 'The Wall', *Esquire* (September 1985), pp. 61–73.

Campbell, N. and A. Kean *American Cultural Studies* (London and New York: Routledge, 1997).

Danto, A.C. 'The Vietnam Veterans Memorial', *The Nation* (31 August 1985), pp. 152–5.

Davis, N.Z. and R. Starn 'Introduction', *Memory and Counter-Memory*, special issue of *Representations* 26 (Spring 1989), ed. Davis and Starn, pp. 1–6.

Ehrenraus, P. 'Commemorating the Unwon War: On *Not* Remembering Vietnam', *Journal of Communication* 39.1 (Winter 1989), pp. 96–107.

Ezell, E.C. *Reflections on the Wall: The Vietnam Veterans Memorial* (Harrisburg, PA: Stockpole, 1987).

Fish, L. 'The Last Firebase', *International Folklore Review: Folklore Studies from Overseas* 5 (1987a), pp. 82–7.

— *The Last Firebase: A Guide to the Vietnam Veterans Memorial* (Shippensburg, PA: White Mane, 1987b).

Foss, S.K. 'Ambiguity as Persuasion: The Vietnam Veterans Memorial', *Communication Quarterly* 34.3 (Summer 1986), pp. 326–40.

Fox, T.M. 'The Vietnam Veterans Memorial: Ideological Implications', in Walsh and Aulich (1989), pp. 211–20.

Franklin, H.B. 'The POW/MIA Myth', *The Atlantic Monthly* (December 1991), pp. 45–81; expanded in Franklin, *MIA, or, Mythmaking in America* (New York: Lawrence Hill, 1992).

Gaspar, C.J. 'Searching for Closure: Vietnam War Literature and the Veterans Memorial', *War, Literature and the Arts* 1.1 (Spring 1989), pp. 19–34.

Gillis, J.R. 'Introduction', *Commemorations: The Politics of National Identity*, ed. J.R. Gillis (New Jersey: Princeton University Press, 1994), pp. 3–24.

Griswold, C. 'The Vietnam Veterans Memorial and the Washington Mall: Philosophical Thoughts on Political Iconography', *Critical Inquiry* 12 (Summer 1986), pp. 688–719.

Haines, H. '"What Kind of War?": An Analysis of the Vietnam Veterans Memorial', *Critical Studies in Mass Communication* 3.1 (March 1986), pp. 1–20.

Hammer, J. 'Cashing In On Vietnam', *Newsweek* (16 January 1989), pp. 31–2.

Harrison, R.P. 'The Names of the Dead', *Critical Inquiry* 24.1 (Autumn 1997), pp. 176–90.

Hass, K.A. *Carried to the Wall: American Memory and the Vietnam Veterans Memorial* (Berkeley, CA and London: University of California Press, 1998).

Hawkins, P.S. 'The Art of Memory and the NAMES Project AIDS Quilt', *Critical Inquiry* 19 (Summer 1993), pp. 752–79.

Hess, E. 'Vietnam: Memorials of Misfortune', in *Unwinding the Vietnam War: From War into Peace*, ed. R. Williams (Seattle: Real Comet, 1987), pp. 262–81. Includes a 1983 interview with Maya Lin, pp. 272–3.

Hubbard, W. 'A meaning for monuments', *Public Interest* 74 (Winter 1984), pp. 17–30.

Huyssen, A. *Twilight Memories: Marking Time in a Culture of Amnesia* (New York and London: Routledge, 1995).

Jameson, F. *Postmodernism, Or, The Cultural Logic of Late Capitalism* (Verso, 1991).

Jeffords, S. *The Remasculinization of America: Gender and the Vietnam War* (Bloomington, IA: Indiana University Press, 1989).

Laqueur, T.W. 'Memory and Naming in the Great War', in Gillis (1994), pp. 150–67.

Mason, B.A. *In Country* (New York: Harper and Row, 1985).

Morrow, L. 'War and Remembrance', *Time* (11 June 1984), p. 27.

Mosse, G. *Fallen Soldiers: Reshaping the Memory of the World Wars* (New York: Oxford University Press, 1990).

National Geographic 'Vietnam Memorial: America Remembers', 167.5 (May 1985), pp. 552–75.

National Review 'Stop That Monument' (18 September 1981), p. 1064.

Neal, A.G. *National Trauma and Collective Memory: Major Events in the American Century* (Armonk, New York and London: M.E. Sharpe, 1988).

New York Times 'The Black Gash of Shame' (14 April 1985), p. 22.

Nora, P. 'Between Memory and History: *Les Lieux de Mémoire*', in Davis and Starn (1989), pp. 7–25.

Oman, A.H. 'The Long Trail of Tears', *Washington Post* (Weekend) (12 November 1982), pp. 53–6.

Pease, D.E. 'Hiroshima, the Vietnam Veterans War Memorial, and the Gulf War: Post-national Spectacles', in *Cultures of United States Imperialism*, ed. A. Kaplan and D.E. Pease (Durham, NC and London: Duke University Press, 1993), pp. 557–80.

Rosenzweig, R. and D. Thelen, 'Introduction', in *The Presence of the Past: Popular Uses of History in American Life*, ed. Rosenzweig and Thelen (New York: Columbia University Press, 1998), pp. 1–14.

Scarry, E. *The Body in Pain: The Making and Unmaking of the World* (New York and Oxford: Oxford University Press, 1985).

Scruggs, J.C. and J.L. Swerdlow *To Heal a Nation: The Vietnam Veterans Memorial* (New York: Harper and Row, 1985).

Sturken, M. 'The Wall, the Screen, and the Image: The Vietnam Veterans Memorial', *Representations* 35 (Summer 1991), pp. 118–42.

Wagner-Pacifici R. and B. Schwartz, 'The Vietnam Veterans Memorial: Commemorating a Difficult Past', *American Journal of Sociology* 97.2 (September 1991), pp. 376–420.

Walsh, J. and J. Aulich (eds) *Vietnam Images: War and Representation* (Macmillan, 1989).

Wolfe, T. 'Art Disputes War: The Battle of the Vietnam Memorial', *Washington Post* (13 October 1982), pp. B1, B3, B4.

Yoneyama, L. 'Memory Matters: Hiroshima's Korean Atom Bomb Memorial and the Politics of Ethnicity', *Public Culture* 7.3 (1995), pp. 499–527.

Young, J.E. *The Texture of Memory: Holocaust Memorials and Meaning* (New Haven and London: Yale University Press, 1993).

5 'I'd Love to Turn You On': The Beatles' *Sgt. Pepper's Lonely Hearts Club Band* (1967)

Gerry Smyth

The purpose of this chapter is to offer a cultural historical analysis of *Sgt. Pepper's Lonely Hearts Club Band* (hereafter *Pepper*), a long-playing record released by the Beatles on 1 June 1967. (I follow most accounts in citing the official release date, although Lewisohn (1987, p. 90) – the nearest there is to an 'official' Beatles historian – writes that it was 'rush-released' five days earlier.) Musically, the album has been enormously influential and is widely cited as the most important, if not the 'best', collection of songs produced in the pop/rock idiom (Frith, 1992, p. 62; Joynson, 1996, p. 46; Macan, 1997, p. 15). Like it or not, *Pepper* is clearly one of the 'works that shaped the century' (McCormick, 1999). At the same time, the album is generally considered to be the most representative text produced by the international counter-culture of the 1960s (Hewison, 1986, p. 142; Caute, 1988, p. 37; Whiteley, 1992, pp. 39–60). Judgements such as these abound both in popular music journalism and in the burgeoning academic discipline addressed to the production, signification and consumption of popular music. Ian MacDonald's effusive estimation, delivered in the context of a by no means uncritical analysis of the entire Beatles *oeuvre*, encapsulates the (currently) general opinion:

> When *Pepper* was released in June, it was a major cultural event. Young and old alike were entranced ... In America normal radio-play was virtually suspended for several days, only tracks from *Pepper* being played. An almost religious awe surrounded the LP ... The psychic shiver which *Pepper* sent through the world was nothing less than a cinematic dissolve from one *Zeitgeist* to another. In *The Times*, Kenneth Tynan called it 'a decisive moment in the history of Western civilisation' ... *Sgt. Pepper's Lonely Hearts Club Band* may not have created the psychic atmosphere of the time but,

as a near-perfect reflection of it, this famous record magnified and radiated it around the world. (1994, pp. 98–9)

Of course, such judgements form part of the 'meaning' of *Pepper* (in terms of reception) and as such will need to be interrogated in their turn. However, the principal attraction of this text from the perspective of cultural history in general and this book in particular is that the Beatles' eighth album clearly speaks to many of the methodological and disciplinary issues broached in Part 1. It would not be overstating the case, for instance, to say that *Pepper* was in part responsible for the consolidation of popular culture as a legitimate subject for serious scholarly inquiry in the final decades of the century. Cross-fertilising with trends deriving from cultural studies, musicology and sociology, the discourse of rock journalism that emerged in response to the album contributed significantly to the development of contemporary popular music studies. As this chapter hopefully will show, the album now functions as the fulcrum around which so many of the analytical discourses – economic, generic, formal, social – of popular music turn.

We could likewise speculate on the text's liminal status in terms of some of the critical-methodological (for example, structuralist and poststructuralist) or cultural-aesthetic (for example, modernist and postmodernist) paradigms explored in Part 1. Whether it be an organic text possessed of an holistic semiotic structure, or a self-deconstructing, avant-garde freak-out demonstrative of a fatal *absence* at the heart of human endeavour, *Pepper* will answer your requirements. In short, this artefact functions as a high-profile site for the contention of various critical systems and cultural meanings. While this has its drawbacks – the sheer volume of relevant material – it does present an opportunity to ground the somewhat abstract discourses of the first part of this book in terms of this easily accessible yet highly evocative text.

With reference to the methodology described in the final section of Part 1, this chapter addresses the cultural and historical contexts of *Pepper* in terms of the evolution of British popular music during the 1950s and 1960s, and the role played by the Beatles in this evolution. We shall also be considering the musical response of the group to the emergence of an international counter-culture, while looking in some detail at the background to the composition and recording of *Pepper* in the early months of 1967. Turning then to the text, attention will focus on the musical and semiotic structure of one selected track, examining the immediate circumstances of its composition as well as the dynamics of its instrumentation, recording and sequencing. Finally, through a discussion of contemporary and subsequent reception, we shall attempt to trace the ways in which *Pepper* has been 'appropriated' and 'productively activated' during the course of its career since 1967.

The Rise of Rock 'n' Roll and the Beginning of The Beatles

Andrew Blake has traced the history of popular music in Great Britain since the nineteenth century, claiming that 'late twentieth-century popular musics were connected to previous musical cultures' (1997, p. 76), indigenous and imported. Given the complexity of these influences, *and* of many of the categories closely associated with popular music (especially that of 'youth'), he goes on to argue that 'there can be no simple narrative of British pop in the 1960s' (p. 103). British pop's inheritance of traditions such as music hall, 'light' classical music, 'Tin Pan Alley', the Hollywood musical and so on, seems clear (an inheritance which will indeed emerge later with reference to *Pepper*). Neither would I wish to deny the troubled status of the many theories of youth and popular music that have been produced in recent times (Cohen, 1972; Hebdige, 1979; Frith, 1981; Willis, 1990; Redhead, 1993). However, the dual assumptions upon which this study is based are that it is specifically against the background of the emergence of rock 'n' roll that the career of the Beatles should be seen, and that this form of music has itself to be contextualised in terms of the emergence of a specific youth market in both the United States and Great Britain in the years after the Second World War, a phenomenon quickly identified by contemporary cultural purveyors and subsequently incorporated as a particularly lucrative niche market in what Blake himself calls the 'political economy of music' (p. 91).

In his book *Understanding Rock 'n' Roll*, Dick Bradley traces the impact of American popular musical tastes on British culture after 1955 and attempts to theorise the elements that contributed to that impact. He highlights three developments as being particularly significant. For many British people, he explains, the first experience of rock 'n' roll came through the movie *Rock Around the Clock*, which featured performances by the American group Bill Haley and his Comets (1992, p. 56). So much about the music and the presentation was comparatively new: the fact that the Comets were definitely a group rather than a dance band; the loud guitar and kit-led sound; the strong rhythm; the vocals that seemed to be shouted rather than sung; the general downgrading of melody; the sheer energy of the performance and the air of semi-improvisation which attended it. All this contrasted sharply with the kinds of popular music with which British audiences were familiar, and as Bradley points out, 'it polarized the reactions of listeners quite dramatically. They either loved or hated it' (1992, p. 55).

Bill Haley and his Comets were in the first wave of rock 'n' roll to hit Britain, lasting from about 1954 to 1957. With its central stress on the rhythm or pulse of the music – or the 'beat', as it came to be called – this kind of music was drawing, on the one hand, on popular twentieth-century African-American styles such as blues, rhythm and blues, and more especially the 'urban electric blues' of the 1940s and early 1950s; on the other hand, it carried obvious resonances of white America's most sucessful twentieth-century popular music – country and western. Harker stresses the sexual metaphors encoded in the song ('rock 'n' roll' was contemporary American slang for sexual intercourse), something which contributed to its status as a dangerous (hence, attractive to teenagers) music (1980, p. 60). Despite this, Haley's music was aimed at white audiences – and not even a white teenage audience, but an adult, dance-oriented audience (Bradley, 1992, p. 58). Although they generated unprecedented scenes of teenage hysteria when they toured England in the mid- and late 1950s, however, the appeal of this group was limited. As Bradley argues, the true achievement of the first wave of rock 'n' rollers was to provide listeners (and especially that new marketing phenomenon known as the 'teenager') with a store of sounds and possibilities that extended their musical landscape and made them more receptive to later developments (1992, p. 60).

The second element impacting on the rise of rock 'n' roll in Britain was the influence of Buddy Holly and his group the Crickets. Besides inspiring John Lennon in his attempt to find a name for his own group a few years later, this influence took a number of forms. For one thing, Holly and the Crickets wrote much of their own material. This was unusual in itself at the time; but songs like 'Peggy Sue', 'That'll Be the Day' and 'Oh Boy' were also formally unusual in so far as they experimented with structure, lyrics and instrumentation. Holly and the Crickets also provided the basic group format of rhythm guitar, lead guitar, bass and drum kit that was to dominate rock music-making for many years. In England, the country and western influence of Holly was adopted along with a particular line of the African-American popular music tradition that, as Moore says, drew from

the Chicago-based rhythm 'n' blues of Howlin' Wolf, Muddy Waters and (later) Chuck Berry, rather than the New Orleans sound of Fats Domino and Little Richard ... this pattern seems first to have been successfully adopted in England by the Shadows, and was later followed right across the early beat/rhythm 'n' blues divide from the Searchers through the Beatles to the Yardbirds and the Rolling Stones. (1993, p. 34)

At the same time, it was clear that neither Holly nor his band were virtuoso musicians and that their musical sound was fairly limited. Even Holly's thick black-rimmed glasses contributed to an aura of simplicity and improvisation. This latter element was perhaps Holly's most important contribution to the development of early rock 'n' roll and related styles in Britain: the idea that anyone with an interest in the music could learn, write and perform it without any specialist training. Bradley points out that Holly was a direct influence on two crazes that hit Britain in the mid- to late 1950s: a boom in guitar playing, and the popular success of what became known as Skiffle music (1992, p. 62). Skiffle was a kind of 'do-it-yourself music' (Nehring, 1993, p. 207) based on improvising with acoustic instruments – guitars, broom bass (or 'tea chest'), washboard rhythm, and so on. Amateurism had been a significant element of British popular music-making since the nineteenth century, and the ethos of a simple, non-virtuoso, supposedly more 'authentic' music continues to impact upon popular musical discourse from time to time (Blake, 1997, pp. 86–90). As the 1950s progressed, music-making as well as music-listening was becoming both more attractive and more accessible (at least for young, white, working- and middle-class boys). In different parts of the country groups of teenagers were experimenting with sounds and composition, because they felt that this was an exciting and valuable use of their time, obviously, but also because changes in leisure and income patterns had rendered such an activity available. The first music-making experience for John Lennon and Paul McCartney was with a skiffle group, and in future years all the Beatles would acknowledge Holly's influence. But by far the biggest influence on Lennon, and on a whole generation of music listeners and makers (and the third element cited by Bradley in his account of the rise of rock 'n' roll in Britain), was Elvis Presley.

Bradley suggests that Presley's initial success was based on two elements that have become integral to the discourse of rock 'n' roll and its various offshoots: sex and the voice (1992, p. 63). In contrast to the rather plump figure of Bill Haley, and to the sensitivity communicated in many of Holly's songs, the earliest Presley records were sending out very different messages to young audiences. His energy, smouldering sexuality, and the suggestive lyrics of many of his early songs, were perceived as a threat by the establishment; but to popular music listeners all over the world in 1956 Elvis was seen as the next, exciting, obvious step in the development of rock 'n' roll. Again, unlike Haley and Holly, Presley was obviously an individual interpreter of music; it was the performance, the delivery and the persona behind the delivery that distinguished the music. Although emerging to some degree from a white country and western tradition (Shepherd, 1991, p. 144), and although consciously packaged to maintain an appeal for that audience (Bradley, 1992, p. 66), Presley's voice and singing technique – foregrounding performance, energy and improvisation – was obviously based on that of black blues singers from both the rural and urban traditions. As such, it was the most obvious instance to date of the ways in which rock 'n' roll, as an exemplary form of popular music, drew apparently unconsciously upon different tradition and styles. This characteristic was something that would survive rock 'n' roll's own demise and resurface in its various offshoots in the years that followed.

So these are the three elements identified by Bradley as being significant in the rise of rock 'n' roll in Britain during the latter half of the 1950s, at a time, that is, when the four teenagers who were to become the Beatles were developing their interest in music. (Another figure worth mentioning is Chuck Berry who perhaps more than any other single artist was responsible for producing the kind of rock 'n' roll – described by Martin as a 'modified blues music' (1994, p. 44) – that was to inspire so many young British boys.) As Bradley and many other commentators point out, however, the implicit threat of blues-inspired rock 'n' roll, given concrete form in the figure of Presley, was very rapidly absorbed, contained and repackaged (Bradley, 1992, p. 71; Harker, 1980, pp. 73–86; Nehring, 1993, pp. 207–9). In America, this process took symbolic form when Presley was drafted into the army in 1959. Emerging after a stint in Germany, he was marketed as a mainstream pop singer with appeal to all age groups and all sections of society (Harker, 1980, pp. 60–1). The raw sexuality that had so disturbed parents in the 1950s was re-presented in the films and songs of the 1960s as natural, wholesome American fun. Similarly, the voice now became fetishised for itself, almost a parody of the excited, emotional rock 'n' roll voice that had so thrilled teenagers, and so frightened parents, back in 1956.

The same processes overtook rock 'n' roll in Britain between about 1957 and 1960. This period was characterised by a kind of 'ersatz rock and roll' (Nehring, 1993, p. 207) which harked back to an older 'show business' paradigm of light music-making, organised around 'entertainment' rather than authentic expression. Middleton writes that '[the] efflorescence of rock 'n' roll, and of the 1960s rock movements, took place against the background of a new socio-historical phase, that of the "long boom", "welfare capitalism" and an ideology of liberal tolerance' (1990, p. 15). If this background was to go on to generate the conditions for an expansive, experimental rock music in the middle of the decade, back in 1960 it provided the context for modern pop music's first major reversal – its capitulation to the forces of the marketplace. ('Sell-out' has been a regular cry in the rock world every since.) Certain elements of the music of Haley, Holly, Presley and others from the first wave of rock 'n' roll were reproduced in adulterated form for mass consumption. Performers such as Tommy Steele, Adam Faith and Cliff Richard emerged as purveyors of a musical practice rather interestingly described as 'neutered' (Harker, 1980, p. 73) and 'castrated' (Nehring, 1993, p. 209). There were only four record companies in Britain in 1960, producing for the most part 'unlistenable ballads by "pretty-boy" singers, covers of the most wretched, contrived American hits, and hideous trad. New Orleans jazz by the likes of Acker Bilk' (Nehring, 1993, p. 208). This is also the case with the two radio networks 'catering' for popular-musical audiences, the BBC and Radio Luxembourg. Constrained by the discursive parameters laid down by the musical establishment, rock 'n' roll in Britain hit its first (though far from its last) crisis.

One of the most significant responses to the 'castration' of rock 'n' roll in Britain in the early 1960s was the rise of what became known as 'beat' music. Many of the elements and attitudes that had been introduced during the 1950s in the first rock 'n' roll wave had taken root in British culture, producing a groundswell of popular music-making which disdained the 'ersatz' product manufactured for mainstream consumption, and taking its ethos from the (perceived) authenticity and (undoubted) excitement of the original American artists instead. This groundswell manifested itself as an army of amateur groups, predominantly male, predominantly based on the group format of the Crickets, and predominantly geared towards live performance. There were literally thousands of these beat groups in the early 1960s (Clayson, 1995), so called because of the emphasis on a strong, syncopated rhythm or pulse that dominated the sound, this being provided by the close unison of the drum kit and the bass guitar. A crucial later development was the use of single-string lead guitar, to give colour and texture to the sound, and the subsequent emergence of the lead guitarist as a sort of modern-day folk hero.

As the name suggests, this was the kind of musical discourse in which the Beatles were participating before they became famous. Their home city of Liverpool was in fact the centre of beat music culture, although it remains unclear why this should have been so. Cohen suggests that the 'wealth of music-making partly reflected an influx of foreign cultures and influences entering Liverpool through its port' (1991, p. 12). Following this well-established line, Martin points to the large number of American personnel passing through Liverpool during the Second World War, and the city's subsequent status as a major site for the importation of American goods, including records (1994, p. 41). As Riley points out, however, the significant thing for the Beatles (and indeed for their fellow Mersey groups) was not so much the derivation of their influences but 'how they digested what came before and turned it into something they could call their own'

(1988, p. 21). In any event, Liverpool became home to a great number of groups producing 'beat' music aimed at young working-class club- and pub-goers. 'Between 1958 and 1965', writes Cohen, 'according to the Liverpool Corporation, the number of teenage "beat" clubs doubled' (1991, p. 13).

The established record companies tended to have little faith in the value or appeal of anything produced outside the capital, however. Having been turned down by the major popular music labels (HMV, Columbia and Decca), the group's manager Brian Epstein finally signed in June 1962 with Parlophone, a subsidiary of EMI run by producer George Martin and noted mainly for comedy and jazz recordings. When the group broke into the charts in October 1962 with their first single 'Love Me Do', it paved the way for an invasion of popular musical culture by beat music in general, and by the so-called 'Mersey Sound' in particular. As one critic remarks, 'the Beatles showed that it was possible to be listened to, and be young, provincial and working-class' (Hewison, 1986, pp. 66–7). The fact that the single was self-penned also had profound implications for the mode of musical production in Britain in subsequent years, precipitating a significant shift from a management/singer paradigm to an author/performer one (Blake, 1997, p. 92). In the meantime, although it did not replace the 'ersatz' pop that had superseded rock 'n' roll, beat became the music of choice for Britain's young, affluent postwar generation. In this respect, many commentators see the emergence of beat music as a temporary reclamation of popular culture by young working- and middle-class people from the big business interests which had dominated popular music production since the end of the 1950s. In fact, some have theorised this as an inevitable pattern: the market leaves a small area within popular culture available for new, romantic, supposedly 'radical' initiatives, so that the old culture can be discarded and a new market, valued by consumers for its supposed uncontamination by material concerns, can in its turn be captured, packaged and sold until the next big thing comes along (Middleton, 1990, p. 39).

In any event, producing a style of music that combined influences from early rock 'n' roll, skiffle, and elements culled from a long British (and American-inspired) popular musical tradition, the Beatles arrived upon the world stage in 1963. The singles 'She Loves You' in Great Britain and 'I Wanna Hold Your Hand' in the United States converted the band from average pop idols into an unprecedented mass cultural phenomenon. While the scenes of hysteria which accompanied the group wherever it went *had* been seen before – for Frank Sinatra, Presley and others – the sheer scale of the Beatles' appeal was something entirely new. In April 1964 they held 'the top five positions in the American chart plus eleven other places in the

Top 100' (MacDonald, 1994, p. 318). 'Beatlemania' was institutionalised when the four group members were enshrined in Madame Tussaud's (the London waxwork museum) in 1964 (Davies, 1968, p. 213), their images being periodically updated with each new change in style. (Some of these discarded effigies turned up subsequently on the cover of *Pepper*, 'paying their respects', as Riley says, 'to their own late live career' (1988, p. 213).) Another significant moment was the receipt of MBEs from the Queen in June 1965 on the recommendation of Labour Prime Minister Harold Wilson in his New Year Honours List. As we shall see, such recognition by the establishment was symptomatic of the ambivalent appeal of the Beatles. On the one hand, with their long hair, their loud music and the hysteria they elicited in their fans, they appeared to embody all that was a threat to traditional values. On the other hand, they seemed quite wholesome compared to 'mod' bands like the Who, or rhythm 'n' blues bands like the Rolling Stones. Likewise, their early music, with its quirky progressions and familiar themes, had a wider appeal than the obviously blues-based music of the Stones or the vitriolic protest songs of Bob Dylan.

It was in fact Dylan who initiated the germ of an alternative attitude among the Beatles, an attitude that would find its fullest expression in 1967 with the so-called 'Summer of Love' and the release of *Pepper*. On 28 August 1964, Dylan and the Beatles met for the first time in the Hotel Delmonico in Manhattan, New York (MacDonald, 1994, p. 98). Before this time the Beatles, typically of the British pop scene, had experienced drugs only in the form of the 'uppers' that they took during their early touring days to keep going on what was an exhausting schedule. That night, however, Dylan rolled the Beatles their first cannabis joint, and the four young men soon became fascinated with the alternative effects it produced compared to the energy surges associated with alcohol and speed. That night the Beatles entered into what might be called their 'marijuana period', and their next two albums, *Help!* and *Rubber Soul*, were composed and recorded under the calming, often stupefying influence of the drug.

Cultural, Political and Musical Contexts

Between 1963 and late 1966 the Beatles continued to have unprecedented popular success, every single, album and both their films outstripping their rivals irrespective of quality. However, by the time they came to record their seventh LP, *Revolver*, many things had changed in their professional and personal lives: 1966 had been a particularly gruelling year, combining death threats in Japan, actual bodily violence in the Philippines, and mass burnings of Beatle materials in the United States in the wake of Lennon's remarks regarding the relative popularity of the Beatles and Jesus Christ (Martin, 1994, pp. 7–12). The exhaustion brought on by years of constant touring was also beginning to take its toll, and all four group members were 'cheesed off', as George Harrison put it (Wonfor, 1995), with both the quality of music they were producing and the quality of life 'Beatlemania' was enforcing upon them. They played their last scheduled live concert in Candlestick Park, San Francisco on 29 August 1966. Collapsing into his aeroplane seat afterwards on a flight back to Los Angeles, Harrison remarked to press officer Tony Barrow, 'Well, that's it; I'm not a Beatle any more' (Turner, 1987a, p. 50).

As Barrow goes on to explain, Harrison did not mean that he was quitting the group, just that the word 'Beatle' was going to have to signify something different in the future. This was an important point, because at the time no group had ever survived solely as a recording entity, and there existed no rationale for a pop group that did not play live shows. The serious possibility existed, therefore, that when the Beatles decided to stop touring the band would simply break up. Their success had lasted longer than anyone, including themselves, had expected, and in late 1966 there was much speculation in the British and American press concerning the imminent demise of the Beatles. During a six-week stay in Spain filming *How I Won the War* with director Dick Lester, Lennon began to address the potentially terrifying question facing all the Beatles: 'What do you do when you don't tour?' (Lennon, 1981, p. 11). If the answer was 'record' (although this was by no means certain in the closing months of 1966), another question presented itself, this time voiced by Martin: 'Could an album, however good, be an effective substitute for a live tour?' (1994, p. 63). A degree of 'reinvention' was necessary, therefore – of themselves certainly, but also of the very idea of pop music – if the band was to continue.

Another major impact on the Beatles during 1966 was their discovery of the hallucinogenic drug LSD (lysergic acid diethylamide), also known as 'acid', and widely considered the single most important factor in the cultural revolution of the 1960s (Stevens, 1987, p. 404; Caute, 1988, pp. 41–3; MacDonald, 1994, p. 145). It is in fact impossible to overstate the centrality of LSD to every aspect of the changes overtaking popular culture during the decade – in counter-cultural organisation, in the growth of the anti-Vietnam political movement, in the fashion for mystical religion, in the development of ecological consciousness, in the emergence of pyschedelic fashion, and in the desire for alternative lifestyles that animated the hippie movement. According to Stevens, the word 'hippie' was invented by the American journalist Michael Fallon in September 1965 during research for an article on former 'Beats' (an American subculture of the 1950s and early 1960s) who had moved to the Haight-Ashbury district of San Francisco (1987, p. 403). Heeding the call of the renegade Harvard psychologist Dr Timothy Leary, significant numbers of the Baby Boomer population of the United States repudiated the values and beliefs of the postwar world and decided, in his famous slogan, to 'Turn on, tune in and drop out'. Always stronger on what it opposed than what it advocated, and disdaining anything so 'square' as a programme, the counter-culture advocated a vague lifestyle politics that was 'international, equisexual, tribal [and] nomadic' in outlook (Neville, 1970, p. 53). The discontent with postwar American life that had been brewing since the early 1960s exploded in the early months of 1967 into a mass popular movement, youth-oriented, centred around the San Francisco area of California, and based mainly on what were believed to be the ego-destroying, liberating qualities of LSD. What followed came to be known as the 'Summer of Love', which saw a number of events or happenings that were to enter popular counter-cultural folklore: the 'Human Be-In' in San Francisco; the Monterey Pop Festival; large anti-Vietnam war demonstrations around the world; the Death of Hippie festival in Haight-Ashbury; and, perhaps most significantly, the release of *Pepper*.

While the Beatles clearly did not initiate this vast disenchantment with established values, it is equally clear that through their own use of LSD and their cosmopolitan lifestyles they were very much in the vanguard of its cultural (although, as we shall see below, not necessarily its political) expression. Lennon later admitted taking about 1000 LSD tabs between 1966 and 1968 (quoted in Goldman, 1988, p. 264), and large parts of 1967 were spent continuously tripping (Turner, 1987a, p. 53). All the other Beatles, too, were using the drug throughout this period, and one of the scandals upsetting loyal Beatles fans during 1967 was when, just a few weeks after the release of *Pepper*, Paul McCartney admitted to *Life* magazine, and subsequently on camera, that he had taken LSD. (It seems McCartney may have actually 'turned on' during the *Pepper* sessions to help out Lennon who was having a 'bad trip' (Martin, 1994, p. 110); if true, as MacDonald points out, it was a 'remarkably brave and loving' gesture (1994, p. 17).) Drugs had hitherto been more associated with 'rock' acts such as the Rolling Stones whose members were harassed by police throughout 1967, or with popular musicians closer in ethos and outlook to the hippie lifestyle. As Harrison puts it, the Beatles were still too 'fab' in 1967 to become victims of estab-lishment reaction (Sheppard, 1987). That was to change, however, after the release of a record so 'fundamentally shaped by LSD' (MacDonald, 1994, p. 199).

Timothy Leary was not the only person to see *Pepper* as 'a complete celebration of LSD' (Stevens, 1989, p. 466). 'A Day in the Life' was banned by the BBC on 20 May – nearly two weeks before the official release date – for what were seen as thinly veiled drug references. 'Lucy in the Sky with Diamonds' was similarly censored on both sides of the Atlantic, although Lennon's story that he took the title from a school painting by his four-year-old son Julian is surely likely if one considers a line from a perennially popular song in British nurseries and pre-schools: 'Like a diamond in the sky' from 'Twinkle, Twinkle, Little Star'. In fact, the so-called 'Summer of Love' is also the year during which the establishment's determination to keep this cocky, affluent postwar generation in line emerged, signalled by developments such as the formation of British regional drugs squads, the suppression of pirate radio and underground press, and the persecution of certain high-profile individuals such as Mick Jagger and John 'Hoppy' Hopkins (Whiteley, 1998, p. 60). It seemed that 'Swinging London' was starting to swing a bit too much for many people's liking.

In fact, the influence of LSD had been apparent on the Beatles' previous album *Revolver*, released on 5 August 1966 and still considered by many to be their finest collection. *Revolver* was different in a number of significant ways from anything the Beatles had recorded up to that point. Anticipating their turn away from live playing, many of the tracks were unreproducible on stage. The Beatles and their crew had been experimenting with recording technology since very early in their career, and *Revolver* was a big step on the road from predominantly live 'pop' group to solely studio-oriented 'rock' band. This album also saw George Martin – their producer, and the 'fifth Beatle', as he came to be known – taking an increasingly important role in the group's sound. The point is, however, that it was only during 1967, when music and lifestyle protest began to coalesce along American lines, that alarm bells began to ring in Britain and the potentially 'subversive' import of the Beatles' musical practices began to be seriously considered.

Being the richest pop group in the world, the post-touring Beatles had unlimited studio time at their disposal and access to the best facilities that British sound engineering had to offer. The latter was, however, technologically far behind its American counterpart in 1967 (Cunningham, 1996). Abbey Road Studios, where the band did most of their recording, was built in 1931 to make classical records for HMV (Goldman, 1988, p. 252). However, rather than restricting the Beatles, as Goldman suggests, these limitations seem to have spurred musicians, engineers and producers to heights of improvisation and innovation. Although still only possessing four-track recording capabilities in 1967, for example, Martin (1994, pp. 59–60) explains how he attempted to overcome such restrictions by running two four-track machines together, thus creating 'the then revolutionary complexity of eight-track arrangements' (Goodwin, 1992, p. 80). And as numerous commentators have noted, many of the musical and recording experiments – here and throughout the Beatles' career – either became standard practice or anticipated later developments.

Nevertheless, McCartney especially was jealous of the facilities available to the top American pop groups, and *Pepper* was conceived partly as a musical response to two albums in particular: *Pet Sounds* by the Beach Boys, released in July 1966, which included one song, 'Good Vibrations', made from 35 separate takes; and *Freak Out!* by Frank Zappa and the Mothers of Invention, which had a 12-minute track on it and possessed a loose thematic unity (Turner, 1987a, p. 57). The Beach Boys had in fact been hailed as the greatest pop group in the world by *Melody Maker* after the release of *Pet Sounds* (Moore, 1997, p. 20). With Lennon beginning his period of LSD-inspired reticence, McCartney determined to lead the group's response. Before *Revolver*, the Beatles had been musicians and songwriters who occasionally went into a recording studio to record their songs. Their first album, *Please Please Me*, was recorded in just a day, and right up to their sixth album, *Rubber Soul*, recording was still a matter of finding time between touring, rushing in to Abbey Road with half-written songs, finishing and recording them on the spot in the least number of takes possible. On *Revolver*, with the help of their technical crew and under the influence of marijuana (and, increasingly, LSD), the Beatles began to hone their studio technique, building up a composite sound, crafting the music track by track and layer by layer, until what emerged was not so much a 'song' as a 'record' – an artefact conceived, composed, recorded and received in ways different from the hits that they had been churning out since early 1963.

The remarkably innovative and ambitious double A-side single comprising 'Penny Lane' and 'Strawberry Fields Forever' was released on 17 February 1967. These tracks had been intended for inclusion on the next album, which in its early stages was shaping up to be a collection of songs about the group's recollections of growing up in Liverpool; indeed, George Martin goes so far as to say that 'Strawberry Fields Forever' in particular 'set the agenda for the whole album' (1994, p. 13). This was a project Lennon appears to have had in mind since writing 'In My Life' for the *Rubber Soul* album over a year earlier (MacDonald, 1994, p. 136). However, under pressure from their manager Brian Epstein (Martin, 1994, p. 25) and record company Capitol (Moore, 1997, p. 20), the two Liverpool songs were requisitioned. Despite offering what many consider to be two of the Beatles' best recordings – Riley thinks 'Penny Lane' is 'as perfect as pop gets' (1988, p. 209) – the record was kept from the No. 1 spot in Britain by Engelbert Humperdinck's 'Release Me', making it the first

Beatles single not to go to No. 1 since 'Please Please Me'. With the character of this recording, however – the brilliant production values, the unusual lyrical and musical quality, the obvious difference in technique and intent between the group's two main songwriters – the Beatles gave a hint as to the musical direction in which they were moving and what people might expect on the next album.

The Text

It is time now to consider that aspect of the analysis which should present most problems for a cultural historian possessed of no formal musical training: the text itself. Although I shall be referring to the whole album at times throughout the remainder of this chapter, as the analysis develops I want to focus on the most famous and celebrated track: 'A Day in the Life'.

On their last tour of the United States in the autumn of 1966, McCartney had been amused by the multi-barrelled names favoured by many West Coast bands, and he began to imagine various extended group titles (Wonfor, 1995). Then, looking around for a direction in which to take the Beatles in their post-touring phase, the idea came to him to release a record under the name of one of these groups. Such a move would be part of the Beatles' refutation of their old 'pop' personas, part of their statement of artistic freedom, and part of the general exploration of identity and expression that was coming to dominate popular culture in the mid-1960s. McCartney said later: 'I thought it would be nice to lose our identities, to submerge ourselves in the persona of a fake group. We could make up all the culture around it and collect all our heroes in one place' (quoted in MacDonald, 1994, p. 184).

At the outset of recording, moreover, McCartney had the idea that this record would not be just a collection of unconnected songs brought together on a long-playing disc, a practice that had characterised all their other albums – and indeed every long-playing record in the 'rock' idiom (with the possible exception of Zappa's *Freak Out!*) – up to that time. This record was to have a degree of thematic unity, a 'concept' running through it which linked all the songs. It was to be a sort of concert on record, a concert taking as its theme the reality of life in the 1960s, and the various ways in which one might juggle with that reality. The record would be a *mélange* of words and sound with something for everybody. It would have characters and situations and stories, it would have comedy and tragedy, realism and surrealism; it would incorporate a wide range of musical styles and genres, odd harmonies, opaque lyrics, unusual instruments and bizarre studio effects. And in its meshing of all these styles and effects – the quasi-heavy rock of the title track, the eerie psychedelia of 'Lucy in the Sky with Diamonds', the classical arrangement and waltz tempo of 'She's Leaving Home', the music-hall nostalgia of 'When I'm Sixty Four', and so on – *Pepper* aspired towards a new phase in the conception and use of popular music.

Opening with crowd noises and the sound of an orchestra tuning up, *Pepper* aimed to create a fictional world within a world, its 'scary comic awareness' (Riley, 1988, p. 213) mirroring and parodying the scary comedy of the Beatles' own career between 1963 and 1966. Amongst other things, that is to say, *Pepper* marks the precise moment at which modern pop music becomes self-aware and begins to reflect upon the discourses within which it is caught up. This turn towards self-consciousness and romantic irony marks the inception of an adult-oriented, progressive rock music, a practice that was to have a profound effect on subsequent popular musical discourse (Blake, 1997, pp. 125ff; Macan, 1997). Once this move is made, moreover, there could be no return to the innocent, adolescent moment of unselfconscious, authentic pop, although this has not stopped many within the pop world – from multinational company executives to garage band hopefuls – from searching for precisely that innocence. In fact, one might speculate that the history of popular music since *Pepper* is marked by an alternation between authenticity and irony, or what Moore terms 'sophistication and simplification' (1997, p. 75), a rhythm that can be discerned throughout popular musical discourse including the key areas of production, performance and consumption.

At the same time, it would be a mistake to read too much intent into anything the Beatles did or said during this period of their career. The compositional technique the group had come to favour at this time was one that they called among themselves 'random', what Martin called 'free-form associative tinkering' (1994, p. 138). This was a technique of artistic free-association that tried to react to the stimulus of present circumstances, to whatever happened to be going on or said, and then to incorporate this into a musical form. Many of the songs on *Pepper* were written and recorded as responses to random, everyday stimuli – a child's painting, newspaper reports, encounters with traffic wardens, a television commercial, and so on. The crazy mosaic of noise in the middle of 'Being for the Benefit of Mr Kite', for example, was achieved by producer George Martin and engineer Geoff Emerick throwing small pieces of tape into the air on the studio floor, and re-recording them randomly for the finished track (Martin, 1994, pp. 91–2). (As Martin's description of the recording of the song reveals, however, this 'random' act was actually the result of a highly calculated process geared towards achieving a series of particular musical effects.)

The extent of direct influence is impossible to trace, but it would seem that 'random' is related to at least two factors bearing on the experiences of the group's two main songwriters at this time: LSD and avant-garde art. As remarked above, Lennon had a prodigious drug habit at this time, and this militated against the possibility of (or indeed the desire for) high-concept projects. Intention, or at least too much intention, smacked of ego, of the 'head', of all those things that the counter-culture and LSD promised to liberate. Lennon's interest in 'random' grew when he met the avant-garde artist Yoko Ono later in the year. In the meantime, McCartney (who had more or less become the band's musical director after 1966) had been listening to the art music of Boulez, Cage and Stockhausen in which elements of chance and indeterminacy played an important part; he too, therefore, was trying as much as possible in the early stages of writing to retain a spontaneous element to his song-writing and music-playing. If these methods could sound like 'chaos' (Davies, 1968, p. 289) to some, and a 'shambles' to others (the classically trained musician Sheila Bronberg who played harp on 'She's Leaving Home'; quoted in Cunningham, 1996, p. 135), nevertheless, for many, the results seemed to justify the method.

Besides the desire to incorporate random stimuli, it seems clear that the idea for a 'concept' album was more or less abandoned in the early stages of recording. As Lennon said: 'It starts out with Sergeant Pepper and introduces Billy Shears, and that's the end apart from the so-called reprise. Otherwise every other song could have been on any other album' (Wonfor, 1995, episode 4). Martin (1994, p. 148) claims that the Beatles approved his track sequencing but were not really involved in the process itself (although this is hard to believe of the perfectionist McCartney). If its credentials as a 'concept' album are suspect, however, *Pepper* was clearly a generational album, an attempt to speak to and for the counter-culture that had emerged throughout the world over the months before its release. As such, it brought that counter-culture and its advocacy of mind-altering drugs into the lives of millions of people (particularly young people) around the planet. Especially in songs like 'Lucy in the Sky with Diamonds' and 'A Day in the Life', the Beatles appeared to be attempting to give form to the possibility of realities alternative to the one insisted upon by the 'straight' establishment.

Pepper was an innovative popular musical text in two other significant ways. The first was its realisation of the widespread desire to engage with musical forms and languages beyond the usual scope of the genre. This involved using instruments and musical techniques from the realms of jazz, classical and avant-garde music. Negus writes that Pepper 'can be listened to as a work that both highlights and transcends the generic boundaries of rock through its flawed synthesis of a variety of generic codes' (1996, p. 156). Related to this was the attempt to develop a lyrical sophistication which would see the words of a song taking on layers of meaning like a poem rather than forming a banal addendum to the music. The Beatles had always used unusual song structures and techniques – this was part of their appeal during the days of Beatlemania. They had also written and sung songs that accorded with the standard pop practice in which the emotions evinced in the song were identified with the singer. As Martin says: 'In most of those early songs, Lennon and McCartney were singing directly to the Female Fan, articulating her daydreams and probably their own' (1994, p. 77). So, for example, when they sang 'I Wanna Hold Your Hand' this was the message that contemporary popular musical discourse encouraged listeners to consume: John Lennon and Paul McCartney want to hold somebody's hand. This allowed for a range of responses to the song, the two most straightforward (in terms of gender) being: (female) John and Paul want to hold *my* hand; or I (male), like John and Paul, want to hold somebody's hand, preferably *yours*. But the Beatles had started to move away from this pop music model of singer-identified-with-song on both *Rubber Soul* in 1965 and *Revolver* in 1966. By the time of *Pepper* we find a multiplicity of 'voices' articulated in a multiplicity of musical styles – pop, rock, jazz, classical, Indian, avant-garde, music hall, and so on – to the point where it is difficult to discern a 'real' Beatles message or indeed a 'real' Beatles song. The lyrics also had moved away from the standard variations on the love song that had dominated the Beatles' early repertoire. Following Dylan's example, the group's main songwriters now attempted to address a range of different themes, and to make the words of their songs resonate, like poetry, beyond any obvious literal meaning.

The Beatles' first album, *Please Please Me*, was recorded in one day and cost about £400; *Pepper* took four months and cost an unprecedented £25,000 (Harker, 1980, p. 35). Even the cover for the new album cost more than the whole of *Please Please Me*. The entire design of the album was revolutionary. Never before had so much time and effort been taken on a record sleeve, and the cover, designed by Peter Blake and Jann Haworth, and photographed by Michael Cooper (all important contemporary British artists), became one of 'the best-known works that pop art ever produced' (Riley, 1988, p. 212). Commissioning, designing and constructing the cover, as well as receiving clearance for all the reproduced images, proved a time-consuming business (Martin, 1994, pp. 117–20); but the fact that over 30 years later it remains probably the most famous album cover in popular musical history proves the Beatles' (or at least McCartney's) instincts to have been correct. Never before had a pop record come with free cut-outs ('Sgt. Pepper' badges, a false

moustache and military stripes); never before had there been a
gatefold sleeve (apart from Zappa's double set *Freak Out!*) or lyrics
printed on the back; never before had a popular musical album offered
the possibility (however spurious) that it might be anything more than
a collection of three-minute love songs. If Bob Dylan was the first
major performer to insist that contemporary popular music should be
taken seriously, *Pepper* would be a vindication of that opinion.
Responses to the album in the weeks and months after its release
constituted the beginning of serious rock journalism, and the end of
the benign condescension with which 'serious' composers, writers and
critics had originally addressed the music of the Beatles. The group
had to produce something that would justify their decision to give up
touring. Also, they had to surpass *Revolver* which, as even contemporaries acknowledged, was a brilliant album. Finally, and perhaps
most importantly, they had to produce something that would
vindicate the larger social, cultural and political issues which had been
preoccupying them in the last few years.

The final track on the album, 'A Day in the Life' (hereafter 'Day'),
has become the focus of critical attention. From the beginning it was
signalled as special. A contemporary *Newsweek* critic felt that '[the]
new Beatles are justified by the marvellous last number alone' (quoted
in Martin, 1994, p. 155). More recently, Moore thought it 'one of the
most harrowing songs ever written' (1997, p. 52), while MacDonald
reckoned that the track 'represents the peak of The Beatles'
achievement ... a piece which remains among the most penetrating and
innovative artistic reflections of its era' (1994, p. 184). It is certainly
the song that has attracted the most comment and seems to be the one
that is most difficult to place in terms of the variety of 'meanings' that
have been attributed to the album. But before we turn to those
meanings and those interpretations, what about the track itself?

In his chapter on the group's working methods, the Beatles' contemporary biographer Hunter Davies describes the genesis of 'Day'.
Lennon talks of 'writing the song with the *Daily Mail* propped up in
front of me on the piano' (1968, p. 290). It is widely believed that
Lennon started by reflecting upon the death of a friend in a car
accident just before Christmas 1966, the Guinness heir and London
socialite Tara Browne, although this is disputed by both Martin (1994,
p. 50) and Lennon himself (quoted in Davies, 1968, p. 290). After
adding other 'random' elements culled from the contemporary press
and his own recent experiences, Lennon brought the bones of the song
to McCartney and the two men worked on various ideas before
entering the studio to begin recording the track on 19 January, a mere
two days after they had finished 'Penny Lane'. 'Day' was in fact
recorded *before* the opening title track for the new album – started on
1 February, at a time, therefore, when the Beatles still had only a rough

idea about the shape and the format of the new album. The track's status on *Pepper* is a problem, therefore, and the fact that it was deliberately sequenced to end the album raises many interesting questions.

'Day' is also interesting in so far as it was certainly the most ambitious project the Beatles and their team had undertaken up to that time. It was two minutes longer than anything they had recorded, at a time when there was little precedent for anything in the pop or rock worlds for anything other than the three-minute single. It employed the resources of 41 classical musicians – only half the full symphony orchestra McCartney had requested of a worried Martin (1994, p. 56). In terms of the musical horizon of the average listener in 1967 it must have been a difficult song with which to engage. It begins very sparsely, with just guitar and voice and loose piano, but it grows in complexity and colour as the song progresses. McCartney added the middle section, a slice of reality from his schooldays which shows the influence of the recent 'Penny Lane' sessions. Just as *Pepper* is a show (by the Lonely Hearts Club Band) within a show (by the Beatles), so 'Day' has a 'song' (McCartney's 'Woke up, fell out of bed') within a 'song' (Lennon's 'I read the news today'), thus multiplying the levels of meaning, irony and confusion. The two orchestral crescendos that come in the middle and the end of the track were an attempt by Lennon and McCartney to actuate the philosophy of 'random' in musical terms. Martin instructed each member of the orchestra to make their way up the scales from the lowest note on their instrument until they reached the highest note possible in the relevant key. This 'freaked-out orchestral orgasm' (Cunningham, 1996, p. 131), entirely original in terms of both popular and art music, was recorded during a party in the Abbey Road studios on Friday 10 February, at the end of which everybody broke out into spontaneous applause (MacDonald, 1994, p. 183). With this track, in fact, it is possible to hear the Beatles and their production team stretching the technology available to them in the Abbey Road Studios beyond its limit. (One of the four Grammies awarded to *Pepper* in March 1968 was for best-engineered album; the others were for best album of the year, best contemporary album, and best album cover (Garbarini, Cullman and Graustark, 1980, p. 159).) Also, given that from about 1964 the famous 'Lennon-McCartney' songwriting partnership was little more than a fiction, 'Day' represented the culmination of their collaboration, as it was the last major number on which they worked together.

Much of the subsequent debate has turned on the issue of the conceptual integrity of the album, and particularly the sequencing of 'Day'. For some, the track is an anomaly on *Pepper* because of the horror of its imagery and, after the generally positive, upward surge of the rest of the album, the pessimism of its vision. Whiteley wonders if the album 'merely constituted optimistic escapism' or whether it offered a more practical engagement with contemporary counter-cultural issues (1992, p. 40). Riley believes that 'Day' represents the return of reality on *Pepper*, writing: 'In the context of the album, the track begins as an encore and winds up a eulogy; it dismantles the illusory world the Beatles entered as Sgt. Pepper's Band. Because "A Day in the Life" sits next to an unabashedly fun set of songs, it sounds all the more stark.' Despite this, 'Day' is 'ultimately hopeful', as it articulates 'Lennon's desire to wake the world up to its own potential for rejuvenation' (1988, p. 229).

There is of course an entirely practical reason for placing the song at the album's end – as Martin says, 'the final chord of "A Day in the Life" was so final that it was obvious nothing else could follow it' (1994, p. 148). Besides this, however, MacDonald (1994, p. 181) points out that the song is the explicit culmination of a subgenre of Lennon compositions going back to at least 1963 – songs like 'There's a Place', 'Rain', 'And Your Bird Can Sing', 'Tomorrow Never Knows' and 'Strawberry Fields Forever' – all of which were concerned with the discrepancy between reality and perception in modern life. Mellers had spotted this when he wrote that 'Day' was 'the Beatles' deepest exploration of their familiar illusion-reality theme' (1973, p. 100). Tara Browne's death, for example, as recorded in the *Daily Mail* on 17 January 1967 (two days before recording began), becomes a mere spectacle, an empty, meaningless event that is incapable of touching anyone, thus draining the incident itself of any meaning. And the music reflects this tired, jaded, dispassionate state, in the next two verses as well, about the English army winning the war and the 4000 holes in Blackburn, Lancashire. Lennon's 'twittery' vocal (Martin, 1994, p. 53) is recorded in such a way as to suggest his bemused gloom, not at these events themselves but at the ways in which they impact, or fail to impact, on people's lives. So, in this reading, rather than being an anomaly, 'Day' is in fact the most typical song on the album, which comes to be seen as concerned throughout with the gap between perception and reality.

Other critics discern a more optimistic alternative to the counter-cultural alienation from modern life, encapsulated in the words and the vocal delivery of 'I'd love to turn you on'. 'Turn on' (as in Leary's 'Turn on, tune in, and drop out'), was part of the hippie argot, referring specifically to the heightened consciousness and ego-death accompanying a good LSD experience. In this reading, 'Day' is seen as a song about the predominant theme of the acid generation, the limits of perception, and the possibility of 'turning on' to a higher reality. One critic suggests that the experience of using LSD is literally encoded in the music (Whiteley, 1992, pp. 42ff). Rather than offering a sober return to reality after the surreal circus frivolities of the rest of the album, the message of 'Day', as MacDonald puts it, is that reality is an illusion, 'life is a dream and we have the power, as dreamers, to make it beautiful' (1994, p. 182). Fantasies are dangerous, we know, but at the same time they are completely necessary human activities. The more positive interpretation is borne out by the upward surge of the music with which the track finishes, with the music rising from fragmentation to a massive, rounded, affirmative last chord: E major, a key that, as Mellers reminds us, 'in the eighteenth century and after, was traditionally associated ... with heaven' (1973, p. 101). Altogether, the lyric, the vocal delivery, the production and the arrangement seem to signify that although emerging from sadness and despondency, 'Day' 'is as much an expression of the mystic-psychedelic optimism' (MacDonald, 1994, p. 182) that characterised 1967 as anything else on *Pepper*.

Cultural history, as has been stressed throughout this book, is concerned not with discovering the 'true' meanings of texts, but rather with accounting for the different meanings attached to texts in different contexts. Coincidentally, this may also be what *Pepper* is about – that is, the human need to impose meaning on phenomena that resist any such reduction. Perhaps, as Moore argues, the album's principal value is its musical and lyrical richness, and in attempting to choose between rival interpretations we begin to deny that which we value most:

> We can ... say what this song is probably about. We can declare that, however partially, it is reducible to mere words. To do so, however, seems to me a cardinal mistake ... [for] in attempting to clarify [references], critics are ultimately misrepresenting the song and, hence, the entire album. (1997, pp. 55–6)

Pepper may address a fundamental contradiction between the need for meaning and the poverty of interpretation; however, this has not stopped people producing a wide variety of interpretations for the text, as we shall now see.

Reception

Pepper has attracted an enormous range of critical and popular attention since its first release. The majority of responses have been positive; even those who mistrust or dislike the album generally concur as to its status as a major cultural text of the twentieth century.

Initial reactions to *Pepper*'s release were almost uniformly positive. For one thing, it sold enormously well, staying 'at number one in the album charts [in Britain] for twenty-seven weeks, in the US for nineteen weeks ... It just kept on selling and selling' (Martin, 1994, p. 151). The American writer Langdon Winner described hearing the album at every point on a drive across the country in the weeks after its release, leading him to the opinion that '[for] a brief moment, the irreparably fragmented consciousness of the West was unified, at least in the minds of the young' (quoted in Whiteley, 1992, p. 39). MacDonald (1994, p. 198) and Taylor (1987, pp. 5, 41) describe similarly awed and effusive responses from May and June of 1967. As remarked in the previous section, much of this must be put down to the sheer innovation of the album and the fact that this was a pop record with such obvious aspirations beyond the limitations of the genre. But perhaps most significantly, *Pepper* consolidated the notion of development and growth in popular music, thus justifying the faith of millions of young people across the planet in the value of both their chosen music and the accompanying lifestyle. After *Pepper*, rock musicians would no longer be tied to a particular 'style', as under the old rock 'n' roll dispensation, but could evolve and develop in the same way as painters, art musicians and writers. The concept of 'reinvention' had entered the rock vocabulary permanently.

Music critics in the 'quality' press were also impressed. In a review entitled 'The Beatles Revive Hope of Progress in Pop Music' published in the *London Times* on 29 May 1967, William Mann referred to *Pepper* as 'genuinely creative ... a sort of pop music master class' (quoted in Thomson and Gutman, 1987, p. 141). In the *New York Review of Books* on 18 January 1968, Ned Rorem compared the music of the Beatles with that of Mozart, Stravinsky, Ravel and other art composers (quoted in Thomson and Gutman, 1987, pp. 106–7). The classical comparisons were taken further in 'The Lennon-McCartney Songs' published on 1 February 1968, in which Deryck Cooke of the *Listener* opined that the Beatles' main songwriters 'will still be remembered when most of our "modern composers" are forgotten by everybody except musical historians' (quoted in Thomson and Gutman, 1987, p. 157); and also by Mellers who thought the band's 'three periods [roughly: youthful passion, responsible maturity, and irony] have a genuine analogy with Beethoven's' (1973, p. 101). Joseph Eger, the Associate Conductor of the American Symphony Orchestra, compared the Beatles with the recently rediscovered American composer Charles Ives in terms of their 'imagination, emotion, and freewheeling individualized expression' (1968, p. 46).

All these commentators, moreover, discerned in *Pepper* an attempt to break away from the confines of the pop album. Mann talked of 'a certain shape and integrity' (p. 141). On 26 June 1967, Jack Kroll in *Newsweek* likened the album to a 'suite of poems', and referred to

'Day' as 'the Beatles' *Waste Land*, a superb achievement of their brilliant and startlingly effective popular art' (quoted in Martin, 1994, p. 155). Mellers found 'a sequence of intricately related numbers, forming a whole and performed without break' (1973, pp. 86–7). An anonymous reviewer in the *New Yorker* of 24 June 1967 wrote that with *Pepper* the Beatles were 'working in that special territory where entertainment slips over into art' (p. 23). Such attentions, and the imputation of a 'serious' intent behind the music, were to rebound on the Beatles. In the meantime, however, it would seem that the 'wave of euphoria' (Macan, 1997, p. 15) that greeted the album was a response on the part of a whole generation of music-makers and music-listeners to the realisation that the Beatles had pushed back the boundaries of what is was possible to do and say within the confines of the idiom.

At the same time as it was receiving these plaudits, however, *Pepper* was also being attacked from a number of quarters. Richard Goldstein of the *New York Times* found the album 'cluttered', 'an elaboration without improvement' on *Rubber Soul* and *Revolver* (quoted in Whiteley, 1992, p. 39). His fellow American popular music journalist Robert Christgau also considered it a consolidation of *Revolver* rather than the great leap forwards it was widely perceived to be (quoted in Turner, 1987b, pp. 69–70). Many within 'the establishment' took exception to what were widely considered to be the album's obvious drug references. As remarked above, 'Day' was in fact banned by the BBC on 20 May – before the official release of *Pepper* (Lewisohn, 1987, p. 90) – and other tracks were later banned on British and American radio. This is ironic, however, in so far as many of the more politicised members of the counter-culture believed that, far from being a great anti-establishment text, *Pepper* represented a domestication, if not in fact a parody, of the radical potential of counter-cultural and LSD-based protest.

Such criticisms grew out of the significant distance, often characterised by antagonism and suspicion, between the hippie counter-culture, with its focus upon personal lifestyle, and those activists dedicated to much more tangible political goals such as supporting the Civil Rights movement and ending the war in Vietnam. As Stevens points out (1989, p. 400), as early as 1965 the Beatles were helping to channel Baby Boomer discontent away from political action towards what contemporary commentators such as Leary and the novelist Ken Kesey understood to be a more radical 'revolution in the head'. Whiteley makes a similar point when she writes that the counter-culture 'diverted attention away from the structural inequalities of capitalist society' (1992, p. 110), and when she pointedly suggests that 'by popularising and commercialising the hippy philosophy, [the Beatles] had contributed towards the softening of counter-cultural politics' (p. 54). By making the attitudes, effects and experiences of hippie culture widely available, and by focusing on interpersonal rather than communal experiences, the Beatles could be said to be leaving counter-cultural protest open to appropriation by the market. This was something the hippies themselves tried to pre-empt by holding a 'Death of Hippie' ceremony in Haight-Ashbury in October 1967, so ending the Summer of Love before it could be exploited as a media event. However, the 'antiquarian fantasy' (Blake, 1997, p. 143) of a criticism founded upon the notion of conscious popular resistance to capitalism is not something with which many would now concur. Moreover, MacDonald argues that because *Pepper* emerges from a peculiarly British context, the criticism that it represents a sell-out to the establishment does not hold (1994, p. 185). Whiteley appears to concur when she writes: 'By wearing the uniform of the past within the context of a psychedelically charged album, Sgt. Pepper undercuts traditional values and the military man becomes yet another showman, a figure of fun' (1992, p. 41).

Related to these criticisms, there were those in the popular music industry who felt that *Pepper* was inauthentic, or 'fraudulent' in Goldstein's words, this time in the *New York Village Voice* (quoted in Negus, 1996, p. 154). Leaving the predominantly teenage, working-class audience of Beatlemania behind (the argument goes), the maturing Beatles started writing more adult-oriented material for a more discerning listener; in the process, however, they lost contact with the roots of the music. Even the album's producer George Martin suspected that it flirted with pretentiousness (1994, p. 150), while a sympathetic commentator such as Mellers agreed that *Pepper* represented the end of rock 'n' roll as a participatory music, and its consolidation as a non-reproducible, electronically manufactured product (1973, p. 86). One of the most significant aspects of *Pepper* in this reading is that it represents the initial 'realignment of rock from its working-class roots to its subsequent place on the college circuit' (Moore, 1993, p. 57), a realignment with which the discourse of rock 'n' roll music is still coming to terms as it approaches its half century.

Although all the Beatles subsequently distanced themselves from the idea of *Pepper* as a 'concept' album, such an apparent consistency of intention and the sort of technical sophistication necessary to realise it has served as the ground upon which the album has been attacked by those who see it as the point where pop music forsook its radical popular roots and began to aspire 'upwards' towards the cultural values of the middle class and the avant garde. Riley accuses it of 'self-consciousness' (1988, p. 204), while Harker sees *Pepper* as the moment in which rock 'n' roll's group/audience relationship (itself an extension of a fundamental blues discourse) was compromised, and technology became the dominant force in popular music-making:

'while audiences were able to listen to significantly more complex music on record, they were simultaneously forced back into what was almost a totally privatized experience' (1980, p. 35). Rehearsing the position set out systematically by Adorno (see pp. 44–6 above) Harker sees this as part of a larger process in which popular culture's subversive potential is systematically neutralised by the capitalist establishment. At the same time, he scorns the notion, so fundamental to the myth of the 1960s, of a counter-culture supposedly liberated from the concerns of profit. On the other hand, although Middleton agrees that 'the supposedly liberated individualist eclecticism of countercultural 1960s rock ... was, in a process of recuperation, rearticulated to the long tradition of *bourgeois* individual bohemianism' (1990, p. 8), he perceives this as part of a more creative process of textual negotiation in which the musical values of the middle class are appropriated by the working class for strategic purposes.

However, both defenders and attackers infer a consistency of intention behind *Pepper* that may be entirely spurious. We have already noted the Beatles' desire to respond to random elements in every aspect of their music-making practice, a point supported by Moore's conviction that *Pepper* 'was not the "all-time killer album" planned in meticulous detail from beginning to end' (1997, p. 24). Goldman refers to a 'clutch of ill-matched tunes' (1988, p. 262), an opinion which accords with his jaundiced view of the entire Beatles phenomenon. It may be, in fact, that the album's so-called unity is largely serendipitous, more to do with a general counter-cultural *Zeitgeist* and the dynamics of studio work than with any masterplan on the part of the Beatles and George Martin to reinvent pop music. In short, although it is widely held as the 'take-off' point for the phenomenon of progressive rock which was to play such a significant role in British popular musical discourse until the mid-1970s, we may be asking too much of *Pepper* if we expect it to support any coherent theory of popular culture.

Besides the critics, many contemporary British and American groups discerned a level of serious intent underpinning *Pepper* and tried in the following years to emulate what they saw as the Beatles' reinvention of 'pop' as 'rock' music by treating it as serious art instead of throwaway, mass popular culture (Macan, 1997). Moore traces *Pepper*'s influence in subsequent developments such as 'progressive rock', the 'concept album', the 'rock opera', and the growth of the album as the predominant unit of pop music currency (1997, pp. 73–5). In this respect, one of the album's most important legacies was to consolidate (if not clarify) the difference between 'pop' and 'rock'. This split had been in the offing for a number of years, with groups like the Beach Boys, the Monkees and the Beatles exemplifying the 'pop' mode, and the Rolling Stones, Cream and the Jimi

Hendrix Experience representing 'rock'. *Pepper* saw the Beatles migrating from the former camp to the latter – 'their definite breach with the pop music industry' as Mellers put it (1973, p. 101) – although not without offering some ironic perspectives on the idea of a 'serious' popular music or without some reminders of their past as the world's premier pop music group.

Subsequent opinion of *Pepper* has moved between these negative and positive estimations. The reputation of the Beatles and of the 1960s in general went into decline after 1975 with the onset of punk and subsequently New Wave (MacDonald, 1994, pp. 1–4). Until the end of the 1980s the hippie lifestyle was the subject of much parody, some of it merry, some bitter. However, during the 1980s both the music and the image of the Beatles began to be rehabilitated with the emergence of a guitar-based independent ('Indie') rock-pop scene, so much so that the CD reissue of *Pepper* reached No. 1 in the British charts in 1987, 20 years after the original release. By February 1998, *Pepper* had sold approximately 29 million copies worldwide (Anon., 1998, 62). The emergence of 'Britpop' during the 1990s, and the worldwide success of Oasis, a 'moptop' band from Manchester playing a kind of music highly evocative of the 1960s, also contributed to the revival of the Beatles. A major television documentary was broadcast in 1995, along with various other initiatives such as the accompanying three double-CD *Anthology* albums (combined sales of which exceeded any of the original albums), and the issue of two 'new' Beatles tracks, 'Free as a Bird' and 'Real Love', which used state-of-the-art technology to blend the three living group members with a demo of Lennon. With 'millennium fever' rampant, *Pepper* featured in all the 'Turning Points' (McCormick, 1999) and 'Best of' polls conducted by various media, although its status tends to vary widely: it made 51 in *Mojo*, 1996; 19 in Sweeting, 1997; 7 in Anon., 1998; 2 in Wroe, 1998; and 1 in Channel Four's 1999 *Music of the Millennium*. The Beatles are fashionable again, it seems, although there is of course no guarantee as to their remaining so.

Conclusion

Moore writes that *Pepper* is probably best understood as 'a failed striving for legitimacy, now sufficiently far distant to be looked on with benign, amused forbearance' (1997, p. 81). From such a perspective, the album may be seen as an attempt to extend the functional parameters of popular music, to engage with other musical forms and styles, and to say something meaningful about the world in which, as a popular musical artefact, it was made and consumed. It was an attempt, in the words of Blake, not only to render authentic but also to romanticise rock by creating 'a new place for the music, on a par with the respect given to the classical music traditions and the more serious side of jazz' (1997, p. 142). As most of the commentators referenced in the present study have pointed out, a desire for authenticity was symptomatic of wider changes in Western culture during the 1960s. The form it took with regard to popular music saw a young, prosperous, well-educated, middle-class audience appropriating the music of the black and white working classes for its own ends. Moreover, *Pepper*'s bid for legitimacy came to form the basis of both its celebration and denunciation. As Negus puts it:

> If *Sgt. Pepper* was heard at the time of its release as a new type of high art by the educated middle class or dismissed as little more than a contrived glossy package by those who believed music should be more direct and spontaneous, so subsequent interpretations have been equally contrasting. (1996, pp. 155–6)

Because of the provenance of these interpretations in such well-established, far-reaching socio-political issues, this particular debate seems likely to continue. In other words, so long as there is contention regarding the relationship between popular culture and society, so long will opinion be divided as to the meaning of *Pepper*.

By way of conclusion, however, it should be noted that Moore's call for a 'benign, amused' view of *Pepper*'s 'striving for legitimacy' is articulated in a text published by a serious academic institution (Cambridge University Press) in a series entitled *Cambridge Music Handbooks*, which contains no other analyses of popular music but focuses rather on a selection of canonical works from the art tradition. This tradition, as articulated in certain intellectual practices and institutional sites, still functions as the sign of 'high culture' in this supposedly postmodern, post-evaluative age. Besides cultural studies and sociology, it would seem that *Pepper* has now cracked musicology 'proper', where it takes its place alongside Bach's *Brandenburg Concertos* and Stravinsky's *Oedipus Rex* as valid cultural capital. *Pepper*, and the rock music tradition it represents, may be said to have truly arrived. If the production of a complex, 'serious' music for a mature, discerning audience was really the Beatles' intention, then it would appear that the album does not represent a 'failed' striving after all but, as evidenced by Moore's own text, a highly successful endeavour. With reference to the previous paragraph, the question once again arises: Was this the result of desire from 'below' or appropriation from 'above'? And, of course, the same question should be asked of the latest discipline to validate *Pepper* by welcoming the album under its methodological wing: Cultural History.

Bibliography

Anon. '*Sgt. Pepper*', *The New Yorker* (24 June 1967), pp. 22–3.

Anon. 'The 100 Greatest Albums in the Universe', *Q* (February 1998), pp. 37–68.

Blake, A. *The Land Without Music: Music, Culture and Society in Twentieth-century Britain* (Manchester: Manchester University Press, 1997).

Bradley, D. *Understanding Rock 'n' Roll: Popular Music in Britain 1955–1964* (Buckingham: Open University Press, 1992).

Caute, D. *Sixty-eight: The Year of the Barricades* (Hamish Hamilton, 1988).

Channel Four, *Music for the Millennium*, 24 January 1997.

Clayson, A. *Beat Merchants* (Blandford, 1995).

Cohen, Sara, *Rock Culture in Liverpool: Popular Music in the Making* (Oxford: Clarendon Press, 1991).

Cohen, Stan, *Folk Devils and Moral Panics: The Creation of the Mods and Rockers* (MacGibbon & Kee, 1972).

Cunningham, M. *Good Vibrations: A History of Record Production* (Chessington, Surrey: Castle Communications, 1996).

Davies, H. *The Beatles* (Heinemann, 1968).

Eger, J. 'Ives and Beatles!', *Music Journal* 26 (September 1968), pp. 46, 70–1.

Frith, S. *Sound Effects: Youth, Leisure, and the Politics of Rock 'n' Roll* (New York: Pantheon Books, 1981).

— 'The Industrialization of Popular Music', in Lull (ed.) (1992), pp. 49–74.

Garbarini, V., B. Cullman and B. Graustark, *Strawberry Fields Forever: John Lennon Remembered* (New York & London: Bantam, 1980).

Goldman, A. *The Lives of John Lennon* (Bantam, 1988).

Goodwin, A. 'Rationalization and Democratization in the New Technologies of Popular Music', in Lull (ed.) (1992), pp. 75–100.

Harker, D. *One for the Money: Politics and Popular Song* (Hutchinson, 1980).

Hebdige, D. *Subculture: The Meaning of Style* (Methuen, 1979).

Hewison, R. *Too Much: Art and Society in the Sixties, 1960–1975* (Methuen, 1986).

Joynson, V. *The Tapestry of Delights: The Comprehensive Guide to British Music of the Beat, R & B, Psychedelic and Progressive Eras, 1963–1976* (1995; 2nd edn., Glasgow: Borderline Productions, 1996).

Lennon, J. *The Lennon Tapes* (Jolly and Barber, 1981).

Lewisohn, M. *The Beatles: 25 Years in the Life: A Chronology 1962–1987* (Sidgwick & Jackson, 1987).

Lull, J. (ed.) *Popular Music and Communication* (2nd edn., Sage, 1992).

Macan, E. *Rocking the Classics: English Progressive Rock and the Counterculture* (Oxford: Oxford University Press, 1997).

McCormick, N. 'Turning Points: 50 Works that Shaped the Century. *Sgt. Pepper's Lonely Hearts Club Band*', *Telegraph* (20 March 1999), p. A6.

MacDonald, I. *Revolution in the Head: The Beatles Records and the Sixties* (Fourth Estate, 1994).

Martin, G. *Summer of Love: The Making of Sgt. Pepper* (1994; Pan, 1995).

Mellers, W. *Twilight of the Gods: The Beatles in Retrospect* (Faber, 1973).

Middleton, R. *Studying Popular Music* (Buckingham: Open University Press, 1990).

Mojo, '100 Classic Albums of the Rock Era', reprinted in Cunningham (1996), pp. 339–48.

Moore, A.F. *Rock: The Primary Text* (Buckingham: Open University Press, 1993).

— *The Beatles: Sgt. Pepper's Lonely Hearts Club Band* (Cambridge: Cambridge University Press, 1997).

Negus, K. *Popular Music in Theory: An Introduction* (Cambridge: Polity Press, 1996).

Nehring, N. *Flowers in the Dustbin: Culture, Anarchy and Postwar England* (Ann Arbor: Michigan University Press, 1993).

Neville, R. *Play Power* (Jonathan Cape, 1970).

Redhead, S. *Rave Off: Politics and Deviance in Contemporary Youth Culture* (Aldershot: Avebury Press, 1993).

Riley, T. *Tell Me Why: A Beatles Commentary* (Bodley Head, 1988).

Sheppard, J. (director), S. Albury and J. Sheppard (producers), *It Was Twenty Years Ago Today!*, (Granada, 1 May 1987).

Shepherd, J. *Music as Social Text* (Cambridge: Polity Press, 1991).

Stevens, J. *Storming Heaven: LSD and the American Dream* (1987; Paladin, 1989).

Sweeting, A. 'Ton of Joy', *Guardian:* Friday Review (19 September 1997), pp. 2–5.

Swiss, T., J. Sloop and A. Herman (eds) *Mapping the Beat: Popular Music and Contemporary Theory* (Oxford: Blackwell, 1998).

Taylor, D. *It Was Twenty Years Ago Today* (New York & London: Bantam, 1987).

Thomson, E. and D. Gutman (eds) *The Lennon Companion: Twenty-five Years of Comment* (Macmillan, 1987).

Turner, S. 'The Story of *Sgt. Pepper*', *Q* 9, 10 (June 1987a, 48–58; July 1987b, pp. 60–70).

Whiteley, S. *The Space Between the Notes: Rock and the Counter-culture* (Routledge, 1992).

— 'Repressive Representations: Patriarchy and Femininities in Rock Music of the Counterculture', in Swiss, Sloop and Herman (eds) (1998), pp. 153–70.

Willis, P. *Common Culture: Symbolic Work and Play in the Everyday Cultures of the Young* (Buckingham: Open University Press, 1990).

Wonfor, G. (director), Chips Chipperfield (producer), *The Beatles Anthology* (Granada, 1995, episodes 1–6).

Wroe, M. 'Hits from the Decade that Taste Forgot: Seventies Acts Dominate Greatest Albums List', *Observer*: News (6 September 1998), p. 13.

Index

Within index entries, the following abbreviations are used: FPU *Address* for *Address of the Female Political Union of Birmingham*; *Pepper* for *Sgt. Pepper's Lonely Hearts Club Band*; VVM for Vietnam Veterans Memorial; *Wigan Pier* for *The Road to Wigan Pier*.